P9-CMP-621

DISCARDED

Making the Grade

Making the Grade

*The Economic Evolution of
American School Districts*

WILLIAM A. FISCHEL

THE UNIVERSITY OF CHICAGO PRESS   CHICAGO AND LONDON

WILLIAM A. FISCHEL is professor of economics and the Patricia F. and William B. Hale 1944 Professor in Arts and Sciences at Dartmouth College.

The University of Chicago Press, Chicago 60637
The University of Chicago Press, Ltd., London
© 2009 by The University of Chicago
All rights reserved. Published 2009
Printed in the United States of America
18 17 16 15 14 13 12 11 10 09   1 2 3 4 5

ISBN-13: 978-0-226-25130-1   (cloth)
ISBN-10: 0-226-25130-6   (cloth)

Library of Congress Cataloging-in-Publication Data

Fischel, William A.
   Making the grade : the economic evolution of American school districts / William A. Fischel.
      p. cm.
   Includes bibliograhical references and index.
   ISBN-13: 978-0-226-25130-1   (cloth : alk. paper)
   ISBN-10: 0-226-25130-6   (cloth : alk. paper)   1. School districts—United States—History—20th century. 2. School districts—United States—Finance. 3. Education—Economic aspects—United States. 4. Educational change—United States—History—20th century. I. Title.
LB2817.3.F57 2009
338.4'337—dc22

                                                          2009018813

♾ The paper used in this publication meets the minimum requirements of the American National Standard for Information Sciences—Permanence of Paper for Printed Library Materials, ANSI Z39.48-1992.

TO MY DAD, WHO WAS ON THE SCHOOL BOARD,
AND TO MY MOM, WHO RAN THE PTA,
AND TO THE MEMORY OF ROSEMARY G. CAMPBELL.

Contents

Preface

Sometimes you can see something new in a familiar object by looking at it from a different angle. Public education is the object, and my different angle is the humble school district. Among education scholars and reformers, school districts are the Rodney Dangerfields of municipal corporations: They "can't get no respect." Almost all social scientists who analyze education issues disdain districts as "creatures of the state" that have no legal ability to obstruct or alter a directive that comes from on high. Education reform, on this view, has to come from the state and federal governments or from the courts.

The theme of this book takes issue with this viewpoint. I submit that ordinary residents of American school districts created a national system of public education that is in many respects an efficient response to the diversity and mobility of the nation. This idea is heretical in at least two ways. The first is that local voters, not state authorities, are responsible for the creation of the system. Educational leaders such as Horace Mann headed parades that proceeded on routes selected by the marchers, not the grand marshal.

The other unconventional idea is that important aspects of the present system of public education that are derided as failures actually have efficiency advantages. A decentralized system of governance not only offers more choices to "vote with your feet" among school districts but also is actually more flexible. The United States is physically large and its population is diverse and spread out, which would make centralized administration problematical. The American population is also mobile, more so than that of any other country, and mobility is an important economic advantage. I offer evidence that a locally controlled system can facilitate mobility and systemic reform without sacrificing self-governance.

The foundational ideas of the present work did not emerge from a vacuum. My previous book, *The Homevoter Hypothesis*, was based on the idea that concern for the value of owner-occupied housing causes homeowners to become the dominant faction in American local government. I was so impressed by homeowners' local political influence that a neologism, "homevoters," seemed appropriate to characterize their role in municipal affairs.

The units of local government that *The Homevoter Hypothesis* focused on were municipalities, the 25,000 cities, towns, boroughs, and townships through which voters govern themselves. School districts were, in my mind, simply adjuncts of local governments. I knew, of course, that "dependent" school districts—those that are actually a department of city or county governments—are rare nowadays. I also knew that school district boundaries only sometimes coincide with municipal boundaries. But I did not regard these as important distinctions. My thesis was that homevoters were in charge and did not care much about the difference between school boards and city councils when buying their homes and then participating in local affairs. After a brief discussion of the differences between cities and school districts, I glossed over the distinction with a sweep of the hand: "A municipality that is touting its charms usually mentions that it has 'good schools'" (Fischel 2001, 22).

The present book is a corrective for my overgeneralization about school districts. The correction was inspired by two musings. One was profound: Why do Americans govern public schools at the local level at all? Almost everyone agrees that an educated populace is a national, not a local public asset. Yet Americans insist on a large degree of local governance and funding for public schools. How did the local school district come about and why does it persist? My preliminary answer to this question was published in *Economics of Governance* as "Why Voters Veto Vouchers: Public Schools and Community-Specific Social Capital" (Fischel 2006a). I thank the editor, Amihai Glazer, for his special encouragement and the publisher of the journal, Springer, for permission to reprint parts of that article in chapter 6.

My second musing about schooling was puckish: Why do schools start their academic year in the waning days of summer and end their academic year at the dawn of a new summer? Like most people, I had thought that that the long summer vacation was a holdover from farming days. It is not. American farm children in the nineteenth century usually attended school in summer and winter. What caused the change, and why does it persist long after air-conditioning has made it as easy to hold school in summer as in winter? My answer to that was first published as "Will I See You in September? An Economic Explanation for the Standard School Calendar" (Fischel 2006b) in the *Journal of Urban Economics,* whose publisher, Elsevier, also granted permission to reprint parts of that article in chapter 4.

Obtaining answers to additional questions and weaving them into this book required much time and the assistance of many other scholars and friends. It has taken me sufficiently long that I cannot recall all those who helped. I hope not to offend those omitted—or improperly implicate those included—by thanking Sarah Battersby, Kelly Bedard, Jan Brueckner, Eric Brunner, Colin Campbell, Tom Downes, Bob Ellickson, Maria Ferreyra, Mike Haines, Michael Heise, Larry Kenny, Daphne Kenyon, Toru Kitahara, Ken Kriss, Robert Leight, Maureen McDonough, Robert Putnam, Martha Reid, Bruce Sacerdote, Cassandra Schug, Jon Skinner, Lisa Snell, Jon Sonstelie, Doug Staiger, Nate Wiewora, Tony Wolk, and Joan Youngman.

I am also indebted to some institutions. Dartmouth College gave me a leave and a grant from its Nelson Rockefeller fund to spend time at a sabbatical at the University of California at Santa Barbara, whose Department of Economics was an especially generous host as I was researching the book. The Lincoln Institute of Land Policy also sponsored part of my leave and several seminars at which I presented parts of this book. Cornell Law School, the Martin School at the University of Kentucky, and the Economics Department of West Virginia University also hosted seminars for my musings. The American Education Finance Association meetings were an especially productive venue for trying out ideas. My largest debt is, as ever, to my wife, Janice Fischel, who has always been willing to listen to my ideas as well as be my partner for more than a third of a century.

CHAPTER ONE

Introduction: Mobility, Property, and Community

"Making the grade" has two connotations for school districts. The more obvious and contemporary is the demand for public schools to conform to high standards of accomplishment. This is not just for educational reasons. Homebuyers are more interested in the quality of schools than in almost any other public service, and prospective home sellers are anxious to have schools perform well. School districts that are not making the grade are penalized in the property market.

The less obvious connotation of this book's title is the historical transformation of school districts. School districts once numbered in the hundreds of thousands, most of them governing a single, one-room rural school. Such schools had a pedagogical method that was much different than that used today. Children were not divided into age-specific cohorts, each of which was taught the same lessons each day. In one-room schools, children were divided into "tutorial-recitation" groups, not grades. Recitation group membership was not by age but by previous accomplishment, typically how far a child had progressed in a reader or speller or arithmetic textbook. Groups were thus composed of students of different ages, and individual students could be in different recitation groups for each subject.

One of my tasks in this book is to explain how the tutorial-recitation method was supplanted by the age-graded method that we now take to be the mark of "real school," to use the telling expression of David Tyack and

Larry Cuban (1995). My main interest is in the process by which this transformation took place. Unlike most historians of education, I do not focus on the education leaders who were eager suppliers of education reform. I focus in this book on the demand side, the resident voters who reluctantly gave up their one-room schools. They agreed to consolidated, age-graded schools, I submit, because the one-room school did not prepare their children for a high school education. Farmers and other rural property owners were penalized if their schools were not "making the grade" and educating resident children in a more systematic way.

1.1 The Mundane Miracles of Mobility, Property, and Community

The themes that cut across the chapters of this book can be summarized as mobility, property, and community. To illustrate their relationship, I would like the reader to contemplate a miracle of the mundane. You have school-age children, and you and your spouse obtain new jobs in a different part of the country. In August, you arrive at a new home and enroll your children in the local public schools. The youngest just completed fourth grade, and the twins are entering high school. After you proffer proof of residence to your new school district, records will be transferred from your children's former school. Your daughter will enter fifth grade and the boys will start ninth grade, and they will almost surely be taught skills and material whose foundation was established in the schools of their previous home, even if it was in a different state.

As parents, you will find that within a month or two you will have numerous new acquaintances and friends in the community. You meet them through some school event or a birthday party or other child-oriented social event. Within six months you will be full-fledged members of a community whose name you may not have known a year earlier, and your kids, once they have gotten over the trauma of change, will be doing as well in their new school as they would have in the old.

These are mundane miracles. The K–12 sequence that makes your kids' new school interchangeable with their former school did not come about from any centralized direction. (Schools are "interchangeable" in the sense that rental cars are interchangeable for most drivers, who can operate the Lexus about as well as the Chevy.) Indeed, there is still no central direction for curriculum at the national level, and even uniform statewide standards are a relatively recent and controversial phenomenon.

The whole system of free public education was developed state by state, and within most states centralized direction arrived only after the general contours of the system had been established by local residents.

The other mundane miracle is the public's financial affection for their local school district. Schools matter for property values. A house built on the favorable side of a school district line may have its value enhanced by 10 or 20 percent, a boundary-line premium that is seldom matched by any municipal boundary unless the city and school district boundaries are the same. Yet almost all social scientists who analyze education issues look upon school districts in the same way that the formal legal system does: districts are "creatures of the state" and have no constitutional ability to obstruct or alter a directive that comes from on high.

If school districts are so irrelevant in a constitutional sense, though, why do homebuyers put so much stock in them? It cannot be just naïveté or inattention on the part of homebuyers; most of them are putting down a good fraction of their life savings to buy a house. Nor is it just low taxes that makes a district attractive. The local school's test scores receive the same sort of scrutiny from prospective homebuyers that earnings reports receive from stock market analysts. Yet the mystery of school districts is compounded by the fact that most homeowners do not have children in schools. True, they know that some of the prospective buyers will have children, but that fraction of the market is going down, not up. Yet school district quality remains probably the most important single indicator of housing prices. Something beyond just schools is involved.

The "something beyond" is, I will argue, the sense of community that local schools provide for residents of their district. Schools are an important source of localized social capital for adults. This is hardly a new insight. What appears to be different is my contention that the communitarian virtues of schools have a spillover effect on the rest of the community. Adults without children in school benefit from the network of social capital that is fostered by public schools.

1.2 Early American Land Policies and the Marvelously Efficient One-Room School

The evolution of modern schools was something akin to a spontaneous order. School districts were so generic and numerous that they can be analyzed as markets rather than governments. I open chapter 2 with a historical argument. Concern about property values drove the establishment of schools and school districts in the nineteenth century. My focus is on the Land Act of 1785, which provided for the measurement and sale of land in most of the nation, and the Northwest Ordinance of 1787, which established a method of governance and progression to statehood. The most notable feature of the Land Act of 1785 was its provision that a square mile of land—the "school section"—in each township be set aside as an endowment for schools for residents of the township.

The school-establishing features of these far-reaching Congressional acts can be best understood as attempting to maximize the value of the government's vast land holdings. The school sections were bait for settlers. The subsequent state constitutional provisions that encouraged education were responses to this same land-value concern. The demand for schools by settlers and subsequent purchasers is what induced the government to establish their education system. It was not something that wise, disinterested public officials tried to impose on an unwilling or indifferent population.

Chapter 2 then goes on to explain the technology of education in nineteenth-century, one-room schools and contrasts it to modern, age-graded education. (I sometimes refer to a general educational technology as a "pedagogy," but the reader should not anticipate discussions of the philosophy or psychology of education along the lines of Johann Pestalozzi, Maria Montessori, and John Dewey.) I argue that each system was appropriate to the geographic, economic, and technological circumstances of its time. Many features of the one-room rural school that are criticized as backward were actually efficient responses to their circumstances. For example, the tutorial-recitation method allowed children to attend school at irregular intervals. If they missed half a term because a family crisis required additional assistance on the farm, they could still make some progress in their texts when they returned. They were not held back a grade, since there were no grades to be held back in.

Understanding the one-room school's unique pedagogy can shed light on some practices that seem peculiar to people accustomed to a modern, age-graded system. Tuition payments, called "rate bills," were often charged to cover part of the expenses in one-room schools. Modern critics of this system often overlook the fact that most rate bills were used mainly to *extend* the term of one-room schools for a few weeks. Low-income children who were deterred from attending during this period were not held back in a grade. They simply had to wait until the tuition-free term began a few months later and continued to progress as before. The only advantage of paying the rate bill was that it enabled children to go through school faster. This explains why the "free school" movement, which abolished the rate bills in most states, appears to have had such a modest impact on educational attainments.

A modern, age-graded system might actually have resulted in less education for the vast majority of nineteenth-century Americans, who lived in low-density rural areas. Grades would have been too small, since rural children could not be transported to a large-enough school. Most farm families' irregular need for their children's labor would have interfered with the continuous and sequential attendance demanded by an age-graded pedagogy. As a result, farm children would have been stuck in an endless loop of grade repetition. By the same token, the nineteenth-century's one-room pedagogy could not produce enough specialized education in the twentieth century, when there was an increase in the demand for workers with skills taught in high school. The drawback of the tutorial-recitation method was that school children spent most of the day in what we would now call study hall, preparing for their brief recitation periods.

Family mobility shaped both systems. One-room schools of the nineteenth century had a generic, standard pedagogy that allowed for each period of attendance, however brief, to advance a child's education. Children could duck in and out of school without fear of failing to be promoted. Twentieth-century schools have a loosely standardized curriculum—the annual progression from kindergarten to twelfth grade. Age grading allows for more specialization by teachers and more attention to children in each grade, but it also demands that schools not be too much different from one another.

1.3 Explaining the School District Consolidation Movement

Chapter 3 uses land-value concerns and economic and technical change to explain the dramatic decline in the number of school districts between 1910 and 1970. At the beginning of the twentieth century, there were probably more than two hundred thousand school districts. By 1970, the number fell below twenty thousand and has since drifted down much more slowly. Almost all the decline in district numbers to 1970 can be accounted for by the consolidation of rural, one-room school districts into larger districts that had multiroom buildings in which children were put on an age-graded track that led to high school.

The process by which rural consolidation and age grading became the norm is widely regarded as the triumph of centralized administrators. Some historians regard this triumph as unfortunate, whereas most others think of it as admirable. But the consensus is that it was accomplished by top-down pressure. For example, Terry Moe (2001, 184) writes (and later qualifies), "From its modern origins in the early decades of the 1900s, America's public education system was designed to be a purely governmental system in which markets play no role at all."

In chapter 3, I beg to disagree. I point out that many standard features of age-graded education that are thought to have been created by national commissions can be seen as generic responses to the need to accommodate mobile families. We would have something like "Carnegie units" for high school credits, even if there had been no Carnegie Commission to establish them. I also argue at length that most "top-down" proposals to consolidate school districts along preexisting political boundaries failed. The district boundaries we see today reflect what were then called "organic communities" rather than arbitrary boundaries.

The political success of the age-graded model was due, I believe, to the recognition by rural voters that their property values would be lowered if they did not get with the age-graded program. One-room, rural schools by 1900 attempted to adopt an age-graded system. This system did not work well in the one-room setting. Whereas students could be sorted broadly by ability and knowledge in the ungraded tutorial-recitation method, they had to be sorted narrowly by age in the new age-graded method. This made for many more recitations for the one-room teacher, and most adopted a compromise that nominally conformed to age stratifications but in practice continued to group children by ability and knowledge.

This compromise would have been tolerable—even admirable—if the only aspiration of public education was literacy and numeracy. The coup de grâce for the rural method was the rapid development of high schools and the growing demand for their graduates in the labor market. Now one-room school teachers had to be able to teach not only a larger number of grades but also a wider and deeper range of knowledge to prepare students for high school. The teachers in the age-graded schools of the city could deal with both of these more easily because they could specialize in subjects and grade levels. One-room schools thus became obsolete. Attendance began to shrink because of declining rural population and because parents of ambitious students moved to age-graded districts. The decline in rural property values that this occasioned in the more backward districts was the prod to do what bureaucratic educators had been urging for decades, which was to consolidate one-room schools into rural age-graded schools. It was this consolidation that accounted for almost all the decline in school district numbers from 1910 to 1970.

1.4 "Will I See You in September?" Labor Mobility and the Standard School Calendar

Chapter 4 offers indirect evidence that school districts were able to evolve from a one-room pedagogy to an age-graded system without a conscious, top-down organizer. My specific example of nearly spontaneous order is the coordination of school calendars, which I take as a marker for coordination of other aspects of school curricula. In reading the history of American education, I found that most rural schools held classes during the winter and the summer. I had always thought that modern-day summer vacation had emanated from the need for farm children to work during the summer. But just a little more thought about farming would have persuaded me that this was not a good explanation, since summer was actually not the time when the unskilled labor of children would be most useful. So summer was indeed a time when farm children attended school regularly in the nineteenth century. A separate winter term also was taught in most rural districts. School was generally not held in the spring and autumn in order to have all hands available for the urgencies of planting and harvesting.

So what does explain the existence of the standard school calendar? In a paper published in the *Journal of Urban Economics*, I argued that it is best explained as a coordinating device (2006b). It allows children and teachers to finish school at one place and move to another school district far away and begin the new school year with everyone else. The now-standard calendar facilitates labor mobility. One bit of evidence in support of coordination is that the standard calendar emerged around 1900, just as the majority of the nation was becoming urban. One-room schools did not require a standard calendar because they had a teaching technology that did not require continuous attendance in schools. But cities were adopting age-graded methods of instruction, and this pedagogy required continuous attendance. When urban, age-graded schooling became the national standard, a common beginning and ending period had to be adopted to coordinate the comings and goings of families and teachers from various districts.

There was almost no discussion in the historical record that directly supports the foregoing account. I instead offer international evidence based on the different seasons in the Northern and Southern Hemispheres. It turns out that the modern school year, which starts near the end of summer and ends at the beginning of the next summer, is a worldwide standard. (Japan is the most interesting exception.) Australian, South American, and sub-Saharan African children usually start school around February and end in November or December. But international schools in those areas that cater to families who must return to Northern Hemisphere countries adopt a Northern Hemisphere calendar, starting in August and ending in June, so that the return to London or New York in July allows their children to enroll in school at the regular time.

In contrast to America's early adoption of the now-standard school calendar (around 1900), several other nations, most notably Germany, did not adopt the mobility-facilitating calendar until the second half of the twentieth century. I use this and some domestic examples as evidence in support of the adaptability of a decentralized system of education. As Claudia Goldin and Lawrence Katz (2008) have emphasized, the United States adopted mass high school education many decades before Europe precisely because high school could be adopted one district at a time. I supplement their insight in this chapter by offering a motive—concern about local property values—that goaded local voters to engage in a beneficial "race to the top" in education.

A standardized system has its drawbacks, however. I demonstrate that the standard calendar and curriculum can act as a ceiling on educational quality, making it difficult to implement desirable reforms. For example, a longer school year adopted by a single state would make its schools less interchangeable with those of other states, thus hindering labor mobility by teachers and parents. I argue that geographical mobility is economically desirable and should not be discouraged by overly specialized education systems. This commends education reforms that extend the period of education both before first grade (to give the disadvantaged a head start) and after high school.

1.5 The Economic Geography of School Districts

In my "bottom-up" interpretation of district consolidation in chapter 3, I argue that voters would agree to consolidations that formed the smallest district that could support a high school. Voters were concerned with governance as much as scale economies. Chapter 5 raises the question of why some school districts are now much larger than would seem warranted by voter concerns. Why do we have the huge city districts of New York, Los Angeles, and Chicago? Why do some western metropolitan areas have large districts in some places but small districts elsewhere? Most puzzling of all, why are Southern school districts so much larger than those of the North?

The South was different, I argue, because racial segregation made the population density of whites and blacks taken separately too low to form efficient school districts. When age grading and high school became desirable, the South herded its white children into consolidated schools and let rural black children stay in the one-room schools. Whites in remote rural areas had to choose between full-time schooling with long bus rides and no school at all. Blacks were not presented with this choice, since the Southern strategy of 1900 was to disfranchise them to keep them from demanding age-graded schools. When it became evident in the late 1930s that blacks would have to be provided with age-graded education and high school, most Southern states reverted to the county as the unit of school administration, since separate age-graded school systems required twice the student catchment area to run parallel K–12 schools. As urban populations sprawled beyond the city, the county became the school district for the suburban South.

The size of urban school districts in the rest of the nation was also dictated largely by rural population density. In the first half of the twentieth century, rural districts everywhere consolidated in order to send their children to more standardized age-graded schools, which gave them access to high school. The minimum size necessary for a rural consolidated district varied regionally. In areas where there was dense rural settlement (chiefly in high-rainfall areas), the land-area of the minimum-size school district could be small. In areas that were arid, mountainous, or otherwise uncongenial to intensive agriculture and a multitude of towns, the resulting district would have to be large in area to get enough children to form consolidated schools.

As cities grew and spread out later in the twentieth century, suburbanites took over preexisting rural school districts. School districts hardly ever break up once they have consolidated, so previous rural consolidation patterns were imprinted on modern suburban districts. In arid and mountainous areas of the country, rural districts were large. In areas with higher farm density, the rural districts adjacent to cities were small. In the South, rural districts became large because of the diseconomies of running separate schools for whites and blacks. Thus two variables, early population density (which I statistically approximate by annual rainfall) and a history of racial segregation, account for most of the national variation in *urban* school district size.

This regional variation affects the competitiveness of school districts in metropolitan areas. A metropolitan area with greater numbers of school districts allows potential residents to "vote with their feet" for the school district they want and also induces school authorities to pay closer attention to effective education. I present statistical evidence that geographic competition is greatest in areas outside of the South that had rural climates that were conducive to high population density.

The other original finding in chapter 3 is the result of my discovery that the mapping program Google Earth can be used to compare municipal and school district boundaries. I found that most cities do overlap with a single school district, even though the degree of congruence is imperfect. This overlap is important because, as I argue in chapter 6, the social capital that is accumulated in the city's school district is also useful in municipal affairs.

1.6 Education Reforms and Social Capital in School Districts

Chapter 6 starts with a modern question: Why don't voters like school vouchers? I motivate this question by first examining the broad trends in school-finance equalization, focusing on the experience of California. Like most other states, California used state-generated funds to offset at least some of the inequalities in education spending that result from school district financing of education. But the *Serrano v. Priest* decisions in the 1970s found that this equalization was not enough, and the California Supreme Court required that local property-tax bases could no longer be the basis for any spending inequalities among school districts.

I argue that this decision and the legislature's implementation of it should have made vouchers much more attractive. Yet statewide voucher initiatives were rejected by large margins in the 1990s in California and in other states. The public seems to embrace other competition-enhancing ideas. Economists' proposals to deregulate airlines, trade pollution standards, and auction radio and TV broadcasting rights have been political successes. Why are schools different?

Education itself is not a public good in the classic sense of the word. Schools can be provided on the private market. There are few technical reasons for them to be run by local public agencies, but voters do not want to give up their public schools. My answer to this conundrum is that local public schools provide localized social capital—the list of people you know locally—for the *parents* of school children. This Rolodex enhancement makes provision of other, nonschool public goods easier to accomplish. If you know more people in your neighborhood, it is easier to get them to help you to lobby city hall for a pocket park or better police patrols. Localized social capital improves the bottom-up provision of true local public goods.

Chapter 6 presents broad empirical evidence in support of the social-capital theory of public schools. (1) States with smaller (and thus more parent-friendly) school districts appear to have more social capital. (2) Demographic data show that the long-term trends in social capital are closely tracked by the average number of school-age children per family. Social capital measures hit their peak just after the peak of the baby boom, and they have glided downward as family size has shrunk since 1960. (3) Contemporary surveys show that parents with more children seem to have more social capital.

It appears that voters do not want to give up their school districts, but overly large school districts are detrimental to both social capital and educational accomplishment. The most obvious reform that this analysis points to is to reduce the size of school districts. Because almost every square mile of the country is already within some school district, this would require some secessions. Creation of larger districts can be done, but making smaller districts from larger units is quite difficult. I illustrate the difficulty by recounting the ongoing saga of residents in Lakewood, California, which sought to form its own school district from the several larger ones into which it had been divided long ago. Lakewood residents appear to have been eager to get a chance to vote on this issue, but the proposed district was blocked by the county and state bureaucracy, apparently abetted by teacher unions. Consolidation of small districts is still undertaken only by mutual consent of the voters of each small district. But they have to think hard about it, since consolidation seems to be a lobster trap: easy to get into, but very difficult to get out of.

One response to the inflexibility of boundaries is vouchers. Most of the ongoing voucher programs focus on students in big cities. The larger trend, however, is the formation of charter schools in large cities. These are publicly funded but governed usually by neighborhood parent groups. Although it is not obvious that charter schools perform better than public schools, it is clear to most observers that parents are more satisfied with their schools. I submit that this satisfaction is an indicator that charter schools promote social capital, which in large cities is more difficult to do than in suburban schools. I thus see the charter school movement as another example of how "bottom-up" governance can emerge even in the most bureaucratized settings.

I close the chapter and the book with the suggestion that a robust system of locally governed—and at least partly locally financed—school districts may be essential for the future of education. The challenge is the decline in the proportion of the population that has children in schools. I review evidence that "elder voters," who are the most numerous childless group, are more supportive of education at the local level than at the state level. The education challenges of the future may best be met with a school system that has strong elements of what most reformers deride as local control.

CHAPTER TWO

Early American Land Policies and the Marvelously Efficient One-Room School

This chapter first offers historical evidence that the provision of American schools was motivated by a concern for property values. I then advance the idea that the one-room school was an efficient response to the pattern of settlement and economic conditions of nineteenth-century America. The latter part of the chapter then addresses the evolutionary question of why the one-room school was so successful that it persisted long after multigrade schooling had been first established. I argue that the system sought by most reformers—an age-graded system with professional instructors, multiroom schools, and centralized finance—would have been much less satisfactory in rural America.

2.1 Schools as Bait for Land Buyers

A major theme of this book is that the development of the American public school system was directed by local voters interested in promoting the value of their property. There are scores of contemporary studies that show that better schools add to property values. Perhaps the most frequently cited (and still one of the best) studies to this effect was undertaken by Wallace Oates (1969). Oates was not interested in school spending per se. He wanted to test whether one of the main conditions of the Tiebout (1956) model was approximated by contemporary local governments. Charles Tiebout had proposed an alternative to voting for public goods in the political system. His alternative has been described as "voting with your feet." Communities set the level and quality of public services—and the local taxes to pay for them—in such a way as to attract residents.

Oates showed that this unlikely sounding model had some basis in reality. Using a 1960 sample of communities in northern New Jersey, Oates found that districts with higher than average taxes had less valuable homes, controlling for size and other features. This demonstrated that potential homebuyers—the people capable of "voting with their feet"—really did notice differences in tax rates. On the other side of the ledger, and more important for the present work, Oates found that communities that spent more than average on public schools, which were the largest local expenditure, had more valuable homes. Turning to local decision making, Oates pointed out that the quantitative size of the tax and spending effects suggested a kind of political equilibrium. Better schools do enhance home values (meaning that potential homebuyers will pay more for the average home), but the higher taxes necessary to improve schools depress home values. The implication was that community authorities, and the voters they responded to, had adopted tax and spending policies with a close eye toward improving the school district's home values.

Oates's article is the most cited and most replicated empirical study in the field of local public economics. His finding that the quality of school districts matters to homebuyers holds up in widely varying geographic areas and under more recent advances in econometric technique. Perhaps the major change over time is the decline in the importance of spending itself and the rise in measures of student accomplishment, such as test scores and graduation rates (Downes and Zabel 2002; Kane, Staiger, and Samms 2003). (I attribute the decline in the importance of spending per pupil to the school-finance-equalization movement that I discuss in chapter 6.) School district boundaries appear to be the most important single determinant of home values in metropolitan areas as disparate as Dallas (Goodman and Thibodeau 1998) and Cleveland (Brasington and Haurin 2006). The migration patterns of families with children in Boston-area communities are largely determined by whether local districts can overcome tax-limitation constraints and spend more on local schools (Bradbury, Case, and Mayer 2001). Real estate salespeople often list the school district as the first quality of the homes they have for sale, and a few actually provide links to studies of home values and school district quality on their Web pages.

Voters in local elections are aware of the importance of school quality and other local services. Several empirical studies indicate that community votes are influenced by the expected impact of a decision on local home values (Sonstelie and Portney 1980; Dehring, Depken, and Ward 2008). My previous book, *The Homevoter Hypothesis* (2001), explored the implications of the idea that concern about property values motivates political behavior. But it would be next to impossible to go back to 1900, say, and show that a vote for or against school reform was motivated in large part by its expected effect on property values. This is in large part because of data limitations; census and other historical data collectors did not ask the necessary questions. My argument in the present work is essentially one of historical inference: if voters in the late twentieth century were interested in the effect of schools on their property values, then voters from earlier eras must have been as well. Because this method is not entirely satisfying, the first part of this chapter offers evidence of a different kind. I will show that the system of local schools in the states admitted to the Union during the nineteenth century was shaped by a desire to maximize saleable property values. Economists would call this macroeconomic evidence, which looks at large trends over time rather than individual transactions within a short time period. The trend I focus on was among the largest in American history, the settlement of the United States west of the Appalachian Mountains.

2.2 Public Land Sales and the Developers' Dilemma

After the American Revolutionary War ended by treaty in 1783, Britain ceded its claims to land from the thirteen colonies out to the Mississippi River and south of the Great Lakes. Some of the original states had colonial-era claims to this territory, but they were soon relinquished under the Articles of Confederation. The new national government as a result became one of the world's largest landowners. What to do with its land was a critical task of the post-Revolutionary Congress of the Confederation.

Citizens in the original states had some ambivalence about selling land out west. On the one hand, rapid settlement of the West would contribute to the depopulation of the East and perhaps reduce property values (Howard Taylor 1922, 13). This anxiety was not unfounded. A Vermont senator complained in the 1860s that his constituents were "well aware how adversely the opening of the Middle West had affected and was at that moment affecting agriculture in his own section" (Paul Gates 1968, 210).

On the other hand, the sale of land would be a source of revenue for the national government. This would reduce the original states' tax burdens. Under the Articles of Confederation, the states were solicited for tax revenues. The national government did not have the power to tax until the Constitution was adopted in 1789, but even then, most taxes would come from residents of the more populous, earlier-settled states. The national government needed money to pay off debts incurred during the American Revolution as well as for its everyday operations.

It was clear that the second consideration—a desire for national revenue—quickly prevailed. It accounts for why the disposal of western land was designed with a close eye toward maximizing the sale value of land. Encouragement of settlement was not by itself the dominant objective until the Homestead Act of 1862, and land sales nonetheless continued long after because the act's burdensome requirements to "prove up" a claim often made "free" land costly to obtain. The early national government also wanted to settle the land as a bulwark against other nations' claims, but as the proprietor of the land, Congress wanted to get the best price it could.

The development of national land-sale policies was informed by some of the same problems encountered by modern developers of large-scale "planned communities." Modern developers seldom build all their homes and then put them on sale. Instead, they build them in phases, using the early sales to help finance and market later construction. To attract early customers, developers unilaterally institute a private governance mechanism, usually by establishing a self-governing "community association." The constitution of the association, which always requires a supermajority to alter, assures early buyers that the developer or other residents will not radically alter the plans after they have bought (Barzel and Sass 1990; Evan McKenzie 1994).

The developer is also subject to a political risk in this early stage. The initial homebuyers who become association members might prefer to have less development than the original plan intended, or they might use their leverage to exact some concessions that the developers did not anticipate. To forestall this, most developers, who own the unsold lots, allocate three voting shares to each unsold lot while granting only one voting share to lots already sold (Uriel Reichman 1976). This means the developer will hold a majority of voting shares in the community association until three-quarters of the lots are sold. Even if all the new owners in a half-built-out community want a policy that alters subsequent development, they will be outvoted by the developer. This assurance that the initial plan can be carried out enables the developer to attract investors and lenders in the first place.

2.3 The Northwest Ordinance of 1787 Enhanced Land Value

The first systematic attempt to dispose of the nation's newly acquired land was the Ordinance of 1784, which provided for the establishment of new states, and the Land Act of 1785, which provided for the sale of the land. The laws can get confusing. The Ordinance of 1784 was superceded by the famous Northwest Ordinance of 1787. Both had to do with *governance* of the territories and the process of admission to the Union. The Land Act of 1785 dealt solely with the surveying and private *sale* of land. Governance and sales were obviously related, and sometimes the 1785 and 1787 laws are collectively thought of as the Northwest Ordinance, but there are reasons to analyze them separately. (My discussion of these laws owes much to Peter Onuf [1987].)

The Ordinance of 1784—the first governance law—was largely conceived by Thomas Jefferson, who was an ardent promoter of an agrarian West, one with land owned by resident farmers rather than distant landlords and speculators. He envisioned a process in which small states with predetermined boundaries were rapidly settled and admitted to the Union. Jefferson's plan called for almost immediate self-government by the pioneer settlers. There was to be no "colonial" period, just a vague and contingent reservation of Congressional authority until the new state was admitted to the union. The constitutions of the new states were also to be more-or-less freely chosen. The Ordinance of 1784 required that a new state's initial constitution and laws use as a template those of an existing state, but there were no restrictions on altering the new constitution or prescribing a bill of rights or governance structure other than that it be a "republican" form of government. Education was not mentioned.

Settlement under this legislation turned out to be much slower than anticipated. One of the problems identified by Jefferson's friend, James Monroe, was that prospective settlers worried about the lack of a governance structure. It was all well and good that new states would be admitted on equal terms with older states, but how would law and order be enforced until they were admitted? For a prospective buyer of wilderness land, lack of interim governance was a serious anxiety. Even the previously established French communities in Illinois, whose ownership rights were recognized, subsequently complained about being left "in a state of nature" that they regarded as unpleasantly Hobbesian (Onuf 1987, 52).

But local self-governance also was a problem for Congress. Its representatives clearly worried that initial residents of the western territories might use their local powers to exploit the remaining unsold land for their own benefit rather than for its owner, the United States. The Ordinance of 1784 recognized this hazard and tried to deal with it by inserting a clause that forbade the new states from interfering with the sale of federal holdings or taxing the government's land. Like modern developers, Congress was concerned that early settlers might seek to use their local government powers to improve their position at the expense of the original owner.

Monroe and other members of Congress (the Articles of Confederation had a unicameral legislature) still fretted that the absence of an initial government in the Ordinance of 1784 was retarding the sale of land. Its successor, the Northwest Ordinance of 1787, addressed these governance problems by setting up an immediate, interim government that temporarily gave most of the power to Congress and its designated officials. In form it looked like a state government, with a judicial branch, a governor, a "legislative council" (analogous to a senate), and a popular legislature. But only the last office was elected by the residents of the territory. All the judges and the governor were appointed solely by Congress, and the appointed governor had absolute veto power over popular legislation. The senate-like legislative council was selected by Congress from a slate of candidates nominated by the popular legislature. (This compresses the population-dependent stages of territorial governance, which are described by Robert Hill [1988].)

Nowadays celebrated as a precursor to the national Constitution that was being drafted in the same year, the Northwest Ordinance was not especially democratic, at least as viewed by the settlers of the new territories. Indeed, even those members of Congress who supported it referred to it as "colonialistic." They defended it as an essential interim step toward the creation of new states. It provided a secure government that settlers could rely on to defend them from external threats and settle internal disputes. But it was also the product of the same anxiety of modern-day community developers. Pioneer settlers might prematurely seize the apparatus of government and adopt laws that would divert the profits of land sales to themselves. The undemocratic temporary government both assuaged prospective buyers and assured Congress that the value of its lands would be preserved by its own representatives.

Looked at in this light, the famed bill of rights in the Northwest Ordinance of 1787 takes on a different function. The tight rein that Congress held on the territories might calm the law-and-order anxieties of prospective settlers, but settlers might reasonably worry that these unelected officials would turn into oppressors. The period between territorial status and statehood was likely to be longer than that which Jefferson had envisioned in the now-superceded Ordinance of 1784, since the minimum population for admission was more than doubled. One way to dampen anxieties about oppression would be to insert some restraints on territorial government action in the form of a bill of rights. The Northwest Ordinance guaranteed religious toleration; proportional representation in the legislature; common-law rights to jury trials, habeas corpus, and bail; moderate fines and punishments; compensation for property taken by the government; and protection of contractual liberty.

The reason for my digression about the origins of the Northwest Ordinance is to establish that its features were consistent with a congressional desire to maximize the value of the public domain. Its influence was greater than that, of course. Many of its features were later turned into "usable history" for opponents of slavery and advocates of religious freedom. (Interestingly, the Northwest Ordinance did not guarantee freedom of speech.) Taken in its immediate context, however, the Northwest Ordinance was an attempt to deal with a problem that is still familiar to community developers: how to create self-government without losing control of your own assets. As will be argued presently, this problem also shaped the establishment of school districts.

2.4 National Land Policies Responded to Popular Demand for Schools

The "Ohio Company," named for the object of its desire, not its members' origin, was the first company successfully organized to purchase land and settle the new territory north of the Ohio River. Many of its members were former soldiers in the Continental Army. Part of their pay had consisted of promises from the cash-strapped Continental Congress that entitled them to so many acres of land in some unspecified area of the newly independent nation. Although it may seem unromantic to say so, this method of payment was similar to modern corporate stock options as pay for CEOs and other managers. The land certificates offered an additional incentive for the soldiers to win the Revolutionary War, because they would presumably be worthless—or worse, evidence of treason—in a British-ruled America.

The Ohio Company's proprietors, who originally numbered about 250, were mostly from New England, primarily Massachusetts, and so were their prospective settlers. As described in the previous section, Congress finally devised the two famous laws that provided a framework to sell the land and establish new states. Both the Land Act of 1785 and the Northwest Ordinance of 1787 were designed to make the federal lands inviting to settlers so as to sell it at the best price. The Northwest Ordinance was designed to appeal to the Ohio Company; indeed, it was largely drafted by its promoters. (The promoters were politically active and keenly aware of congressional debate about how best to settle the West, so one should not assume that they were truly the authors of the Northwest Ordinance.) Even before the Ohio Company appeared, however, the Land Act of 1785 made provisions for the sale of land that were based on a New England model (Dennis Denenberg 1979). New England had the excess population and scarcity of arable land that made its residents the most likely settlers of what we now call the Old Northwest, which includes the modern states of Ohio, Michigan, Indiana, Illinois, Wisconsin, and part of Minnesota.

The Land Act of 1785 initiated the national survey, which divided the land into square "townships" of thirty-six square miles each. Townships were surveyed so that they could be sold as entire units to groups of settlers or purchased as one-square-mile parcels (still universally called "sections") by individuals. This vast effort resulted in the square patchwork of land that one can see from an airplane (or via Google Earth) when flying almost anywhere west of the Appalachians (Ardo Linklater 2002).

The township method of settlement had originated in New England in the seventeenth and eighteenth centuries. Colonial authorities would grant large parcels of land, usually on the order of six-by-six miles in size, to groups organized as "proprietors" (Roy Akagi 1924). Early proprietors were usually also settlers of the new towns, but both resident and nonresident proprietors made it their business to make *Profits in the Wilderness* (1991), as the title of John F. Martin's book cleverly puts it. (Proprietors were distinguished from other town residents by their corporate entitlement to profit from the use and eventual sale of the remaining "common" land in the township.) New England proprietors would attempt to get other settlers, often connected to a parish church in a previously settled town but not necessarily religiously motivated, to purchase subdivided land within the new town. As an inducement to settlement, colonial authorities and early town proprietors regularly promised, and sometimes delivered, essential public infrastructure such as roads and land whose rent was earmarked to support churches and schools.

For almost two centuries before the Land Act of 1785, both public and private developers of wilderness lands used education as bait for attracting settlers. In the seventeenth century, the colonies of Virginia, Maryland, Massachusetts, and Dutch New York used land grants for education as inducements for settlement (Lawrence Cremin 1970, 177, 306). Fledgling towns in Massachusetts often sought to have land grants donated for schools by the colonial authorities, the better to promote settlement. Both the larger colony and the towns' proprietors stood to gain from further settlement of their towns. Dedication of particular parcels of land within the town for financial support of education was a device by which prospective land buyers could be assured that they would not be stuck with lots in an uncivilized wilderness.

The process could be competitive. The Susquehanna Land Company in 1768 offered settlers of the Wyoming Valley (the environs of Scranton, Pennsylvania) the benefit of land grants to support schools and colleges (James Wickersham 1886, 75). Eleazer Wheelock, the founder of my home institution, Dartmouth College, was given five hundred acres of land for the college by the colonial governor of New Hampshire as a way to encourage settlement in the then-untamed wilderness of the upper Connecticut River Valley. Wickersham in his Pennsylvania history noted that the Susquehanna Land Company had also tried to lure Wheelock to the Wyoming Valley with a land grant. (And to think I could be writing this in Scranton!) In his review of the practice, Benjamin Hibbard (1924, 309) concluded that "the principle of giving land for educational purposes was well established before the adoption of the Ordinance of 1787."

The principle continues to this day. The main draw for many buyers of homesites in the Disney Corporation's new town, Celebration, Florida, was the promise of a new and innovative public school (Frantz and Collins 1999). Disney went to the extraordinary trouble of persuading Osceola County to relinquish control over schools in the new town in order to be able to hand over management of its school to a group of progressive educators. Many people bought homes in Celebration primarily for the school.

It initially turned out to be problematic. Parents were less than delighted by the nonstandard schools that were started on the Disney dime. They were surprised to learn that progressive education did not involve tests, report cards, age grading, or curricular standards. The Celebration parents—allied with homeowners who had no children but regarded the school as an important asset of the community they had bought into—in short order ousted the education theorists and worked hard to make the school into a good example of the universally interchangeable schools that homebuyers actually want. (Celebration's experience is a microcosm of a larger story about the failure of progressive education methods in the United States, as described by Tyack and Cuban [1995].)

2.5 The School Section Was an Endowment, Not a Campus

Schools in the late eighteenth century were not necessarily publicly funded, but it was important to settlers of original New England towns that some provision be made for them. As a result, Congress thought it a good idea to include a subsidy for schools in the Land Act of 1785, since New Englanders were the most likely settlers. The national government had no money to spare, so its inducement came in the form of the currency it had in great quantity: land. The Land Act of 1785 specified that for each new township surveyed, one of the middle-most of the thirty-six square sections should be reserved "for the maintenance of public schools, within said township." This was the "sixteenth section" or "school section" of the townships laid out and numbered by the public land survey system (Linklater 2002). The location of the school section is indicated in figure 2.1. Many states later created political units and school districts along the lines of their congressional townships, and these political townships were often modified to account for geographic and settlement patterns that did not conform to the uniform survey grid.

Many people today assume that because of its central location, the sixteenth section was intended to be the campus of the school for the township. This illustrates how difficult it is to recreate in out minds the conditions of two hundred years ago. Not only were there no motor vehicles, but roads were very poor and draft animals could seldom be spared to haul farm children to a central school site. So children had to walk to school, and a

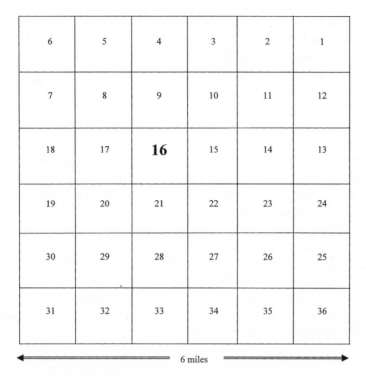

6	5	4	3	2	1
7	8	9	10	11	12
18	17	**16**	15	14	13
19	20	21	22	23	24
30	29	28	27	26	25
31	32	33	34	35	36

◄——————————— 6 miles ———————————►

FIGURE 2.1 Location of the sixteenth section dedicated to schools in the congressional township of the public land survey system.

walk of more than two miles over irregular terrain was not considered to be acceptable.

Instead of transporting the children to school, schools were brought to the children in the small, one-room school houses that were dotted across the township. Thus there would have been anywhere from five to twenty one-room schools within the township, depending on terrain, the population density, and neighborhood amity. The default arrangement in the upper Midwest was nine school districts in the thirty-six–square mile township, which yielded districts of about four square miles and walking distances of less than two miles from the farthest farmstead to the school (Wayne Fuller 1982, 44). Most of these schools were governed by a separate school district rather than by the township or county.

The function of the sixteenth-section reservation, then, was not as a campus for schools but as an endowment for the schools within the township.

Land within the designated section could be rented to farmers or other land users, and the income was dedicated for education. For states admitted to the Union later in the nineteenth century, the federal school land donation was pushed up to two or more sections, apparently to compensate for the low value of land in arid states (Fairfax, Souder, and Goldenman 1992). As the century wore on, states were permitted by Congress to sell the land outright and use the money for a "perpetual fund" to support education.

The congressional township and the sixteenth-section reservation predated the admission of western states. The federal government initially expected to sell land to groups of settlers who would then populate the township, as had been the colonial-era practice in New England. But that happened only occasionally in the new American territories, and land sales did not live up to Congress's hope. With a great deal of land sitting on the market and generating no revenue for Congress, the government soon agreed to sell land in units smaller than sections to individuals. Surveyors subdivided townships into quarter sections (160 acres) and even quarter-quarter sections of forty acres, and sales of the public domain improved early in the nineteenth century (Linklater 2002).

As a result of piecemeal sale of land within a township, residents did not necessarily have much in common with one another except for their collective entitlement to the revenues from the sixteenth section to support local schools. Unlike New Englanders, who from the beginning saw their township (or, as it is called here, the town) as a comprehensive unit of government, purchasers of the western public domain formed municipal governments from geographic configurations that often did not conform to the borders of a township. School districts for one-room schools were often formed across township boundaries (Fuller 1982, 44). The nearest neighbors who would join a school district might be just down the valley but in a different township or even a different county. For example, schools in Iowa and the Dakotas were originally organized along township lines, but as settlement proceeded, subdistricts were formed within the townships and eventually ignored township and county boundaries (Paul Theobald 1993, 61). Even state boundaries were not necessarily sacrosanct. One-room school districts in Daggett County, Utah, originally drew students and revenue from neighboring Wyoming and Colorado (Donald Baxter 1959). (Two modern interstate school districts will be described in section 5.2.)

Another reason for fragmentation was that the township's sixteenth-section endowment was often not available until the township itself became settled, and schools were demanded before that time. Settlers often started schools on their own without public funds. In his detailed examination of an early-nineteenth-century settlement in Illinois, John Faragher (1986, 126) concluded that "the most reliable support for education came from parent subscriptions, often paid in butter or eggs. A prospective teacher circulated among the households in the area with a 'subscription paper,' and parents put down the number of scholars they wished to send, at a set fee for the three-month term." The school was later replaced by a public school financed by taxes and the school-section endowment after enough land had been sold. Sometimes a school was established with the specific understanding that public support would be available in the future. An enterprising Kansas pioneer in the 1880s started her own school and school district with private subscriptions in anticipation of public money being forthcoming when enough homestead land was "proved up" to generate local taxes (Joanna Stratton 1981, 161).

2.6 "Religion, Morality, and Knowledge" Assured New England Land Buyers

The process by which new states were formed was initially governed by the Northwest Ordinance of 1787, and its successor acts were largely true to its principles. Like its predecessor Ordinance of 1784, the Northwest Ordinance advertised its anxieties that residents of the new territories would adopt schemes contrary to the national interest. Congress worried in particular that territories and new states might try to interfere with the disposal of federal lands by, say, giving in-state residents more favorable title conditions than out-of-state buyers. By so limiting the market, the federal government's land would sell less readily and at a lower price. So Article 4 of the Northwest Ordinance forbade the territories or subsequent states from such interference, declaring in part:

> The legislatures of those districts or new States, shall never interfere with the primary disposal of the soil by the United States in Congress assembled, nor with any regulations Congress may find necessary for securing the title in such soil to the bona fide purchasers. No tax shall be imposed on lands the property

of the United States; and, in no case, shall nonresident proprietors be taxed higher than residents.

Perhaps to mitigate the impression of a Scrooge-like grasp on its land, Congress in the Northwest Ordinance pointed out that the new territories and the states formed from them could offer an education. The first sentence of Article 3 (not part of the Ordinance's bill of rights) reads: "Religion, morality, and knowledge, being necessary to good government and the happiness of mankind, schools and the means of education shall forever be encouraged." This was lifted almost verbatim from the Massachusetts Constitution of 1780 and was aimed at the Ohio Company and successive settlers to help market their land.

The "religion, morality, and knowledge" clause in the Northwest Ordinance has since been taken to be a commandment to establish public schools. The exhortation is prominently carved in the entablature of Angell Hall at the University of Michigan and doubtlessly on other temples of public education in the Midwest. Because the clause is restated almost verbatim in numerous state constitutions that followed, the Northwest Ordinance has been regarded as the fountainhead of education in the West (Harold Hyman 1986). This is a bit doubtful. A cynic might note that the education clause was paired in Article 3 with an even more elaborate exhortation to deal fairly with the Indians, and one might infer from subsequent events that Congress did not expect either to be honored too strictly.

The not-so-cynical reason for doubting its foundational importance is that the "religion, morality, and knowledge" phrase, which found its first expression in the Massachusetts Constitution, was not actually a guarantee of public education, let alone a founding principle. Schools had been long established in the Commonwealth, largely because, as I have previously noted, settlers in New England towns wanted schools. The Massachusetts clause seems instead to have been a way of promoting nonsectarian Protestant religious values via the schools rather than by government-supported churches (Nathaniel Wiewora 2007). Both the Northwest Ordinance and the Massachusetts Constitution of 1780 had separate and almost identical clauses for religious toleration. But Massachusetts was not yet ready to break all ties between religion and the Commonwealth, which, after all, had started out as a Puritan theocracy and continued to allow support of Congregational Churches with local tax revenues into the nineteenth century. The "religion, morality, and knowledge" clause served as a conservative balance. The step toward religious toleration was balanced by a constitutional assurance that public schools could still instill faith-based virtues in the young.

Thus the education clause of the Northwest Ordinance served the same purpose as the Land Act's school-section grant. Both were designed to make prospective settlers from New England feel that their native institutions would be easy to reestablish in the new wilderness. The clause did not establish education as a right. Education was already widely established, and few people thought of it as a "fundamental right" deserving inclusion in state or federal bills of rights. Summarizing the congressional debates about the Land Act of 1785 (which established the "school sections"), Howard Taylor dryly concluded, "The thought of laying a permanent foundation for a public school system seems not to have entered into the discussion of the matter" (1922, 13).

By all accounts, education was intended to make land more attractive to the yeoman settlers who would most enhance the value of the land. Congress worried that less-reputable settlers would threaten the security of its holdings, and the school-section donation and the incantation of "religion, morality, and knowledge" were indicators that ruffians and adventurers were not welcome. Noble sentiments in this case also served to increase the sale value of the land. Of the 1787 Northwest Ordinance, Taylor concluded, "the provision for education in the ordinance was one of the special inducements which encouraged the purchase of lands and settlement in the Northwest Territory" (1922, 52). Secretary of the Treasury Albert Gallatin argued at the time of Ohio's admission (1805) that congressional donation of school lands to the new state "would increase the value of the remaining lands and hence would involve no loss to the [federal] government" (quoted in Gates 1968, 289).

Education was not the only aspect of the 1787 Northwest Ordinance that was designed to lure New England settlers. The prohibition against slavery almost surely served the same purpose. It was not inserted by Yankee abolitionists over the objections of Southern slave owners. It was inserted by a committee of five representatives, three of whom, including the chair, were from the South and owned slaves themselves (Taylor 1922, 40). The reason had little to do with congressional scruples about slavery. It had much to do with federal revenue from land sales. Prospective buyers of land, particularly the Ohio Company from Massachusetts, did not want to settle on land with slave owners and slaves as neighbors. Historian Peter Onuf (1987, 111) concluded that "because slavery might deter

industrious settlers from New England—the best available source—
southerners did not hesitate to vote against the extension of slavery across
the Ohio." (Slavery also discouraged settlement by white freeholders in
the rural South, as I discuss in chapter 5, and undermined the establishment of local schools in that region.)

Given the influence of the "religion, morality, and knowledge" clause,
one might ask why the 1785 Land Act did not also reserve land for the
support of churches, as had been common in New England town grants. A
church grant was in fact proposed by the drafters of the ordinance and its
predecessors. However, as Daniel Elazar (1988, 2) explained, "The proposition failed by a narrow vote—not because religion was not to be encouraged, but because of the denominational pluralism anticipated among
the new settlers." Church lots worked as settlement subsidies in early,
monoreligious New England, but they would either be too costly (because
of the number of possible sects) or create too much discord in what Congress knew would be a multireligious (or at least multisect Protestant)
West. Schools had the virtue of appealing to a wide range of denomina-
tions and so were the most common denominator to attract settlers. Later
congressional land grants in territory west of the Mississippi supported
court houses, prisons, and universities, all of which had appeal to potential
settlers, and all calculated to attract a broad spectrum of land buyers.

2.7 Statehood Created Tension about the Control of Congressional School Lands

The Northwest Ordinance provided a framework for admission of new
states to the union, but admission was not automatic. Territories that met
the minimum population required for statehood were granted enabling
acts by Congress to write a state constitution. The constitution had to be
approved by two parties. One was the inhabitants of the proposed state,
and the other was the Congress of the United States. This set up a tension
with respect to unsold federal lands remaining within the proposed state.
As noted above, the ordinance itself in Article 4 attempted to forestall
new-state opportunism by forbidding territories and states from interfering with federal land sales.

A conflict more difficult to resolve in advance was the vesting of school
lands. The 1785 Land Act specified that the school-section reservation
was only for the benefit of residents of the township. But this was not

an especially fair or efficient way to fund schools. In a typical example, the school section of the Illinois township examined by Faragher (1986, 127; described in section 2.5 above) happened to be a fertile, well-drained square mile, and its rental and eventual sale provided generous support for township schools by the mid-1800s. But the school section of the township just south of it was barely arable and incapable of even half the revenue of its richer neighbor. For a time, children from the poorer township were allowed to attend the schools of its richer neighbor, but only if they paid a supplementary tuition. School-finance inequality started early in American history.

It was soon clear to most authorities that it would be better for a unit of government larger than the township to manage and distribute the funds derived from the sixteenth section. Steps were taken in that direction over time, but the ultimate, seemingly most sensible step, was to simply vest the school lands in the state government when it came time to grant the territory statehood (Gates 1968, 289). The logic of state control was obvious, but it risked the possibility that the state might use the federal school-section funds in a way that did not benefit the lands still owned by the federal government. If Ohio, for example, were given the right to control school-land funds without qualification, the state might spend a disproportionate amount of it on schools in the Cincinnati area, leaving the rural areas north of the Ohio River, where the unsold federal lands were located, with little or no benefit. The sixteenth-section grant would still benefit the state of Ohio, but it would not necessarily help the federal government get the best price for its unsold land.

Evidence that the federal government cared about this is from rejected proposals by new states to use any part of the school lands to support education outside of their original locus. Missouri, for example, proposed using half the school-land revenue for an academy of higher learning in St. Charles County, which is next to St. Louis (Taylor 1922, 106). Congress would not grant its permission, insisting that teaching basic skills was more important. Equally important, one might infer, was that a remote academy would not help sell as-yet undeveloped federal lands. An attempt to obtain land grants for county seminaries (which offered more advanced education) in Arkansas was similarly rejected (Gates 1968, 297). Inverse evidence of the federal concern about keeping school revenues local was its treatment of college and university grants. The endowments for these were initially entire townships and, after the Morrill Act of 1863, simply any federal land the state wanted to use as its "land scrip"

(Vernon Carstensen 1962). The national government expressed little concern about the location of the university itself, since it was expected to benefit the entire state, and not just a locale where Congress still owned unsold land.

An exhaustive work by Fletcher Swift (1911) detailed the progress of the school-lands issue over the next hundred years, when most of the remaining states were admitted. Statehood was always a negotiated event, and negotiations were greatly influenced by larger events, such as the controversy over the extension of slavery, the Mexican War, discoveries of gold and silver, the Civil War, and the development of railroads and cities. (These are described for each state by Gates [1968], who does not, however, mention much about how school-land revenue was to be distributed within the state.) The constant of prospective-state negotiations with Congress that Fletcher Swift highlights was whether the school lands were to be vested in the township or in the state government.

Initially, the township remained the sole unit that benefited from school lands. With the admission of Michigan in 1835, Congress allowed the state to assume control of the school lands and pool the profitable with the barren sections in various townships for the benefit of common schools. But Michigan's admission did not establish an invariable rule. Some later states were admitted with the previous township-vesting rules. It was clear that Congress still cared about how the funds were distributed within the state. Yet it was also obvious that township-specific school funds were a cumbersome way to assist education.

2.8 State Constitutions Assured Congress about School Lands

One resolution of the tension about vesting seems to have been for the new states to declare their commitment to an evenhanded distribution of education funds in the constitutions that they submitted for approval to Congress. Mimicry was one way of showing commitment. Tyack and James (1987, n.p.) note that in the years after the Northwest Ordinance, "at least 17 states adopted language about schooling in their constitutions that closely resembled that of the Ordinance of 1787 and the Massachusetts constitution of 1780." Tyack and James go on to explain, "In part, this copying was an obligatory bow towards their patron, Congress, acknowledging the purpose of the public lands granted to new states for schools." My addendum to Tyack and James's insight is that insistence on this "obligatory bow" was prudent because Congress still had land for sale whose value was partly contingent on the local availability of schools.

It is possible, of course, that such clauses would have been inserted even if the federal government had sold all its land in the state and cared little about its future value. Most states wanted to attract more settlers, and perhaps inserting a popular clause in their constitutions would attract more prospects. But other provisions in the constitutions of new states are more explicit about federal land issues. In addition to inserting the "religion, morality, and knowledge" clause, state constitutions formed under the Northwest Ordinance added language assuring that federal endowments would not be diverted to other purposes and that the school system would not show partiality to one group or region within the state. Ohio's original Constitution of 1802, stated in Article 8:

> that no law shall be passed to prevent the poor in the several counties and townships within this state from an equal participation in the schools, academies, colleges and universities within this state, which are endowed, in whole or in part, from the revenue arising from donations made by the United States, for the support of schools and colleges; and the doors of the said schools, academies and universities, shall be open for the reception of scholars, students and teachers, of every grade, without any distinction or preference whatever, contrary to the intent for which said donations were made.

Clauses like this appeared in the first constitutions (which had to be approved by Congress) of several states. The language addressing the use, preservation, and equitable distribution of revenue from federal school lands is explicit in Indiana (1816, art. 9, sec. 1), Mississippi (1817, art. 6), Alabama (1819, art. 9007), Michigan (1835, art. 9023.0), Arkansas (1836, art. 7, sec. 1), Florida (1839, art. 10), California (1849, art. 9, sec. 2), Minnesota (1857, art. 8), Kansas (1859, art. 6, sec. 3), South Dakota (1889, art. 8, sec. 2), and Oklahoma (1907, art. 11, sec. 2). (These were located online from the National Bureau of Economic Research/Maryland State Constitution Project: http://www.stateconstitutions.umd.edu/index.aspx).

In addition to these commitments, states inserted education clauses into their constitutions that would assure that settlers would be treated equally in school matters. Terms like "thorough and uniform" and "uniform system" and "thorough and efficient" cropped up with remarkable regularity in the constitutions of the newly admitted states (William Sparkman 1994, n.22). Given how little uniformity there actually was among the common schools before and after the new states were admitted, the constitutional rhetoric can best be interpreted as a commitment device. A commitment to a uniform, statewide system of education, even if it remained only an aspiration, was additional assurance to Congress that its school-section donation would still be available to attract buyers for its remaining land. (The clauses are important nowadays because many state courts have seized on them as a way to justify their role in the distribution of school funds.)

The enthusiastic tenor of the state constitutional clauses for education was vastly different from the crabbed view such documents had toward most other state enterprises, which were typically subject to detailed fiscal and procedural constraints. Tyack, James, and Benavot (1987, 45) document education's special constitutional regard with a sense of wonderment. The original thirteen states' constitutions had none of this enthusiastic language about equality and thoroughness in education, even though they were composed in the fervor of revolutionary equality. As Sparkman (1994, 572) remarked, "only six of the original thirteen states made any general reference to schools in their initial constitutions, although all states ultimately added an education article at some point in their history."

Tyack, James, and Benavot concluded that American states just regarded education as being a whole lot different than other government functions. My view is not necessarily contrary. Education was important, but not because state constitution drafters came up with the idea that it was important. Their constitutional enthusiasm was induced by the need to convince Congress that giving the state control over federal school-land revenue would not result in devaluation of federal land holdings. And the reason the federal government wanted to keep schools in the picture for every township was that settlers continued to be attracted by school subsidies. Thus what looks like a top-down subsidy was really a sensible, perhaps inevitable, response by those at the top (Congress and state constitution drafters) to the ubiquitous, bottom-up demand for local schools by prospective settlers.

2.9 The Decreasing Importance of the School Sections

Although control of funds from the school lands was a part of every state's admission negotiation, the importance of the school lands for funding education steadily declined throughout the nineteenth century. Even when rural land was an important source of wealth, it was unlikely that its annual rent accounted for more than 20 percent of national income. (It is now less than 10 percent.) A single section was 1/36 of the township area, so at best it would generate income equal to about one-half of 1 percent of a township's income (1/36 times 20 percent is 0.55 percent). Public education (K–12) nowadays takes about 5 percent of national income. Adjusting that downward for nineteenth-century school conditions (shorter terms and fewer years of schooling, but more children per family) might mean that as little as 2 percent of township income would be required for regular public schools. Thus even on this optimistic scenario, the sixteenth-section grant would cover a little more than a quarter (0.55 percent divided by 2 percent equals 27.5 percent) of then-reasonable education expenses.

Covering one-quarter of expenses would not have been bad, but in fact the school funds were badly mismanaged both at the state and local level. (This is dealt with in detail by Swift [1911].) Many states would sell the school land and invest the proceeds to generate "perpetual" income. They would often attempt to earn interest by lending it to specific borrowers. Many of these loans did not work out, not least because some were politically motivated or just plain stolen or, in the case of the South, lost during the Civil War. If states relied on renting the sixteenth-section lands and pooling the revenues, they created a commons problem. The townships would become indifferent to how much revenue was generated from the sixteenth section it happened to control, since their share was a small fraction of the total pool. Local lessees of school land would lobby the township and the legislature for favorable (to them) rents, thus reducing the income (Oscar Davison 1950; Taylor 1922, 94). By 1840, funds in the midwestern states resulted in revenues that were barely sufficient to "keep school for two or three weeks a year" (Fuller 1982, 28). The desirable norm at the time would have been about twenty weeks of schooling.

Financial mismanagement along with the declining share of agricultural land rent in the economy and the increasing support for education from other sources meant that the school lands became a trivial fraction of education finance by the end of the nineteenth century. Swift (1911, 198) gives figures suggesting that it was less than 5 percent even in states where the fund had not been badly mismanaged. (Swift's work remains the definitive book-length work on the subject most probably because of this decline.) Florida's school-section money dropped from 29 percent of school spending in 1870 to 2.2 percent in 1905. So small was the amount that in Indiana—one of the states in which income from the school lands had remained vested in the townships—the state's other funds were sufficient to offset any advantage that an especially rich school section conferred on a township (*Quick v. White-Water Township*, 7 Ind. 570 [1856]).

Nowadays the remaining school lands—those that had not been sold or otherwise alienated—are such a small source of education revenue that serious thought has been given to converting them to park and conservation lands in the eight far-western states that still hold significant acreage (Fairfax, Souder, and Goldenman 1992). The trustlike constitutional language that designates the school lands as a source of "perpetual" funds for education nonetheless stands as a barrier to that diversion. Parks and wildlife reserves do not directly generate much school revenue.

It should be clear, however, that the original mission of the school-lands to encourage land sales is obsolete, since the federal government seems uninterested in selling the balance of the public domain, most of which constitutes the forests, rangeland, deserts, and mountains of the West. The original purpose of the trustlike limitations on the school-section grants has been fulfilled, as every state provides for schools in even the most remote corners of its territory. The role the school section had in promoting development has run its course, but its history is testimony to the public awareness of the role of schools in promoting land values.

2.10 The Efficient Schools Hypothesis and Land-Survey Determinism

An efficient social institution is one that allows people to accomplish their goals in the least costly way, given resources available to accomplish those goals. The "given" is critical. If we had wings like birds, flying to nearby destinations would usually be more efficient than walking. But given that we are not endowed with wings, walking is the best we can do with what we have. The technological and geographic endowment of most nineteenth-century Americans is the "given" from which we must judge whether the one-room school was an efficient institution.

For most of the nineteenth century, one-room schools had terms that were irregular, attendance that was spotty, and teachers who were hardly trained and who seldom stayed on the job for more than a year or two. Most jarring to twenty-first-century Americans are the accounts of discipline in many of these schools. It was strict and physical. Questioning the material, let alone "authority," was rarely tolerated. Yet I maintain that this was an efficient system for the people who created it. A better system could have been had only by sacrifices which they could not reasonably make. My reason for belaboring its pedagogy is to help readers appreciate how radically different the present system of education is. The ungraded one-room school offers an alternative universe from which we can view modern school reforms.

Defending the one-room school on economic grounds is an uphill battle. For much of the nineteenth and twentieth centuries, nearly all professional educators—state superintendents of schools, faculty of teacher-training ("normal") schools, and various blue-ribbon commissions charged with solving the problem of rural decline—regarded the ubiquitous one-room schools and their methods as horribly inefficient (Paul Monroe 1940, 279). The one-room school was by 1900 regarded by educationists as an embarrassment. Theodore Roosevelt's 1908 Commission on Country Life singled out the one-room school as a drawback to rural progress and urged consolidation of rural schools into larger districts, each with at least one multiroom, age-graded school (Mabel Carney 1912). Even early nineteenth-century educators had little respect for it. Horace Mann, the still-revered state superintendent of schools in Massachusetts from 1837 to 1847, tirelessly worked for the consolidation of school districts and the establishment of age-graded schools throughout the Commonwealth and not just in urban areas.

Most of the American population in the nineteenth century was rural, and nearly all rural schools were one-room schools. (I will refer to them as "one-room schools," but the official statistics often called them "one-teacher" schools, since a few had small rooms for storage or recitations in addition to the main classroom.) Almost all one-room schools were the only school in their district. At the beginning of the century, almost every adult was a farmer, and as late as 1880, half of all American workers were engaged in agriculture. American farms were larger than those of the old country—land-extensive farming was long a basis for the nation's comparative advantage in international trade. As a result, American farmers seldom lived in villages. A farm operator's daily trek from village to farm would have been wastefully long and tiresome, and so farmers lived in widely spaced farm dwellings. Thus the local density of settlement was low throughout most of North America.

The survey system created by the 1785 Land Act divided territory west of the Alleghenies into squares instead of the European long field or some other, more communal layout. This has sometimes been held responsible for the isolated farmstead (Lowry Nelson 1949), but such surveyor determinism seems to overlook that the land system itself was a response to long-standing American demands for large farms. Immigrants to North America wanted to own land in fee simple and in large quantities (James Ely 1992). Quaint European villages and commons agriculture were what they were escaping. The descendents of peasants expelled from their common lands by European enclosures became among the most eager seekers of American land, for "none knew better than the dispossessed the urge to own a farm that could not be taken away" (Linklater 2002, 42). American land is also highly fungible. Had a different agricultural system been desired after settlement, the official township squares could have been reconfigured by private surveyors.

Land-survey determinism also fails to explain why irregularly shaped midwestern villages were carved out of the township squares without much trouble (John Reps 1965; see especially his account of the aptly named Circleville, Ohio). Traditional north-south street plans, said to be in the Cartesian grasp of the national survey, were also often altered when railroads went through a nascent town at a northwest or northeast angle. This is still seen in the obliquely oriented street plans of the older parts of such cities as Fresno, California; Billings, Montana; and Salem, Oregon, not to mention innumerable railroad towns such as Lincoln, Illinois; Elba, Nebraska; and Donnelly, Minnesota, whose modern street maps I compared to maps of nineteenth-century railroad locations. The villages' original streets parallel the railroad, in defiance of the original survey orientation, to facilitate cross-town movement of surface traffic.

2.11 The Pedestrian Logic of One-Room School Districts

Although railroads revolutionized long-haul transportation by the time of the Civil War, rural roads remained poor until the popularity of bicycling and automobiles goaded local officials to improve them around 1900 (Hal Barron 1992). Even if rural roads were passable, few farmers could afford to transport their children to school in horse-drawn vehicles. So children of all ages trudged on foot to one-room schools.

The necessity of walking gave the one-room district school its dimensions and dictated its ungraded pedagogy. With the possible exceptions of Abraham Lincoln and your great-uncle Harry, children could not be expected to walk more than two miles to school. Keep in mind that this walk was not on sidewalks with crossing guards. Snow-drifted, dusty, or muddy paths (depending on the season) were more the rule. Besides this, children were still important contributors to the family economy, and a long walk to school kept them from their chores and tired them as well. Wisconsin's first school law exempted property owners who lived more than two miles from the nearest school from district taxation (Lloyd Jorgenson 1956, 95).

Having to create a school within walking distance of rural homes also promoted coeducation. Historians remark with some wonder at the early and persistent mixing of boys and girls in the same schools. This was not because of any view that girls and boys should be treated the same (Tyack and Hansot 1992). Within one-room schools it was usual to seat boys and girls in separate parts of the room, and there were sometimes separate entrances for boys and girls (Vinovskis and Bernard 1978, 865). Coeducation was probably the rule because a separate school for the boys alone (or girls alone) would have required too great a catchment area and hence required too long a walk. This calculus carried over to the creation of age-graded schools. When Rochester, New York, established age-graded schools from its one-room districts in 1849, the question arose of whether to have separate schools for boys and girls. It was rejected not for enlightened reasons about gender equity but for economy. Separate schools would be more expensive (Lois Rosenberry 1909, 262). (As I will describe in chapter 5, the South's insistence on racial segregation was a diseconomy of scale that promoted oversize school districts and fewer opportunities for education for both whites and blacks.)

School districts in nineteenth-century America were truly neighborhood affairs. A typical example of school district configuration is illustrated by the 1871 map of Middlebury, Vermont, in figure 2.2. The town's land area is thirty-nine square miles (three more than a congressional township), so its thirteen numbered school districts would average a little less than three square miles each. (Some of the town's territory was not in a numbered district.) Population growth in a rural township during the nineteenth century would normally warrant more one-room schools and school districts rather than a larger school. Unlike modern school districts, one-room school districts seem to have subdivided fairly often (Carl Kaestle 1983, 113). For example, District 13 on the southern border of Middlebury (figure 2.2) is squeezed between Districts 1 and 2 and may have been a subdivision of them. District boundary changes were so common that an early history of Middlebury exempted itself from making an inventory: "The changes have been, and promise to be, so frequent, that it is more than the object is worth to trace here their boundaries" (Samuel Swift 1859, 367).

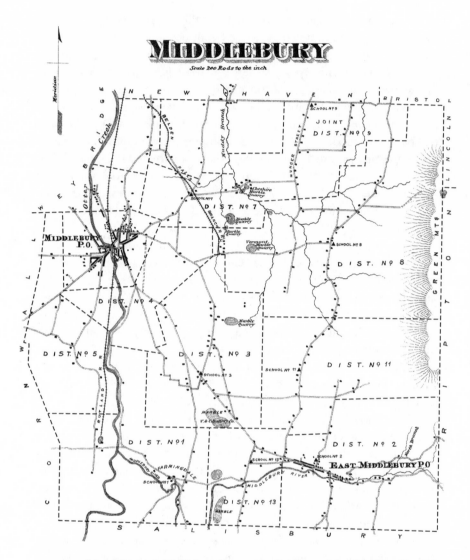

FIGURE 2.2 School districts in Middlebury, Vermont, in 1871 (Beers Atlas of Addison County). Digitized version courtesy of the Vermont Collection at Middlebury College Library and modified by Harp and Company, Hanover, NH.

Even in New England, where the township was the foundational political organization (rather than just a surveyor's convenience), neighborhood school districts could spill over town lines when practical geography warranted. An example in the northern part of Middlebury is "Joint District No. 9," whose schoolhouse is directly adjacent to the border with neighboring Bristol and New Haven, rather than centered in the populated part of the district. Some other Middlebury districts have no schoolhouse indicated on the map (e.g., on the western borders), and their children probably attended schools in neighboring towns or in the village of Middlebury.

2.12 The One-Room School's Ungraded Pedagogy

Aside from their generic and flexible district boundaries, the most important difference between one-room schools and modern schools was their method of instruction. Modern Americans have usually seen preserved examples or reproductions of one-room schools, with their tiers of benches or old desks, wood-burning stove, and the teacher's high desk. What is less widely known is their educational technology. Indeed, I have read sophisticated historians who referred in passing to the one-room schools of the mid-nineteenth century as having "all eight grades" in a single room.

There were no grades in rural one-room schools before 1870, and age grading continued to be more of an ideal than reality for most one-room schools up to about 1940 (Angus, Mirel, and Vinovskis 1988). Thus there was no "first grade" in rural schools in 1850, at least not in the sense that we now think of "first grade" as a time when six-year-old students are introduced to reading and other subjects. In rural schools before 1870, there were no promotion and graduation requirements from the common schools. Students just came and learned textbook lessons until the time spent out of school was more valuable to them than time spent in school. As one education historian summarized it, "Rural pupils worked their way through the available textbooks, recited what they knew to the teacher, and called it an education" (William Reese 2005, 67).

When children arrived at the beginning of a term at a one-room school, they typically brought their own textbooks. Although educators regularly decried the lack of uniformity in textbooks, publishers usually strove not to make them too different from one another (much like introductory texts in colleges today) in order to encourage their adoption. Historian Diane Ravitch (1995, 168) remarked that it was "striking how similar" various common-school textbooks were. The success of the McGuffey Readers, by far the most popular reading textbook in the late nineteenth century, had less to do with the quality of McGuffey's selections—though they were quite serviceable—than with their being so familiar that almost all parents would know that their children's teacher would use it. McGuffey and his publishers should be classified with Alexander Graham Bell and Bill Gates as entrepreneurs who created a network standard.

Within the first week of the new school term, the teacher (who was also often new to the school) would quiz his or her charges about how far they had gotten in various textbooks (readers, spellers, and arithmetic books) in the previous term they had attended or in their previous school. After obtaining this information and perhaps orally testing the students about their subject mastery, the teacher would sort students into recitation groups. Sometimes the "group" in a more advanced subject would consist of a single student, but more often there were five or six.

Membership in a recitation group was based on students' current knowledge, not their age. A six-year old who learned his ABCs at home could be placed in a more advanced recitation group than a nine-year old who had come to school for the first time and had had no home training. (The latter would be referred to as an "abecedarian" from his need to be taught the alphabet.) A ten-year-old girl who had gone to school every day in every term might be in an advanced geography group, while her older brother might be in a more elementary group because farm chores kept him from attending regularly. This method continued throughout the century with remarkably little change (Barbara Finkelstein 1989, 136). A former student in a one-room school in Kansas, circa 1880, recalled that "At the beginning of the term the teacher had to arrange the pupils in classes, for we had no formal grades. A new teacher sometimes asked each pupil what reader he was in the last term and classified him temporarily in that way, subject to promotion or demotion at some later time" (Marshall Barber 1953, excerpted in Tyack 1967a, 171).

The illustration in figure 2.3 below captures both the heterogeneity of age groups—at least the girl is clearly younger than the three boys—as well as the basic technique of recitation. The children seated in the background are studying lessons that the teacher had previously given them. They have to keep quiet so that the teacher can hear the recitations of the four before her. The four children in the foreground are being quizzed by the teacher. If she is unusually competent, she is asking them to explain what they read, correcting their errors, and perhaps offering an oral elabo-

FIGURE 2.3 An early-nineteenth-century one-room-school recitation group. Reprinted from Edward Eggleston, *The Circuit Rider* (New York: Ford, 1874), 270. Modified by Harp and Company, Hanover, NH.

ration of the material they have covered. If the teacher is more typical, she simply demands that they recite what they have read from memory. This particular teacher is drawn to look kindhearted, so perhaps she would not impose a physical punishment or public humiliation on students who fail to recite their lessons to her satisfaction. But if so, she would be un-usual among teachers, and the parents of her charges might complain to the school trustees on that account. Punishment was widely regarded as a necessary correction for academic failures, not just for social misdemean-ors (Finkelstein 1989, 96). One should not assume, however, that teachers could inflict punishment arbitrarily, and some were dismissed by the school board—or by the older boys—for excessive zeal in this department.

The subjects that were taught depended largely on what the teacher knew. They included at least reading and spelling, basic arithmetic, and writing and pen making—a teacher was expected to help students make their own from feather quills. Beyond the basic subjects, the list could vary, and as the nineteenth century progressed, the expected material could be quite broad if not deep. In the 1880s in California, the county-administered test to qualify one-room school teachers included arithmetic, grammar, geography, U.S. history, physiology (centering on the ill effects of alcohol), penmanship, composition, reading, single-entry bookkeeping, word analysis, spelling, music, and "practical entomology" (mainly crop pests in California). (The list is from May Cheney [1888].)

It is unlikely that many teachers actually had much knowledge about the aforementioned subjects. For most rural schools up to 1870, the minimum qualification for teachers was simply that they had attended a school like the one they were hired to teach in and had gone through the textbooks they were about to teach. Some rural teachers apparently did not meet even these minimal qualifications. One-room schools had a common pedagogy—memorization and oral recitation—but the only thing that brought any uniform standards to the curriculum was the use of common textbooks (Larry Cuban 1984, 19).

2.13 American Local School Directors and India's Truant Teachers

In the decades before the Civil War, the teacher's qualifying examination was usually conducted by one of the three locally elected school directors. The exam could thus be idiosyncratic, and a homegrown applicant usually stood a better chance of getting the job. This was not necessarily a bad thing. School directors themselves were often not well lettered (Fuller 1982, 83), so their examination was not an especially good filter against teacher ignorance. In these circumstances, choosing an applicant whom they knew had gone through the local school successfully—one outward sign of success would have been doing well in public spelling bees—may have been safer than an apparently more knowledgeable applicant whose pedigree was unknown. As the century progressed, the examination to qualify for a common-school teaching certificate became more standardized and centralized, usually at the county level. Teacher certification was an important function of the county superintendent, but arbitrary disregard of local preferences would make his tenure brief.

Local school directors in American one-room school districts were expected to monitor the performance of the teachers they hired. Their physical presence in the school was only occasional, but their role as paymasters had a benefit that underscores what people really meant by "local control." To illustrate this, I pass along a modern story from a developing country that faces issues in its rural areas that are similar to those of nineteenth-century American districts.

Rural elementary schools in India are often ungraded, and the school terms adjust to the rhythms of agricultural life, as in nineteenth-century America. However, the schools in India have a problem that I never heard of in my extensive reading about American rural schools. India's problem is that the teacher often does not show up to teach his or her charges (Michael Kremer et al. 2006). India's rural teachers are paid by a nonlocal government agency, typically the state. The pay is low but regular, and it is difficult to fire teachers without proof of misfeasance. The state government is remote and has few other representatives in the area. So when the teacher finds a more profitable activity for the day, he or she often does that instead of teaching school. Children show up for school, but the teacher is playing hooky, getting paid for being a teacher but not actually teaching.

American rural teachers, who were even farther removed from state supervision, were never truants of their own school. The reason is that the local school board was the paymaster. An unexcused absence of even a day would be immediately noticed. The local school board would be informed by taxpaying parents, and the teacher would be docked a day's pay. This was in the early part of the nineteenth century taken to the extreme of deducting Christmas Day from teachers' pay if they declared a holiday. Teachers often did give their pupils the day off (sometimes under the threat of student rebellion), but it was truly a gift from the teacher, since it meant one day's less pay. (A fictional but realistic account of this custom is Edward Eggleston's *The Hoosier Schoolmaster* [1871, chapter 8].)

2.14 Young Women Displaced Men as One-Room School Teachers

Many beginning American teachers had recently completed—that is, ran out of textbook material to learn—the same school in which they had been students a few months earlier. It was not uncommon for a female teacher to have male students who were older than herself, as girls attended more regularly than boys, who were expected to work on the farm after age ten or so. Even girls who did not become teenage teachers would often complete a common-school education at a younger age than boys. The more regular attendance of girls in one-room schools has consequences that historians need to take into account.

A count of young people enrolled in school at age sixteen and older in 1850 indicates at least 25 percent more boys than girls (Goldin and Katz 2008, 152). One might infer from this that boys at the time were getting a more advanced education. This cannot be rejected out of hand, but it should be kept in mind that some of those older boys were there because they had attended school only during the winter terms, while girls would often attend both summer and winter terms. The missing older girls may have just completed their common-school education sooner, and a few might even be teaching school.

Teaching was not well paid, but most evidence suggests that the wages were comparable to beginning wages in other occupations for which a "common school education" was a qualification. Joel Perlmann and Robert Margo (2001, 96) demonstrate that female teachers became the norm almost everywhere after the Civil War. The transition varied by region, with the more settled and educated regions embracing a female labor force sooner and more thoroughly. Women were almost always paid less than men, and the disparities persisted well into the twentieth century. The wage disparity was said by contemporaries to be due to the greater ability of men to physically control unruly boys, and men were most often hired to teach in the winter terms, when older boys who worked on the farm in other seasons were able to attend. I want to suggest an additional factor to account for the wage disparity and the displacement of men by women.

I had long thought that battles between boys and male teachers was a colorful legend, but nearly every sober account of rural teaching up to 1880 or so mentions this phenomenon (Finkelstein 1989, 95). The existence of physical conflicts between teachers and students so offends our modern image of education that we are apt to dismiss all aspects of the one-room school as barbaric relics (e.g., Theobald 1993). This may be too harsh, and it could reflect an anachronistic imposition of modern mores onto an earlier society. An account by a neophyte male teacher, D. S. Richardson (1883), indicates that the fighting was more ritualistic and less vicious than we might think. (I culled this from a Web site called "School Tales" [http://www.schooltales.net] created by David Safier, a retired teacher, and it is thick with similar stories, for which Mr. Safier provides useful context and commentary.)

Richardson spent a summer sometime in the 1870s (he was not specific) teaching thirty sons and daughters of ranchers at a one-room school in Lake County, California, 120 miles north of San Francisco. It was his first and apparently only term of teaching. As often happened to male teachers in one-room schools, Richardson was locked out of his school by the bigger boys and girls early in the term, and he had to fight to regain control. But instead of being a no-holds-barred contest, Richardson's account of the event sounds more like a game of "capture the flag" or "king of the hill." (See also Finkelstein 1989, 121.) After his first attempt to get back in failed—he readily conceded that the older boys were stronger than him—the girls who were locked inside with the boys actually helped him get in through an open window. Once he gained entry, he wrote that the "healthy, rosy lasses" helped him regain control of the building from the boys. Richardson noted that the battle, while strenuous and damaging to his clothing, was all pushing and shoving. No fists were thrown, and no weapons were brandished, even though the older boys routinely brought their guns to school and stacked them in a nearby shed.

After the teacher finally prevailed, he magnanimously forgave the boys for their trespasses—as they appear to have expected. The only real casualty was his clothing and some school fixtures. As the girls mended his rips, the boys repaired the schoolroom, and he later called a holiday and paid for some treats. After that, Richardson's summer of teaching went smoothly. He related that both he and his charges were tearfully regretful when the three-month term came to an end and he departed for his new career as a magazine writer.

It is hard to say how many schoolroom takeovers were done in this spirit—the mettle and humor of the teacher surely had a lot to do with it—but what sound to modern ears like educational catastrophes seemed to have been taken as part of the job by the men involved. But that prospect could have something to do with the rapid feminization of teaching from 1840 onward. (The fact that Richardson was able to place his story in a prominent magazine suggests that by 1883 such battles had become as unusual as men teaching in summer term.)

I encountered no stories of women fighting with or being assaulted by their students. In their book about the history of coeducation, Tyack and Hansot (1992, 68) confirm the near absence of physical intimidation of women by students. The universal norm of respect for women may have had an effect on the gender composition of the teacher labor force. Men had to endure the threat of student violence. Even when the violence was "friendly," it surely made teaching a less attractive job for many men. It could be that male teachers demanded a hazardous-duty premium, and school boards eventually decided that it was less costly and educationally more effective to hire women.

It is true, however, that multiroom, age-graded schools, which were developing in the late nineteenth century, hired at least one man to be the "principal teacher." One of his duties was to discipline troublesome boys that women teachers could not keep in line (Perlmann and Margo 2001, 94). This would seem to contradict my explanation for the feminization of one-room school teaching—the absence of conflict between boys and women teachers. But the most serious discipline problems in one-room schools were more easily avoided by having the student not attend for the term. He might be expelled or, more likely, just come to the conclusion that school attendance was not worth the conflict with that particular schoolmarm. The pedagogy of one-room schools allowed him to resume his studies where he left off when a more agreeable teacher (or a more mature student) appeared in some future term. Age-graded schools, however, required continuous attendance, for which compulsory attendance laws were eventually adopted (section 2.19 below). In an age-graded system, conflicts between boys and women teachers could not as conveniently be resolved by having the boy not attend.

2.15 Women Teachers Had to Stay Unmarried and Men Had to Keep Moving

Despite the common complaint about low wages by educational commentators, the teacher labor market seems to have regularly cleared. Teaching in a one-room rural school was for most of the nineteenth century regarded as a starter occupation, a way station on the road to another career. For women, the later career was almost always marriage and homemaking.

Married women seldom taught school. Most one-room school boards had rules against hiring married women and often made new hires agree not to get married during their teaching term (Perlmann and Margo 2001, 114), though there seem to have been exceptions in especially labor-short areas (Mary Cordier 1992, 88). The usual explanation for the practice was that teaching should be reserved for the breadwinner, so that a married woman would seem to be double-dipping. (This rationalization was actually more common in the twentieth century, especially during the Depression.) Given the legendary parsimoniousness of one-room school districts, this explanation is unconvincing. Excluding any fraction of the potential supply of teachers was surely costly to penny-pinching school boards. Gender prejudice seems unlikely to account for the practice, as *unmarried* women were increasingly employed in rural districts as the nineteenth century wore on.

A more plausible explanation is that being a farm wife—and, in short order, a mother—was a full-time job. Most farm wives were essential to their family's economic survival, and household management and child rearing before the arrival of rural electric power was a strenuous, full-time career. One-room school teaching was also a strenuous and time-consuming job. (For details on how strenuous it was even in the early twentieth century, see the teacher survey discussed in section 3.18.) So the prohibition on marriage may have been similar to modern-day teaching contracts, which usually prohibit holding two full-time teaching jobs simultaneously. The reminiscences of women who taught in one-room schools often remark on the antimarriage rule (Diane Manning 1990), but even feminist historians suggest that women teachers did not think it was entirely unreasonable (Kathleen Weiler 1998, 183). Perhaps they knew that attempting to do both jobs would have shortchanged at least one of them.

For men, a career after teaching could be almost anything that required literacy, but there were some who persisted as itinerate school teachers. They had to move because it was unusual for any teacher to stay at the same one-room school for more than a year or two, and most districts usually hired different teachers for the summer and winter terms, even after it became common for women to teach in both terms. This turnover rate seems to have persisted into the twentieth century. The one-room–school states of Nebraska and North Dakota were reported to have annual teacher turnover rates of 61 and 54 percent, respectively (Frank Bachman 1933). The states with the fewest one-room schools in Bachman's 1930 survey, Maryland and Virginia, had turnover rates of 13 and 16 percent.

School directors were said to prefer turnover, and it may not have been just a way to save taxpayers money or avoid teacher burnout. Turnover may have had some educational advantages as a risk-reducing strategy. In a modern, age-graded school, a student who does not learn much from a given teacher will usually not have that teacher in the following year. But in the ungraded one-room school, it is the disagreeable teacher who must be encouraged to move on, since students could be in the same classroom for several years.

Routine turnover had its drawbacks, of course, since it meant losing good as well as bad teachers. However, even a competent teacher's style could be helpful to some students and not to others. I read several accounts by former inmates of one-room schools who attributed almost all their education to one or two terms with a sympathetic teacher. John Swett (1900, 121), the first state superintendent of schools in California, gratefully recalled how a handful of his several one-room school teachers in his native New Hampshire taught him most of what he learned. Rapid turnover of teachers might have been a reasonable way of assuring that pupils who spent several successive terms in the same school would get one or two teachers from whom they would learn something.

2.16   Path Dependence? "The Most Unfortunate Law"

An enduring story about the creation of independent one-room school districts within townships and counties holds that it was just a political mistake. New England towns, those irregular prototypes of the six-by-six mile township created by the federal survey, were originally commanded by their colonial legislatures to create town-wide schools. The invariably cited source was a 1647 edict from the theocrats of Massachusetts. It is referred to by words extracted from its stated purpose as "the old deluder Satan" act (Cremin 1970, 181). The law required all towns above a certain size to establish schools—not necessarily publicly financed—so that children could learn to read the Bible and succumb not to the delusions of Satan but rather to the truths of the established church.

New England towns, goes the story, were originally settled in compact areas around a central common, and a single school was located there, financed by the town as a whole. But later settlers strayed from Eden and built houses and farms far away from the town center (Macy Campbell 1927, 281). The remote settlements—perhaps we would call them "rural sprawl"—were too far from the original school for their children to walk. Some towns dealt with this by establishing a "moving school," a town-supported institution that operated in different sections of the town at various seasons of the year (Monroe 1940, 118). Most towns, however, dealt with decentralization by establishing subdistricts—"common school districts"—within their boundaries with a more-or-less permanent school house in the center of each district. Although these were town institutions and entitled to some degree of town and state support, their separate districts soon became fairly independent in their governance, and they added local taxes, parent contributions, and volunteer labor as support for their local school (Reese 1995, 25). Variable educational outcomes were the inevitable result.

Horace Mann (1847, 37) lent credence to the fable of a lost ideal when he mourned as "the most unfortunate law on the subject of common schools" a 1789 statute that authorized Massachusetts towns to create submunicipal districts and tax themselves for schools. The impression given is that the one-room district school and its mostly self-financing governance was purely the product of legislation and could have been prevented had the lawgivers foreseen its consequences. In a formal sense, this may have been true—taxes could not easily have been collected without state authorization—but in a practical sense, the legislators had little choice given the distribution of the population. In any case, the law did little more than validate a system that had been developing for more than a century in Massachusetts (Burke Hinsdale 1898, 12).

Many of Mann's followers, who invariable advocated a more centralized system, lamented the growth of the decentralized settlement patterns elsewhere in the nation, which resulted in the political demands for submunicipal school districts (Davison 1950). Such a view overlooks the realities of an agricultural community in a country with a large amount of land. Farms had to be spread out in order for farmers to make a living, and the district system was a logical consequence in Massachusetts and every other state. Every state, including the South, had a generic version of the district system for most of the nineteenth century (Kaestle 1983; James Leloudis 1995). They were not slavishly following the "most unfortunate" example of early Massachusetts, as some historians continue to imply. There wasn't any other way to do schooling in rural America.

Voters' preference for local taxation and local control could nonetheless be thought of as a path-dependent outcome, even if the Massachusetts 1789 statute that Mann lamented was not its source. That is, the much-replicated system of district schools could have resulted from decentralization being a default position that no one had thought to challenge. The system would have evolved differently, this argument goes, if voters had been presented with a truly statewide system of finance at the outset.

Evidence to the contrary comes from what I would regard as a "natural experiment" that was brought to my attention by Kirk Stark (1992, 805). A decision by the Indiana Supreme Court, *Greencastle Township v. Black*, 5 Ind. 56 (1856), effectively outlawed the collection of local taxes for schools. The court's reason was not that schools should be discouraged, but that the legislature could not authorize localities to raise or lower local taxes for township and district schools. The newly adopted Indiana Constitution of 1851 authorized taxation for public schools, but it also had a separate clause that prohibited "special and local" legislation. Legislation authorizing localities to tax themselves to support local education ran afoul of this principle, said the *Greencastle* court.

What is relevant to the present task is that the *Greencastle* decision made state—as opposed to local—support for public schools the legal status quo. The legislature could have complied with the decision by raising a uniform statewide tax in support of schools. This it did not have the political will to do. Historian Emma Thornbrough (1965, 473) described the upshot:

> As a result, cities and towns drastically curtailed their educational efforts or abandoned them entirely. In some places public school buildings were rented to groups who operated them as private schools. In others, there were efforts to keep the schools open by soliciting voluntary contributions to supplement the funds contributed by the state, but these were largely unsuccessful. Many teachers were dismissed, and there was a general exodus of trained superintendents and principals to other states.

Voters clearly did not want to rely solely on a statewide tax system for education, even when they were presented with a choice between statewide funding and almost no public education at all. The preference for localism cannot have been a preference for doing the same old thing over and over again, since the *Greencastle* decision had taken that off the table. From this experience, it appears that the path-dependence story does not work.

Even the eventual restoration of local control in Indiana supports the idea that local voters actively supported education only if they could use local funds for it. According to Thornbrough, schools gradually revived after 1860 as some towns and cities used local taxes for public schools without the benefit of an enabling law. (How such taxes were collected without the enforcement power of the state courts was not made clear.) After the legislature failed to pass a constitutional amendment in 1863 to overrule *Greencastle* (it could not muster the necessary supermajority), the legislature in 1867 "simply adopted a law which re-enacted features of the laws previously invalidated" (Thornbrough 1965, 475). Most schools reopened and public education expanded. A challenge to this ad hoc defiance of the 1856 *Greencastle* decision belatedly reached the state supreme court in *Robinson v. Schenk*, 1 N.E. 698 (Ind. 1885). The *Robinson* court simply reversed *Greencastle* and similar cases, conceding that the legislature had largely ignored them and that the schools had prospered as a result of local support (*Robinson*, 1 N.E. at 699–700). It is difficult to imagine a modern court being so candid about its predecessor's misconceived decisions.

2.17 Mobility and One-Room Schools: Of Laura Ingalls Wilder and Abraham Lincoln

An underappreciated fact about nineteenth-century rural life is the great mobility of the population. Household mobility was actually greater than it was in the twentieth century (Claude Fischer 2002). Pioneers were by definition movers, but even the population of areas that had long-established farms relocated often. Early settlers encouraged immigration for the straightforward reason that it raised the value of their land. A study of western pioneers in the 1860s demonstrated that this was not a vain hope—early settlers' wealth was considerably greater than that of latecomers (David Galenson 1992). Farmers traded up to better land as they acquired more skill and capital, and immigrants from abroad added to the restless rural population.

An example of this mobility was one of America's most famous nineteenth-century families, that of Laura Ingalls Wilder, author of the semiautobiographical "Little House on the Prairie" series. I invoke her here because her books (or at least the TV adaptations) evoke in many people an image of rural stability. Laura was born in 1867 to a pioneer family in Wisconsin. Her parents moved eight times from the time she was born to the time of her fifteenth birthday. During her childhood, Laura entered a new school four times, though one was a return to a school previously attended.

Laura's attendance was irregular because of the family's moves, which were hardly unusual, and because she sometimes had to work to help make ends meet, an obligation that also was characteristic of family life in that era, as her biographer points out (John Miller 1998). Like many literate teenagers, Laura taught in one-room schools for a few short terms at age fifteen. She then continued her own schooling in a local institution that was an early version of high school. After she married Almanzo

Wilder at age seventeen, the couple moved at least four more times, finally settling in Missouri. Despite all this moving around, Laura's education cannot have been too bad. She started writing later in life and eventually wrote (with help from her daughter) the "Little House" books that made her an enormously successful author in the 1930s.

A better-known fact about farming in the 1800s was that it involved a great deal of child labor. Children were an important part of the family farm's labor force, and schooling usually had to fit into work on the farm. This plus the vicissitudes of weather, illness, and family crises all made for irregular and discontinuous attendance in rural schools. The one-room school's pedagogy was well adapted to these conditions. It was actually far better educationally than an age-graded system would have been, had such a system been practicable in the first place.

To illustrate its efficiency, consider the self-deprecating example of Abraham Lincoln. He once officially pronounced his education "defective" and said it amounted to little more than his learning to read, write, and "cipher to the rule of three." But this was actually pretty good for an American born in 1809. (The arithmetic skill he mentioned was a rule for solving proportions—"2 is to 4 as x is to 10"—and enabled those who mastered it to use carpenter's plans, compute total costs from partial information, and do elementary surveying.) As David Donald (1995) points out, Lincoln's education was actually better than that of most other Americans of the time. Professor Donald surmises that Lincoln deliberately downplayed his schooling in public statements in order to remind voters of his humble origins and not dwell on the fact that he was one of the most successful lawyers in Illinois.

Lincoln's formal education illustrates the strengths of the one-room school's ungraded pedagogy for the era's rural children. At ages five and six, Lincoln acquired basic reading skills in two short (less than three months) terms in a Kentucky school near his parents' homestead. His family then moved to Indiana, where Lincoln, age ten, attended a three-month term at a one-room school about a mile from the family cabin. His education was interrupted by the death of his mother and his father's need for him to work on their Indiana farm. At age fourteen and again at age fifteen or sixteen, Lincoln walked the fabled five miles to another school, attending only irregularly but nonetheless acquiring enough skill to continue his education on his own. He later taught himself enough practical math to become a surveyor, and still later he read law under an established attorney to embark on his career as a lawyer and legislator. For recreation during his two-year congressional career, Lincoln taught himself formal geometry by studying Euclid's *Elements*. His "Gettysburg Address" is commonly regarded as the best short essay in the English language. Some defective.

Had modern age-graded schools existed in Kentucky and Indiana at the time the Lincolns lived there, it is unlikely that young Abraham could have learned nearly as much as he did during his childhood. He would have left each school without completing a single year, and as a result he would always have had to start the same grade all over the next time he tried to attend. But his teachers in the ungraded one-room schools only had to find out how much he already knew about various subjects, and they could place him in the proper recitation group. The five separate school terms that he attended all gave him additional knowledge and skills. He never had to waste time by repeating the same grade.

Lincoln's experience was not exceptional; Lawrence Cremin (1980, 499) called it "a characteristic frontier education for its time." Children all through the nineteenth century attended school at irregular intervals, and the length and frequency of school terms themselves were subject to local discretion. The one-room school's pedagogy was well adapted to this pattern. For all their nonstandard features, American one-room schools had by 1850 produced the "most educated youth in the world" (Goldin and Katz 2008, 163).

2.18 One-Room Pedagogy and the Returns to Education

The point of the Wilder and Lincoln stories is not to extol the flexible virtues of the ungraded school's method—though it does have its modern enthusiasts. What I want to emphasize is that the one-room school and its ungraded pedagogy were efficient adaptations to the conditions of rural life. An age-graded system would have required too much walking to a distant, centralized school, which would have been necessary to assemble enough students to make up grades. Irregular attendance was the inevitable consequence of a mobile population and a labor-short farm economy.

Other characteristics of the rural ungraded schools are less easy to defend on efficiency grounds. The recitation method of teaching is by itself unexceptionable in a classroom whose students necessarily have widely varying abilities and accomplishments. The drawback of the method is not for those who are reciting, but those who are not, which in a heterogeneous classroom includes the vast majority of students. They have to be engaged in quiet study, which is not by itself bad, but in this case "study hall" constituted most of the school day. (This may be why I encountered no recollections of "homework" by former students of these schools.) Children who attend an age-graded school do not have nearly as much time outside of the teacher's attention. The one-room school-teacher's need to have most students quietly working may also explain why disciplinary issues frame so many accounts of the one-room school. (Nostalgic recollections about older children assisting the younger students seem to have derived from twentieth-century versions of one-room schools, in which the number of students was usually far smaller and more manageable than in the nineteenth century.)

Another drawback of the ungraded system was that so many teachers were poorly trained or personally unsuited for teaching. Before 1860, most teachers were young people who had little more academic training than their most advanced students. The early normal-school graduates usually headed directly to the cities and taught the age-graded classes for which they received their training. After the Civil War, some rural schools obtained recent high school or academy graduates (usually young women) as teachers. This was an improvement, but even then the rapid turnover of teachers persisted as a norm and discouraged much personal investment in teaching as a profession. In retrospect, the best way to have improved teaching in the nineteenth century one-room school would have been to hire better teachers and pay them wages that would encourage them to stay in the profession (if not in the same school) for more than a few terms.

Yet even this modest improvement might not have been cost effective in the rural setting. The economic returns to having more than a basic education were not especially high until the latter part of the nineteenth century (Goldin and Katz 2008, 167). The low return affected both demand and supply of teachers. Rural parents wanted their children educated enough to read, write, and manage some arithmetic, but going beyond that did not have much of a payoff. The modest expectations for education meant that most teachers were themselves modestly educated. Prospective teachers saw little return to obtaining more education themselves in order to teach in one-room schools, and few regarded it as a profession. The fledgling Iowa State Teachers Association, established in 1854, would not even accept one-room school teachers as members (David Reynolds 1999, 63).

2.19 The "Common-School Revival" Affirmed a Logical Trend in Education

One of the most famous movements in the history of American education was the "Common School Revival" of the 1820–50 era. (This was sometimes called the "Common School Crusade.") It was occasioned by concern that public education had fallen onto hard times after the American Revolution and was not meeting the expectations of the new republic. Its best-known leader was Horace Mann, but it included numerous others, such as Henry Barnard in Connecticut, Caleb Mills in Indiana, and John Swett in California, who were, like Mann, among the first heads of newly formed state departments of education. (Every state seems to have had at least one early leader who is "the Horace Mann of ___.") As described by David Tyack (1967b), the movement had four important goals. They were to establish the following:

1. public governance rather than private schools;
2. schools with all economic classes in attendance rather than separate public schools for the poor (no "pauper schools");
3. schools that did not preach any particular religion but still promoted nondenominational Protestant values, somewhat like twentieth-century YMCAs; and
4. schools funded entirely from public funds rather than based partly on tuition payments or "rate bills."

The Common-School Revival was successful in achieving these goals largely because, as Tyack contended, it was preaching to the choir: "The movement was more remarkable for the consensus it secured than for the conflict it aroused" (1967b, 121). Such opposition as there was came from taxpayers (at both ends of the wealth spectrum), proprietors of private schools, and religious and linguistic minorities. But opposition was sporadic and ineffective. National political figures of all persuasions endorsed public schools. It is true that state controls were sometimes resisted—the office of state superintendent of schools was occasionally dismantled during the century—but that was a reaction to what voters regarded as excessive state meddling in local school districts (Kaestle 1983, 115). The basic system advocated by Mann and his contemporaries had a life of its own. They got credit for leading a parade that was under way even at the beginning of the movement (Albert Fishlow 1966). Indeed, there is doubt

whether the quality of schooling in Massachusetts—Mann's home state—
had in the early 1800s suffered any significant decline, which supposedly
had triggered the "revival." Much of the contemporary complaining had to
do with the decline in the teaching of Latin, which practical-minded school
directors outside of Boston were unwilling to finance (Reese 1995, 25).

The school-founding elements of the Land Act of 1785 and the Northwest Ordinance of 1787, which preceded the crusade by a generation, were
the product of popular demand for education. This demand resulted in
the system desired by the crusaders largely because landowning voters
regarded public schools as essential for attracting buyers of their property. In rural conditions at the time, having special schools for different
religions, for boys and girls separately, or for rich and poor separately did
not make economic sense. There weren't enough people within walking
distance to set up separate schools. Even the town schools of seventeenth-
century Massachusetts, which were ordered to offer different levels of instruction, usually had too few students to run separate schools and instead
melded the entire student body, including girls, into a single one-room
school (Cremin 1970, 186).

Public funding also had widespread support. It had long been an element in school support in part because public and private life were not
strictly separated early in the nineteenth century (Cremin 1980, 165). Private academies, which were precursors to high schools, received considerable support from local and state governments throughout the nineteenth
century (Bruce Leslie 2001). Nor was religion a serious barrier. There was
little anxiety about using taxes to support sectarian schools before 1860
(Kaestle 1983, 119). The "Blaine Amendment" movement, in which most
state constitutions prohibited public aid for sectarian schools, did not arise
until after the Civil War. The Common-School Revival's campaign to raise
the public ante in the pre–Civil War era was building on a well-established
base of public support for education.

In almost all cases, there were at least two and sometimes three levels
of public funding. At the top was the state government, which distributed
state revenues from general taxation and earmarked endowments—funds
from the school sections—to local districts. (Over the course of the nineteenth century, Congress made supplementary donations to allow eastern states to share in the public-lands largesse.) The basis for the state's
distribution was usually the "school census," an annual count of district
residents who were eligible to attend public schools (Fuller 1982, 86).
Sometimes there was a minimum entitlement per school to account for

very sparsely settled areas, but the main basis was simply capitation. The typical age range for the school census was five to twenty-one. This makes it look as if children attended school for a very long time, but that imposes a twentieth-century "age-graded" view of schools on the ungraded one-room schools on the nineteenth. Children in that age range were eligible to attend school, but they did not have to attend school at any particular time.

To assure that state funds were not diverted to other uses, most states required that the receiving districts actually hold school for a minimum number of months. Again, there was little assurance that children would attend that long. Fuller (1982, 87) describes as typical a Wisconsin district that in 1882 had an enrollment of twenty-nine but an average daily attendance of thirteen. But continuous attendance was not all that critical in the one-room school. Later in the century, states began to adopt laws that compelled children to attend school for a minimum period. The impetus for such laws was concern that the children of immigrants and the poor, who often labored in mills rather than on family farms, would not be educated otherwise. Compulsory attendance laws started in New England and spread through the North and West, with the South adopting them only around the turn of the twentieth century.

The original compulsory attendance laws had a feature that looks puzzling to modern eyes. The early laws required attendance for what today seems like a laughably short period of time. Connecticut's 1872 law required children between ages eight and fourteen to attend school for at least three months of the year, at least six weeks of which were to be consecutive (Stephen Lassonde 2005, 33). Massachusetts in 1867 had a similarly short requirement (Gary Courchesne 1979). Three months per year was a typical standard, hardly enough to complete even half of a now-standard grade.

In an age-graded school system, minimum compliance with the law would seem to condemn students to endless grade repetition. But in the ungraded, one-room school that was familiar to all state legislators of the period, three months of school was a useful advance for any student, even if the school was in session for six or even nine months of the year. Occasional attendees could find appropriate recitation groups for whatever subjects were being taught. Even as late as 1910, many states had different compulsory attendance laws for rural and urban schools. Only in cities, where age grading was increasingly the norm, was the child required to attend continuously (Monroe 1913, vol. 1, 289).

2.20 The District "Rate-Bills" and Their Opponents

The bottom layer of public support for local schools was the local school
district itself. In New England and other township-governed states, this often constituted two layers. The town or township would provide funds, and
the several school districts within the town would supplement the town's
funds with a local tax, usually on property within the district. In addition
to general taxes that everyone had to pay, many local districts adopted
"rate bills."

The rate bill was the nineteenth-century name for tuition payments
to attend the public schools. In most of the midwestern states before
the Civil War, the rate bill was the original method of financing public
schools (Fuller 1982, chapter 2). The same was true in New York, where
it accounted for most of the financing of rural schools up to 1850 (Nancy
Beadie 2008). Although almost all the new states admitted under the
Northwest Ordinance made grand constitutional promises about education—usually, as I argued earlier, to persuade Congress that its school-
section donations would not be diverted from their role as enhancements
to congressional land holdings—they were slow in financing them. Districts were authorized but not initially required to raise taxes. They would
instead collect what state revenues were available, usually through the
school-section funds, and then use rate bills to finance the rest of the term.
Rate bills were collected through the tax system, which had the enforcement advantage of making them liens against the property. But the only
residents of the district who had to pay were those who sent children to
school, and their payments were usually proportioned to the number of
children per family who attended.

Rate bills were not originally a system specifically authorized by the
state. The system was a spontaneous response to the demand for education in rural areas (Beadie 2008). Nonetheless, abolition of the rate bill
was one of the defining goals of the Common School Revival. Modern
commentators either applaud its abolition as a clear-cut affirmation of
public education or deplore it as a regrettable example of state suppression of local demands. In this and the following section, I will explain why
both views are based on a mistaken conception of rate bills.

Many modern commentators conceive of the rate bill through the eyes
of age-graded school experience. Thus the payment of tuition via the rate
bill is implicitly assumed to be necessary for students to receive *any* education. But this was seldom the case. Rate bills were usually charges that

the local district made to *extend* the regular school term (Kaestle 1983, 117; Goldin and Katz 2008, 140). The district might have enough public money from state and local tax sources to run a three-month winter term and a three-month summer term. Some families might want their children to attend several weeks longer, and so the teacher would agree to stay on if they paid tuition. The tuition was collected from parents as part of their property taxes, which were then called "rates." The rate bill thus enabled children whose parents had the means to do so to proceed more rapidly through school. It did not mean that poor children had no access to school at all.

Evidence for this is that the abolition of rate bills in Massachusetts was followed by a slight *decline* in the enrollment rate of children under age nineteen in the following decades (Goldin and Katz 2008, 145). This makes it look as if free schooling had a perverse effect on education. But free schools enabled more children to attend continuously and so complete their "common school education" at a younger age. A drop in enrollments among older teenagers could simply have been a consequence of their finishing school sooner and should be counted as a success of the "free school" movement.

Even during the extra weeks of school financed by rate bills, poor children were usually given need-based waivers of rate bills to attend the extra sessions. However, the obligation to claim "pauper" status to get the waiver was said to deter many prideful parents from sending them during this period. (One might think, though, that the failure to send their children would also be an admission of poverty.) In any case, parental inability to pay a rate bill or unwillingness to risk a tax lien on their property did not apparently deny poor children of the core months of school that were financed from general funds. (I say "apparently" because "rate bill" occasionally referred to general taxes rather than those specific to parents of school children. Early historians such as Ellwood Cubberley [1919, 47], who would have been most familiar with the recently abolished practice, indicate that rate bills extended the free term for those willing to pay, although Swift [1911, 26] indicates that in some states it referred to general school funding, not just to extending the term.)

My task here is not to defend the rate bill from its critics. I want to offer an alternative explanation for its demise. The best documented political decision to abolish the rate-bill system was in New York in 1849. New York's use of the rate bill, as described by Samuel Randall (1871, 251), who is the main contemporary source, leaves open the possibility that nonpayers did not have a basic term that was free. (This is also the position of Monroe [1940, 316].) However, a modern historian whose dissertation on New York's schools covered the entire period in which the rate bill was used, says: "In practice, all students could attend school for free until the public funds ran out, usually after three months. The remaining five months or so of schooling were tuition based, with voluntary local provision made for the education of those who could not afford to pay the rate bill" (Thomas Mauhs-Pugh 2003, 13).

The decision to abolish the rate bills in New York State was controversial, and the legislature authorized two extraordinary referenda to test public sentiment. (The state courts in *Barto v. Himrod*, 8 N.Y. 483 [1853] held that the referenda were unconstitutional and the legislature had to make the call, but the legislature's decisions were plainly driven by the voters' preferences.) The first referendum was held in 1849, and it passed by a large margin, seemingly dumping the rate bills forever. After a year's experience without the rate bills, however, voters in rural areas objected strenuously to its loss. The state's plans to use public funds for what the rate bills had formerly financed had been only partially successful.

Another statewide referendum was held in 1850. Abolition of the rate bills in New York was again upheld, but this time by a much smaller margin. Almost all rural counties voted to repeal the ban on rate bills. Nor was New York unique. Rural support for the use of rate bills existed in other Northern states at the time, including Michigan and Wisconsin (Kaestle 1983, 150). Perhaps because the majority of New York's counties actually voted to reinstate the rate bills in 1850, the legislature implemented its abolition in a phased manner that allowed some local discretion, and the rate bills were not completely gone until 1867.

2.21 Why Cities Wanted Rural Schools Not to Have Rate Bills

The nineteenth-century demise of the rate-bill method of financing schools is celebrated as a triumph of educational enlightenment (Monroe 1940, 320) and criticized as undermining freedom of choice (Edwin West 1967). Both positions overlook an oddity of the New York State referendum in 1850. The larger cities in the state had already abolished their own rate bills. This was not peculiar to New York. Goldin and Katz (2008, 144) point out that many larger cities, including those of the South and the Midwest, had established free public schools, not supplemented by rate bills, before the Civil War. The second New York referendum, which seems to have more accurately reflected public sentiment, succeeded only because of the wide margin of votes favoring abolition of rate bills in counties that contained the larger cities of the state (Randall 1851, 77; Cubberley 1919, 148). It was plain that cities that already had free schools wanted to impose this obligation on rural counties.

Why would cities that already had free schools vote to prevent *other* school districts from using rate bills? One could say that it was general public spiritedness, but that would require explaining why that quality was so much greater in New York City, whose residents voted overwhelmingly to abolish the rate bills in other places, than in any of the rural counties of the state. New York City had enjoyed free schools (no rate bills) since 1832. Nothing in the 1850 referendum to repeal the free-school act threatened its status, since rate bills were always adopted only by local option. (It is possible that urban voters might have feared that rate bills would later be required, though that seems unlikely given that rate bills were to supplement the term's length, and most city schools by that time were open almost all year [Finkelstein 1989, 272].) The reason that the free-school cities wanted other places to abolish rate bills may have been more self-interested.

I speculate on this here because it introduces an ongoing tension between rural and urban school systems that became more pronounced later in the century. By 1850, most of the sizable cities in New York State and elsewhere had age-graded schools. Grades were not necessarily divided into single-age cohorts; most age-related divisions were more coarse. But these systems did require a sequence of knowledge from one year to the next that all children beginning the academic year (itself a new idea) had to have. Dropping into school for a few weeks, out for a month, and back in for another month, which was possible in the ungraded schools of the countryside, would be disruptive for the newly age-graded city schools.

The city schools did not have the luxury of dealing with a static population. Most of their populations were growing, and much of the increase came from families from rural parts of the state. In a study of a special 1855 census of Buffalo, New York, Laurence Glasco (1978) found that a majority of urban immigrants were families who had come from outlying counties in the state. The rural areas that such families left did not lack for schools. School enrollment and literacy in rural New York were at least as high as in cities (Easterlin, Alter, and Condran 1978, 34; Kaestle 1983, 25). But the rate-bill system in rural areas created a cohort of children who had a more haphazard education. It was not that they had attended bad schools or that they lacked all academic skills. Poorer children did not have enough school *for their age*. They were more likely to have attended rural schools only for the three- or four-month "free" term and been withdrawn for the extra schooling that was financed by the rate bill in most areas.

As poor families moved from rural areas to cities, many of their children would have been enrolled in free schools. But with less schooling than their contemporaries of similar age, poor immigrant children would have been a drag on the age-graded system. They would have to be placed in grades with younger children, which would have subjected them to ridicule and perhaps made them into classroom bullies. Being "overage" was not a problem in the rural, ungraded one-room school. The many boys who continued in the rural common schools into their late teens were not regarded as "retarded"—the official term for held-back students in urban, age-graded schools. (The modern word is "retained.") Every rural school patron knew that some boys had to work for their families more often than others, and that was why they could not attend as regularly.

In effect, the rate-bill districts may have created a negative externality for the cities. Age-graded systems were more difficult to manage with undereducated children coming into them. Requiring that the rural schools be made tuition free, as the New York vote did, could be regarded as a small step toward making them conform to the nascent system of age-graded education in the growing cities. City voters wanted the country kids to fit into their system when they arrived.

The rural-to-urban problem was noticed in other contexts. Writing about late-nineteenth century schools generally, William Reese (2005, 109) concluded, "Only in graded classrooms of the larger towns and cities was there anything approaching a uniform curriculum. And even there age-grading was confounded as ill-prepared rural youth, the children of immigrants, and home-grown youngsters of uneven preparation and differing ambition made teaching anything but uniform." The twentieth-century urban migration of Southern blacks, who had largely been confined to one-room schools (as will be described in chapter 5), created the same difficulties for age-graded schools in the North. Their spotty educations often caused blacks to be placed in grades in which they were considerably older than white and city-born black children, who had begun within the graded system. The seeming backwardness of immigrant blacks in turn fed racial stereotypes, and even some sympathetic school administrators promoted

segregated classrooms and schools, despite their illegality in most northern states (Davison Douglas 2005, 155).

The problem continues to this day. A report in the *Los Angeles Times*
(November 2, 2005) found that Southern California schools that enrolled
a large number of Mexican immigrants did not have much of a problem
educating students who had come from urban parts of Mexico. It was children from remote rural areas, where school attendance was irregular, who
were most difficult to integrate into the American (and urban Mexican)
age-graded system of education.

The evidence for the New York urban-school motive in the 1850 vote is,
of course, highly circumstantial. My main reason for advancing this explanation for the vote is to illustrate the implications of having two parallel
systems of education, rural ungraded and urban graded. Once the systems
are seen as different and in some ways incompatible, it is easier to explain
the struggle to establish an age-graded system of education in the twentieth century. Criticism of the one-room school by turn-of-the century reformers was not so much motivated by the schools' failure to educate as
it was by the poor fit of their students in the modern age-graded systems
of urban areas. The free-school saga of New York may have been an early
marker of a shift that would require voters to accept a vastly more centralized and standardized school system all over the country.

2.22 Rate Bills Survived as "Boarding Around"

Even after rate bills had been abolished, an "in-kind" version of them appears to have survived and even been widespread in states that had long
ago established free schools. Part of the compensation for many one-room
school teachers was free room and board with the parents of enrolled students. This by itself would constitute something of a rate bill, since the
teacher usually did not board with taxpayers who did not have children in
school. This form of rate bill would have been a significant fraction of the
cost of schooling. Food and shelter might have been one-third to one-half
of a teacher's full compensation. Another in-kind tax that was important
for winter schooling was the obligation to provide firewood for the school
stove. This again could have been apportioned to families whose children
attended school for the longest period.

Massachusetts was among the first of the states to have abolished rate
bills, banning their use in 1826 (Goldin and Katz 2003, table 4.1). What is

not widely noted, however is that in-kind rate bills for teacher boarding
and schoolroom firewood persisted, as indicated in the statewide summa-
ries of school district income sources (Kaestle and Vinovskis 1980, table
A7.5). The category "board and fuel contributed" amounted to 7.7 percent of the category "taxes for wages of teacher, board, and fuel" in 1840.
(This was for the entire state, and the board percentages would surely
have been larger in the rural districts than in Boston and other cities,
where teachers could live at home.) The percentage of user contributions
steadily declined to 2.1 percent in 1860, but the category disappeared entirely from the reports only in 1880.

There was another feature of "boarding around" that made it seem
even more closely tied to benefits received. Many people who commented
on the system mentioned that the teacher usually boarded with several
families during the term. Parents with the most children attending the
teacher's school typically were obliged to feed and house the teacher for a
longer period (Stratton 1981, 161). Boarding around thus seemed to have
operated much like a tax in proportion to benefits received, just as the
rate bills were used. Boarding around could also tax the teacher, for the
households with the most children were likely to have the least bedroom
space and the most mouths to feed. On the other hand, I read several
reminiscences by teachers as well as families that it was not all bad. Most
families tried to show their best to the teacher, and teachers got to know
their pupils and communities better, which often helped them deal with
in-school problems.

Thus as long as there were one-room schools in rural areas, there were
opportunities to impose in-kind support for the schools in proportion to
usage. Accounts of "boarding around" seemed to have died out by the
turn of the century. Whether the practice increased after the rate bills had
been abolished in various states cannot be determined, since the evidence
is mostly from scattered reminiscences of the practice. I have learned,
though, not to underestimate the ability of local districts to work around
state-imposed constraints on their activities and financing.

2.23 Conclusion: Efficient in the Nineteenth Century, Obsolete in the Twentieth

This chapter has examined the one-room school system that grew up more
or less spontaneously across the continent in the hundred years after the

American Revolution. The important features of this system are obscured at times by nostalgic antiquarianism and contemptuous modernism. My interest is not in bringing the system back as an educational model. I have sought only to examine it as an institution in terms of its success in the time and economic context in which it flourished.

Within the limits imposed by geography—a big country—and a dispersed population whose local transportation remained crude through most of the nineteenth century, the one-room school system and its incremental pedagogy have to be judged a remarkable success. A population that demanded the rudiments of literacy and numeracy was largely well served by the system. Its ungraded pedagogy allowed children to acquire increments of skill and knowledge while meeting their families' demands for their labor. One-room schools made use of a minimum amount of resources. Buildings did not need to be complicated, governance could be undertaken by locally interested parties who could monitor teacher effort, and the curriculum could be taught by relatively untrained young adults using widely available, more-or-less standardized textbooks.

The system did its job efficiently in spite of the celebrated educational leaders of the nineteenth century. Many of their proposed policies would have been counterproductive for the rural population that constituted the majority of the nation. Reformers sought to impose urban ideas such as consolidated and age-graded schools, a uniform curriculum, and a professional teacher corps on a rural population that was not ready for it. Had the reformers been successful in their own time, it is possible that the educational attainment of the American people would have been retarded, not advanced. Consolidated schools would have required longer walks for rural children, and their attendance would have suffered. Age grading would have entailed multiple grade repetitions for the majority of students who could not attend full time. Requiring the employment of professional teachers and suppression of tuition-like contributions would have raised the fiscal cost and reduced the willingness by local voters to pay for basic education.

Fortunately, the American political system gave the reformers voice but not power. That resided in the voters, and they almost always rejected reforms that were inappropriate for their time and location. Yet the more uniform system that the nineteenth-century reformers urged was finally triumphant in the twentieth century. The next chapter examines how this transition took place. Its success was less a matter of persuasion by educational leaders than the changed conditions of rural life and the higher payoff to education in the new century. The relative and eventually absolute decline in farm populations coupled with improved roads and automotive transportation persuaded rural voters that they had to adopt the age-graded system that was being fitfully developed in urban schools. Coupled with the enormous increase in the demand for high school training, rural voters eventually accepted the consolidation of school districts and the bureaucratization of school administration that had been fruitlessly urged on them for almost a century.

CHAPTER THREE

Explaining the School District Consolidation Movement

The previous chapter advanced the idea that one-room schools and small districts in the nineteenth century were actually efficient institutions. But if they were efficient, why did they die out? The conventional answer is that the twentieth-century school bus and the road improvements that motor vehicles induced made it possible for rural children to attend a larger school. But why was a larger school desirable, and how did it come about? On this I will argue something more controversial. The demands of age grading and high school made one-room schools obsolete, and local voters then agreed to the consolidation of school districts. Almost all accounts of this transition emphasize that the local districts had to be dragged into consolidation against the will of the locals. I argue the contrary. Consolidation was locally desired by a majority of voters because it plugged them into what was developing as a national system of age-graded schools that led to high school.

In one sense, what I am arguing for is a "demand side" view of the transition. The state school establishment—such as it was—had always been an eager "supplier" of centralized institutions, particularly age-graded schooling and the bureaucratic infrastructure that this system entailed. But age grading and its accoutrements could not be put in place until there was a widespread shift in the demand for access to high school that was facilitated by age grading. District consolidation required in most cases the consent of the local voters, who had to be persuaded that consolidated, age-graded schools were desirable.

My thesis is not that educational leaders were unnecessary or irrelevant. Leaders explored the many ways by which education could be standardized within the age-graded format and were ready with plans—not all well conceived—when voters were ready. But they could not proceed until local voters made up their minds that a more systematic education was necessary for their children's success in life.

The flip side of these questions is why it took so long for one-room schools to finally consolidate. Here my answer is more tentative. I advance circumstantial evidence that in remote rural areas where child labor was still essential for the family farm, the one-room schools allowed children to proceed with school on a part-time basis. Forcing all these districts to consolidate into regularly age-graded schools would have caused many children to drop out altogether. Only after mechanized agriculture entirely displaced labor-intensive farming was it sensible for voters in the most rural areas to give up their one-room school.

3.1 School District Decline Was Caused by the Extinction of One-Room Schools

If the one-room school was so efficient for low-density areas, why is it not still around? Figure 3.1 illustrates the dramatic decline in the number of schools and districts since 1916. One-room schools went from more than two hundred thousand early in the century to near zero in 1972. This graph is relevant to three distinct points that will be addressed in this chapter.

The first point is that the decline in the total number of school *districts* appears to have been largely accounted for by the decline of rural, one-room schools. Most one-room schools were the only school in their district (Fuller 1982, chapter 3), so the number of districts in the period before 1938 can be approximated by the number of one-room schools. Consolidation of several one-room schools almost always meant consolidation of several districts. From this we can infer that school districts moved a decimal point, from over two hundred thousand to fewer than twenty thousand, in the span of sixty years. The downward trajectories of one-room schools and districts in figure 3.1 are almost perfectly parallel from 1938, when data on district numbers were first kept continuously, to 1972. Moreover, after 1972, when virtually no one-room schools remained, the

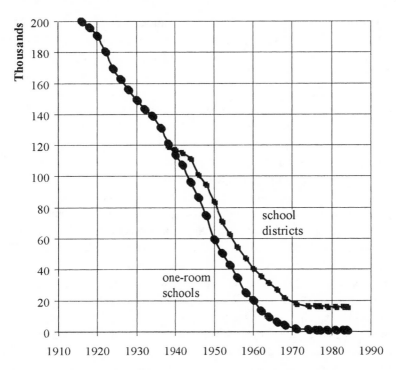

FIGURE 3.1 Decline in the number of one-room schools and school districts, 1916–2000. Adapted from Nora Gordon (2002).

decline in the number of school districts slowed to a trickle. No other unit of American local government followed this trend. The count of counties remained constant over this period, and general-purpose municipalities increased in numbers—mostly by proliferation in the suburbs—but one-room school districts virtually disappeared.

A second point is that the smoothness of the decline in school district numbers in figure 3.1 masks considerable state-by-state variation. The pattern for individual states seems to have been a punctuated equilibrium, with one-room schools and districts declining only slowly for a decade or so within a single state, then a mass die-off within three or four years of a school district reorganization effort. For example, Illinois undertook a push to consolidate its 9,459 school districts in 1948 and reduced them to 3,413 by 1952, while Wisconsin in the same four-year period declined by a much smaller number, going from 6,038 districts in 1948 to 5,463 in 1952. But after that, Wisconsin went on a consolidation binge and had "only"

739 districts in 1964, whereas Illinois had almost twice that number. (Data are from Hooker and Mueller [1970].) Without some organized campaign, one-room schools and their districts tended to persist. These pushes typically involved financial carrots rather than regulatory commands. As I will show in more detail below, consolidation almost always required a concurring vote of the residents of the districts involved.

Third, the one-room school did not die quickly. If we assume that most one-room schools constituted a single district, the one-room school accounted for almost half of all districts (but far fewer than half of the students) up to 1960. Only by 1972 do they become virtually extinct. There is something deceptive about figure 3.1, however. The one-room schools of the twentieth century already were different from their nineteenth-century counterparts. Around the turn of the century, most one-room schools had at least nominally adopted an age-graded curriculum. The ungraded curriculum and flexible attendance terms that made one-room schools efficient adaptations to their circumstances in the nineteenth century were gradually displaced by city-bred standardization.

As I will explain presently, one-room schools struggled with age-graded education. In the period after World War II, this led to consolidations that, for a time, left some one-room schools as essentially dispersed classrooms within a larger school district. School buses would distribute the district's children to their one-room-school classrooms. For example, first and second grades would be in the Wood School; third and fourth in the Field School; and fifth and six in the Mountain School. These were "one-room" *buildings* with a single teacher, but they were not traditional one-room schools because the teacher had to manage only one or two grades. Robert Leight and Alice Rinehart (1999) mention that school districts in southeastern Pennsylvania adopted this scheme after World War II, and parts of the district whose schools I attended nearby also did this. I cannot determine the extent of this trend around the nation—the national data do not make the definition of a "one-teacher school" clear—but if it were widespread, it would mean that true one-room schools were becoming extinct more rapidly than the data indicate.

Data from a special study by the U.S. Bureau of the Census (1960), one of the earliest that listed the number of school districts by county, confirm that district consolidations in the last forty years continued to be almost entirely rural. The 1960 study listed the number of districts for each county in every state, and one can compare the statewide declines to the year 2000 to those of urban counties in the state. Consider the states with the nation's three largest metropolitan areas, New York, Chicago, and Los Angeles. Between 1960 and 2000, the number of districts in New York State declined by 582 (43 percent of its 1960 total), but the suburban counties adjacent to New York City, Westchester and Nassau, had exactly the same number in both years.

Between 1960 and 2000, the number of districts in Illinois declined by 657 (62 percent of its 1960 total), but during this period the number of school districts in counties closest to Chicago—Cook, Dupage, Kane, and Will—was virtually unchanged. California during the same period had a net loss of 666 school districts (39 percent of its 1960 total), but the eight largest urban counties (Los Angeles, Orange, San Diego, San Bernardino, Riverside, Santa Clara, Sacramento, and Alameda), which had two-thirds of the state's population, accounted for only 19 percent of the decline. (This probably overstates the loss in urban areas, since several of California's urban counties are very large in area—San Bernardino is the nation's largest—and contain much rural territory.)

The same pattern exists in other states that experienced considerable district decline since 1960. Indiana went from 930 districts in 1960 to about a third of that number in 2000, but Marion County, which contains Indianapolis and its suburbs, had almost no net change. (The creation in 1970 of "Unigov," a municipal-service body that encompasses Marion County, did not alter school district boundaries.) Wisconsin went from 2882 districts in 1960 to 459 in 2000, but Milwaukee County (containing the state's largest city and its close-in suburbs) had the same number of districts, 24, in both years. Consolidations in urban and suburban areas account for very little of the overall decline in the total number of districts.

A previous attempt by economists to explain the decline in the number of school districts does not put as much emphasis as I do on the switch from one-room schools to graded schools. Larry Kenny and Amy Schmidt (1994) statistically explain the tail end of the decline, from 1950 to 1980, as the result of the decline in rural populations, the rise of teacher unions, and increased state funding that displaced local funds. (David Strang [1987] reached a similar conclusion.) Rural population decline figures in my story, too, but there is more to it than that. As I will explain presently, consolidation of rural schools was impelled by voters' demand for age-graded education, which the formerly ungraded one-room schools could not adequately provide. Kenny and Schmidt and most other scholars regard consolidation as a top-down story, but I will show that it was almost entirely consensual. The rise of teacher unions and the growth of state aid are, in my opinion, results of and not causes of school district consolidations. Teacher unions had almost no political power before the late 1960s (as described in section 3.14 below), and by then most of the decline in the numbers of school districts had already taken place. State aid was the carrot that made consolidation acceptable to local voters. It was given conditionally on consolidation—districts sometimes negotiated for it—and so it was not an independent cause.

3.2 Rural School Districts Declined along with Local Financing

The decline in school district numbers was financially facilitated by an increase in state aid to local education. The peak of local funding seems to have been around 1920. Carter Alexander (1921) decried the falling share of state aid (and rise in the local share) for education up to that time. He indicated that in 1890 state aid was 18.4 percent of public school revenue but declined to 13.7 percent in 1918. Alexander expressed the common sentiment among education professionals that the state share should be increased, and indeed it was. As table 3.1 indicates, the local share of funding—almost all from property taxation—was steadily displaced by an increasing state share over the rest of the twentieth century.

The two most rapid declines in local financing were occasioned by the Great Depression (1930–1940) and by the 1970s property-tax revolts, mainly that of California. Both these events pushed financing responsibility to the state governments, not the federal government. The federal government's role grew in the 1960s with "Great Society" grants (which also facilitated desegregation) and after 2000 with the "No Child Left Behind" legislation, but it remains a bit player.

The increase in state funds was not necessarily caused by state initiatives. Districts would often demand increased aid for facilities and transportation as compensation for their agreement to consolidate. For example, the U.S. Commissioner of Education (1910, 214) reported that Rhode Island offered one hundred dollars to each graded school for each ungraded school with which it consolidated, and Virginia appropriated twenty-five thousand dollars to "encourage rural graded schools of two, three, and four rooms." However, it should be noted that the local share of spending continued to decline after 1970, when one-room schools had become statistically extinct and consolidation slowed to a trickle. Consolidation was facilitated by state aid, but consolidation clearly was not the only reason for the greater fiscal

TABLE 3.1 **Historical trends in local, state, and federal financing of K–12 public schools, 1920–2004**

School year ending	Local (percent)	State (percent)	Federal (percent)
1920	83.2	16.5	0.3
1930	82.7	16.9	0.4
1940	68.0	30.3	1.8
1950	57.3	39.8	2.9
1960	56.5	39.1	4.4
1970	52.1	39.9	8.0
1980	43.4	46.8	9.8
1990	46.8	47.1	6.1
2000	43.2	49.5	7.3
...	...	...	...
2004	43.9	47.0	9.1

Source: U.S. Department of Education, National Center for Education Statistics, Digest of Education Statistics, table 32.

involvement by the state in education funding. (I will suggest in chapter 6 that the post-1970 centralization of funding was driven in large part by the state courts.)

3.3 Farm Mechanization and Better Roads Facilitated Consolidation

The more obvious factors that accounted for the decline in one-room schools are demographic trends that are familiar to students of American history. The famous 1890 announcement by the U.S. Census that the American frontier had disappeared roughly coincides with the peak of one-room schools, but that is too pat. One-room schools existed in every rural area in 1890, not just on the western frontier of the United States. The rural population of mostly urban states such as Connecticut and Maryland continued to attend one-room schools well into the twentieth century (Edward Starr 1926; Bachman 1933).

The more important factors associated with one-room school consolidations are the steady trend in urbanization, as shown in table 3.2, and the concomitant decline in farming. The farm population declined from 39 percent in 1900 to 15 percent in 1950, and it now hovers around 1 percent. Not only did the number of farms decline, but the average size of farms rose steadily after 1870. Rural birth rates, like those in cities, declined throughout the nineteenth century and most of the twentieth, although

TABLE 3.2 **U.S. population in urban areas, 1870–1950**

Year	Urban (percent)	Big city (percent)
1870	25.7	12.9
1880	28.2	13.5
1890	35.1	16.9
1900	39.7	21.2
1910	45.7	25.0
1920	51.2	28.9
1930	56.2	31.8
1940	56.5	31.6
1950	59.0	32.3

Source: Schnore and Petersen (1958).
Note: "Urban" is a place with a population ≥2,500, and "big city" has ≥50,000.

rural rates have always been above urban rates. These trends were in turn the result of mechanization of farm work, which made large farms viable and reduced the demand for child labor (Deborah Fitzgerald 2003). For all these reasons, the number of rural children per square mile declined, so that the number of children within walking distance of a given school decreased.

As school enrollments declined, a one-room school could not easily cut costs. Since there was only one teacher, the only cost-saving possibility was to consolidate with another school nearby. This sometimes did happen, but it meant even longer walks for rural children, and a long walk was the most important deterrent to attendance and regular progression through school (George Reavis 1920). Further consolidation in rural areas could only be accomplished by using nonhuman transport.

As I mentioned in section 2.11, vehicular transportation was limited by the quality of rural roads. By the late nineteenth century, road quality had improved. The improvements were often specifically motivated by the need to get children to consolidated schools. David Reynolds (1999, 61) mentions that Iowa school districts sometimes maintained roads to facilitate access to schools. Clayton Ellsworth's history of consolidated schools in the Ohio Valley insists that improved roads had an "inseparable connection" with school consolidation (1956, 122). William Link (1992, 236) likewise emphasized the importance of roads for Southern states' consolidation efforts. In rural Tennessee, "school reformers were among the strongest advocates of better roads" (Jeanette Keith 1995, 126).

It is tempting to say that the now-ubiquitous yellow school bus was the catalyst for consolidation, but that would be premature. Books that discussed consolidation of rural schools from the early twentieth century show photographs of horse-drawn "school wagons" (e.g., Foght 1910, 328; Cubberley 1914, 236). Reformers gave advice to district school boards on how to outfit them and what sort of teamster should be hired to drive them. The motorized school bus came into general rural use only after 1920, when school consolidation was under way as a national movement. A contemporary source that detailed the establishment of rural consolidated schools in the late 1920s listed the mode of transportation by which rural pupils got to school (Macy Campbell 1927). The great majority were on motorized buses, but horse-drawn wagons were still in occasional use in the Midwest.

3.4 Costs and Benefits of Consolidation

Better roads and school wagons made it possible to consolidate rural schools, but why would local voters agree to consolidate into districts large enough to do graded schools? If two adjacent one-room districts lost half their students over thirty years, they could just join together and run another one-room school at a convenient location. This would preserve the one-room school and allow about half the students to continue to walk, with only the more distant children being transported a few miles. Schools would remain close to the neighborhood, and local control by both elected school board members and informal contacts between parents and the teacher would be preserved. Sometimes this did happen, but the more durable type of consolidation was to join several (from four to eight) one-room districts into a district big enough to create an age-graded school. Rural school consolidation was not just about transportation. It represented a decision to adopt multiclassroom, age-graded education.

I will argue presently (section 3.15 below) that consolidation of rural one-room schools into larger, graded school districts was mostly done with the consent of the residents of the districts. Their representatives in the state legislature were attuned to their concerns and not those of the education establishment. As an overview of what follows, it may be useful to try to reconstruct the general economic calculations that voters in one-room districts might have considered in weighing the costs (the balance of this section) and benefits (in the next section) of voting to consolidate.

On the negative side of consolidation, transportation, political control, and community identity seemed paramount. Transportation was costly in two ways. One was that wagons and buses and teamsters and drivers had to be paid, an expense not necessary in the neighborhood one-room school district to which all children walked. Less obvious is that the time spent on the school wagon or (later) the school bus was a loss of the children's time. Harold Foght (1910, 322), an advocate of consolidation, offered an example of a consolidated district in Kansas in which children spent as much as an hour and a half on the ten-mile trip to school. The school bus was faster, but it also made for larger districts and longer rides for those living on the periphery.

The lost hours were an economic cost to the parents as well as the child. Although children in the early twentieth century were less critical in the daily operation of a farm, their labor for chores and seasonal activities like harvesting and planting was still important. Greater distance between school and home reduced the remaining economic contribution that children could make to family farms and household management. However, this cost should not be overstated. One of the advantages of the rural consolidated high school was that students from remote areas no longer had to "board out" in the town that had a high school (Foght 1910, 318). If there were a rural high school, the daily commute to school might be long, but students could still live at home.

The second great negative of the consolidated school was the dilution of political control over school governance. The one-room school district has been celebrated as the most democratic of the public institutions that were widespread in the United States. Wayne Fuller (1982, chapter 3) emphasized the importance of the one-room school in teaching ordinary people how to govern themselves. The (usually) three school directors were seldom professional educators or professional anything else, for that matter. The majority of voters got exactly what they were willing to pay for, and there was considerable variance in the quality of education.

This variance was not especially harmful in the past. The nineteenth-century one-room school's pedagogy allowed each district to be an island unto itself. State legislation imposed modest floors on length of term, student attendance, teacher credentials, and curriculum, but beyond that it was up to the local board and the voters to whom they answered to decide how good school would be. Joining with other districts would surely dilute the influence of each former district. And professional educators made no secret of their desire to further dilute local influences. The professionals invariably wanted more rigorous statewide standards for length of term, attendance, teacher qualifications, and curricular offerings.

A third disadvantage was loss of community. One-room schools were an important locus of social capital, a place where people of different religions and stations in life could get to know one another (Fuller 1982, 7). The loneliness of rural life was mitigated by the dispersed schools and the teachers who were involved in their communities. I offer contemporary evidence in support of this benefit in section 3.18 below, but I do not want to oversell it. The consolidated age-graded school also provided opportunities for governance and social-capital building. The same road and transportation improvements that enabled children to be transported to a consolidated school also liberated their parents from the walking-distance neighborhood.

In a 1925 essay, the daughter of Laura Ingalls Wilder, Rose Lane, marveled, "Neighborliness goes now on rubber tires and takes in, more swiftly, a wider radius" (quoted in Miller 1998, 169). An enthusiast of age-graded schooling in North Carolina wrote, "There is no equal to a consolidated school to build up a powerful public spirit in the community; cooperation in public schools on this plan does almost as much good to the parents as to the children. The consolidated school is the great permanent unifying center of social and intellectual life for the people" (Charles Dabney 1936, 232). Wilbert Anderson (1906, 252) observed that New England townwide consolidation induced residents to pay more attention to town affairs, as opposed to purely neighborhood concerns, and develop what I will call in chapter 6 "community-specific" social capital.

3.5 Age Grading Was the Primary Benefit of Consolidation

The negatives of district consolidation were offset by the promise that taxes would be lower and education would be better in consolidated schools. Many if not most rural school districts were depopulating by the 1920s. In the late nineteenth century, it was not uncommon for a one-room school to have an enrollment of fifty students or more. In that era, it was a good thing that daily attendance fell considerably below enrollment, because there would have been no place to seat everyone who enrolled. A teacher-pupil ratio of one to fifty was also highly economical, especially if the teacher was paid to match his or her modest qualifications. But as the population of rural areas declined, such desperate economies were no longer possible. By 1940, Illinois, the state with the most one-room schools (more than nine thousand), reported that 2,211 of them had fewer than seven students (Leon Weaver 1944). More than half the one-room schools in Kansas had fewer than nine students in 1942 (National Commission 1948, 184). To the extent that local taxes had to fund these schools, the cost to taxpayers began to rise. If the state provided the funds, local voters might seem insulated, but taxpayers at the state level (or potential recipients of state funds for graded schools and nonschool projects) would rebel.

But tax savings were seldom realized by consolidating schools and restoring the larger student-teacher ratios in an age-graded setting. There was an undeniable economy in classroom size in consolidated schools, but this was offset by a more profound change in education. The continuously variable school year, the curriculum tailored to local preferences, and the locally good-enough teaching staff of the one-room school yielded to the insistent demands for uniformity. This resulted in the age-graded system that we now take for granted as "real school," to use David Tyack and Larry Cuban's expression from *Tinkering toward Utopia* (1995). This universal system swamped the local economies of the age-graded classroom by dramatically increasing the *amount* of schooling that students had to have.

Age-graded schooling required regular attendance, and its logical culmination was high school. Ungraded one-room schools were cheaper not just because the teacher and building were less expensive, but because students could take as much or as little as they wanted of what the school had to offer. In contrast, age-graded schools could not count on absences to make a thirty-seat one-room school accommodate a sixty-child enrollment. A twelve-year-old who went to work on the farm for three months could come back to the one-room school later and master his last reader. In the age-graded school system, he was a dropout and would have to repeat his most recent grade from the beginning.

The multiclassroom, age-graded school was, of course, the product of increased demand for education by both rural and urban voters. Voters surely knew that the consolidated schools would mean more expenditure, even if the labor cost per unit of education (teacher-wage per student hour) was lower. The tide of age-graded schooling swept away local resistance to consolidation by making one-room schools obsolete. Just as the word-processing computer has vacuumed up even the most dedicated users of manual typewriters, age-graded schooling created an irresistible impetus to greater school expenditures.

3.6 Age-Graded Schools Required Coordination of Curriculum and Schedules

Age grading is an idea whose origins continue to be debated. Several American education reformers had independently observed or heard of the idea in Prussia (Frederick McClusky 1920a), but many historians still regard age grading as an idea that cropped up without apparent antecedents in many different states. (Cubberley [1919], whose claims McClusky specifically attacked, was a prominent proponent of the "native genius" of the age-graded system.) The Prussian origins' story perhaps became popular because people who disliked age grading—and they were numerous—for its factory-like standardization could attribute to it the undemocratic overtones that the name "Prussian" evoked (Patricia Graham 1974, 17). Even if the idea had not first been invented in Prussia, the economic advantages of age grading were sufficiently powerful that it surely would have been invented in the United States and other urbanizing nations soon thereafter. The method of private voting that we call "Australian" was indeed imported from Australia around 1880, but no one would argue that our individual ballot choices would still be made in full view of others had the Aussies not adopted it first.

What is not debated about age grading is that it was first adopted in cities (Angus, Mirel, and Vinovskis 1988; Reese 1995). Cities had sufficient population density to enable a large number of children to be assembled in a single school building and divided by age group into classrooms of homogenous age groups. It should not be assumed, however, that dividing children by age was the immediate response to the opportunity to create scale economies in formal schooling for urban children. An early experiment, circa 1820–40, was the factory-like monitorial system of Joseph Lancaster. Hundreds of city children would be taught by a single schoolmaster who supervised dozens of young "monitors," who imparted the instruction (Carl Kaestle 1973). It was not an age-graded system; students were sorted by knowledge, not by age. Something like it survives in large universities, where graduate teaching assistants are supervised by a senior professor, but its popularity in public education died out before the Civil War era.

Cities that first created multiroom schools did not instantly adopt age grading. Instead, each teacher simply taught as if he or she were in a one-room school. An important element of Horace Mann's famous battle (c. 1847) with the traditionalist Boston school teachers was his attempt to introduce the age-graded classroom (McClusky 1920b, 139). Mann won that battle (many of his other reforms, such as consolidation of districts within towns, were not adopted until after his death), but even if he had lost, age grading would soon have become the standard urban method. Its economic and educational advantages—the division of labor in teaching and the more continuous attention to students—were too compelling to be overlooked.

Although the idea of age grading took hold fairly early, the details had to be worked out over a long period of time. It was clear to almost every educator that reading had to be taught first. This involved learning the alphabet and phonetic sounds and then words and sentences, usually in that order. (Mann was actually an opponent of that sequence and advocated a method that taught whole-word recognition rather than phonetics [Hinsdale 1898, 189].) But it was not obvious to everyone how other skills and subjects should be introduced. An early division of students among classrooms was by subject matter (McClusky 1920a, 36). Up to 1855 in Boston, one room in a multiroom building would be for teaching reading, and students would be divided within the room by reading-skill groups, through which they progressed until they had mastered enough material to be sent to another classroom in which writing would be taught (Garrett Rickard 1948). The now-prevalent idea that each early grade should impart some of every skill was not immediately obvious. The eight years of elementary schooling and four of high school did not become a national norm until the twentieth century (Rickard 1947). Indeed, a few local variations persisted for some years. Salt Lake City's schools took eleven years to high school graduation, adopting the standard twelve only in 1944 (John Moffitt 1946, 194).

These antique issues are relevant for my task because they required coordination between classes within the same school and among other schools. All the teachers in a multigrade school had to agree to the curriculum in each grade. The sole teacher in a one-room school could teach skills and subjects in just about any order. In most cases, teachers just followed textbook order, but they could select which textbook subjects would be studied. Variety in subject matter did not matter much because each time a new teacher arrived (which was often) or each time a child entered a new school (which also happened frequently), the child's lessons would start from the point where he or she had left off in the textbook. Rural teachers in one-room schools did complain about irregular attendance.

or their very existence. The same is true for other municipal corporations, although the "creature" theory seems to be applied more stringently to school districts than to municipalities (Roald Campbell et al. 1990). But this merely states a necessary condition for state power to revise school district boundaries and authority. The relevant question is under what conditions would the state legislature actually do this without the consent of the local districts.

The answer is . . . hardly ever. Writing of mid-nineteenth-century consolidation proposals, William Reese (1995, 69) observed, "Legislatures, dominated by rural constituencies, pushed reform measures more slowly than educators precisely because they had to answer to the electorate." Even those historians who champion the top-down view of consolidations concede that the legislature almost always obtained the consent of local school district voters or their representatives.

The federal government's authority over schools is said to be limited by the Tenth Amendment, which reserves powers not specifically granted to Congress to the states. Since control over education was not granted to Congress (unlike, say, coining money or establishing post offices), it would seem that the federal role would be very narrow. But the spending power that the Constitution grants to Congress opens an alternative route to federal control. Congress can put regulatory conditions on its disbursement of funds. It can make eligibility for federal funds conditional on some reform, such as desegregation or accommodation of the handicapped. As a result, the chief limitation on the federal role, like that of the state, is political, not constitutional (James Ryan 2004).

Why the disconnect between state supremacy in theory and local self-determination in practice? The answer is the method by which state legislatures are selected. Every state elects both houses of its legislatures (and the unicameral Nebraska legislature) by geographically contiguous electoral districts. No American state has at-large elections for legislatures, as some other nations do. Some states do have multimember districts. In my hometown of Hanover, New Hampshire, I vote for four representatives to the legislature, not just one. But that is simply an accommodation to the tiny districts that would be created by having single-member districts in a legislature composed of more than four hundred members. (We joke that in New Hampshire, we don't really need elections; we could just take turns.)

The geographic basis of state electoral districts was perturbed in the 1960s by the U.S. Supreme Court rulings that resulted in the "one person, one vote" rule, *Baker v. Carr*, 369 U.S. 186 (1962). Before the Court's re-

Reassigning returning students to recitation groups was not seamless, and long-absent students did forget much of their former lessons. My point is only that irregular attendance did not have nearly as adverse effect on the rest of the students, nor was it as educationally catastrophic for the truants, as it would be in age-graded systems.

Age-graded schooling could tolerate much less variety among classrooms. Within the same school it was essential to have curricula in the upper grades follow from material taught in the immediately preceding grade. A contemporary discussion of these issues was contained in a book by William Wells (1877), the Chicago superintendent of schools who introduced citywide grading in 1856 (Mary Herrick 1971). From its first edition in 1862, Wells's influential book emphasized that standardized age grading, uniform textbooks, and teacher supervision were essential to facilitate mobility among schools. The idea caught on quickly. Quoting an 1881 editorial in the *Indiana School Journal*, William Reese (1998, 38) wrote that "grading would cut costs, allow a teacher or a pupil to transfer to other schools more easily, 'and find classes corresponding to the ones he left.' It seemed 'essential' that the country school abandon their ungraded plans and promote a more uniform state system."

Age grading in turn required parallel standardizations that had been less critical to educational success in the one-room school. Foremost was that attendance be more regular. The chief advantage of an age-graded classroom was that all students could be taught the same, age-appropriate material. A student who missed two weeks of school was in this setting a far greater liability to the rest of the class. The teacher would have to spend time with the truant to get him up to the level of the rest of the class, and this time subtracted from the overall pace of the class. If time could not be spared, the former truant would have to limp along through material that often involved cumulative knowledge, some part of which he now lacked. In the worst case scenario, the truant would waste most of the rest of the school year and have to repeat the grade again next year, also wasting much of that time.

3.7 Rural-to-Urban Migration Pressured Rural Schools

By 1900, most large urban schools had something that looked like modern, age-graded systems and a curriculum that allowed students within the same district to move from one school to another and fit in with their classmates. Coordination of graded curricula and schedules among *differ-ent* districts, however, would be more difficult to achieve. It was likely that city schools within the same state could do this, as their local superinten-dents were subject at least nominally to state supervision. Another influ-ence was the professional contacts among urban teachers and supervisors at the innumerable county and state events. By 1920, most urban schools were following a standard thirty-two- or thirty-six-week schedule that be-gan in September and ended in June.

But why would *rural* schools feel compelled to get with the age-graded program? When the movement of students from one school district to another was mainly among one-room schools, differences in the previous school's curriculum and the student's mastery of it were easily managed. Stu-dent mobility did become a problem, however, once rural students moved to urban areas with age-graded schools. A ten-year-old former farm boy who arrived at an age-graded urban school complicated his own education and that of other children. He might read at one grade level, do arithmetic at a higher level, but know no more geography than an eight-year-old in his new school. He either receives a lot of remedial attention or has to settle into a lower-than-age-group grade, in which he will often be aca-demically bored and socially out of place. (I speculated in chapter 2 that dealing with this problem may have motivated New York's urban counties to vote to abolish rate bills and impose more uniform schools on rural areas of the state.)

When most of the American population was rural, children whose par-ents moved most likely went to another rural area. (Joseph Ferrie [1997] shows that in 1850–70 the vast majority of those who moved fit this cat-egory.) Even if families did go to an urban area and sent their children to age-graded schools, the consequences were mitigated in the nineteenth century by the coarse fabric of most age grading. Age-graded schools circa 1870 usually had wide bands of ages contained in two, three, or at most four "grades." Even the numbering of grades was not standard; in many cases, the most elementary grade was given a higher ordinal number than more advanced grades (e.g., Wells 1877, 39). In this setting, the irregulari-ties incurred by a student's attendance in an ungraded, one-room school were less detectable and easier to accommodate.

But consider what happened when a majority of children in the United States attended urban, age-graded schools, and grading itself became more closely aligned with a single birth year. Now the rural-to-urban migrant had a more serious problem of adjusting to the new school, and age-graded schools found that nonstandard immigrants were more disruptive. By 1915, one-third of urban residents were native-born immigrants from rural areas (Glaab and Brown 1967, 136).

I propose that there arrived a "tipping point" at which the proprietors of rural schools and rural voters realized that their ungraded schools were a liability. This tipping point did not arrive simultaneously in all regions of the country, to be sure, but it did arrive long before the last one-room school went out of existence. Consolidation was one rural response to age grading, but another was to continue with a one-room school but adjust its methods to mimic age grading.

3.8 Problems of Age Grading in One-Room Schools and the High School Tipping Point

The period during which ungraded schools became obsolete corresponds roughly with the trends in urbanization. As indicated in table 3.2, between the 1910 and 1920 census, the number of Americans in rural areas was surpassed by the number living in "urban places." A census-designated urban place is a closely settled locale, usually but not necessarily an incorporated municipality of at least 2,500 people. A town this size would be able to assemble enough children to make a multigraded school, especially if nearby rural children could be induced to attend it. At about the same time, one-room schools were attempting to fit themselves into the garb if not the reality of age-graded education.

One-room schools did not make the transition to age-graded education very well. Teachers with students in each of eight grades simply did not have time to give a separate recitation lesson in their individual grades. A teacher with students in each cohort would have to cover on average six subjects in each grade. That would be forty-eight separate recitations per five-hour day, or six minutes per lesson (Cuban 1984). In theory, students would be in "study hall" for seven-eighths of the school day. In reality, teachers usually compromised by grouping many students, as they had in the ungraded schools.

Some official sources attempted to deal with these problems by encouraging one-room schools to teach odd-numbered grades in one year and even-numbered grades in the next year. The Vermont Department of

Education (1921, 14) promulgated an elaborate system of alternate-year curricula for one-room schools so that "the number of daily recitations is decreased materially." It is not clear how extensively Vermont's plan was implemented, but its existence illustrates contemporary awareness of the difficulties of age-graded education in one-room schools. Rural Missouri schools of the same era tried a similar plan (David Burton 2000, 23). Such creative compromises were perhaps the best they could do, but in a world in which students came and went from one school to another, the compromises were sure to show. A student who had completed second grade in a previous school and was ready for third grade had a problem if she came to a school that was teaching "even-numbered" grades that year. She would have to either stretch for fourth grade or repeat second grade.

Age grading created other complications. The one-room school teacher who had to teach each grade could no longer put off those topics that she actually did not know herself, as she could in an ungraded situation. ("Latin? Miss Cousins will surely cover that in the winter term.") She had to know the material in all eight grades (as they were eventually to number). One of the advantages that urban teachers now had is that they could specialize in the material for certain grades or certain subjects. There were inspired rural teachers with both the erudition and the energy to teach eight grades well, but by the 1920s, many such energetic and able mentors found that pay and working conditions were more attractive in the growing number of urban and consolidated schools.

The lore about resistance to rural school consolidation is full of quotes from hayseed types who disparaged the need for consolidated schools. No doubt there were such types, but another force was drowning out their complaints. High schools had, like age-graded schools, originated in larger cities. But up to about 1870, public high schools had a curriculum that mimicked their private competitors, the classical academy. Whether private or public, secondary education was undertaken only by a small minority, and its content reflected elite aspirations to attend college and enter the ministry or another learned profession. Classical languages and history occupied much of the curriculum. Some academies did cater to a middle-class clientele and offered more general studies, and many were partly supported by local taxes in the hope of making their towns more respectable, but there was no systematic streaming from common schools to these protosecondary schools (Bruce Leslie 2001).

After 1870, the American economy began to demand a large number of workers who were numerate and literate to a degree that went beyond the typical common-school curriculum. This demand grew rapidly after 1900 (Claudia Goldin 1998). Those with the ability to read blueprints, write contracts, do some algebra, keep account books, and draft business letters with that new word processor, the typewriter, were widely sought and well rewarded. These skills were not typically produced by the classical academies. Public high schools of the latter quarter of the nineteenth century transformed themselves to be able to produce graduates with these skills. In doing so, they put most of the private academies out of business, often taking over their former buildings (Leslie 2001). Elite colleges and universities, led by the example of public land-grant universities, eventually had to modernize their formerly classical curriculum to attract applicants from the new high schools. Pressure for modern curricular reform came from the public schools to the colleges, not vice versa (Cubberley 1919, 234).

The role of high schools in my present inquiry is that their growing popularity put pressure on the rural, imperfectly graded, one-room schools. High schools required a standardized preparation, to which the eight grades of primary school were increasingly attuned. Voters in rural school districts could not ignore this pressure even if their own children had no interest in high school. In 1870, the small town of Franklin, Indiana, established a high school program. Upon establishing its high school, Franklin simultaneously created consolidated, age-graded schools, because "in the one room school no teacher could be expected to conduct classes for all eight grades in six subjects" (Graham 1974, 38). Small towns in Iowa followed a similar path after about 1870 (Reynolds 1999, 64), as did those elsewhere in Indiana (Reese 1998). Local boosters everywhere regarded graded schools as essential to the town's growth. In a report for the World's Columbian Exposition of 1893 in Chicago, Kansas educators proudly pointed out that cities with a population as small as two thousand had graded schools that could stream their students into high school (Kansas State Historical Society 1893). North Carolina towns began adopting age-graded education in the 1880s in a conscious effort to become centers of the new market economy (Leloudis 1996, chapter 1).

3.9 Property Values Responded to Proximity and Systemic Effects

The economic factor that induced rural voters to support multiclassroom, age-graded schools was the threat of declining property values. We know from many twentieth-century studies of urban areas that declining school quality is bad for home values. The threat of such declines usually motivates voters to support school spending when it appears to be efficiently allocated. Rural voters earlier in the century had an even greater incentive to pay attention to factors that affected property values, as it constituted both their business—mainly farming—and residential wealth.

Many historians of public schools would assign a different direction to the role of property values. They would rightly point out that one of the most frequent objections to consolidation that rural voters voiced was that removal of the old district school would reduce their property values (Ellsworth 1956, 124; Link 1986, 146). The New Hampshire Superintendent of Public Instruction (1900, 272) got so tired of hearing it from local school boards that he felt compelled to declare in an official report, "The public school was not established, nor is it demanded, by our state laws for the purpose of enhancing the value of property in the vicinity of the schoolhouse." It is important, then, to divide the influence of schools on property values into two components: proximity effects and systemic effects.

As I emphasized in chapter 2, the size of the rural school district was governed by the distance a child could reasonably be expected to walk. But within the district, some children had to walk farther than others. A homestead located close to the center of the district (the center usually being the location of the school itself) had an advantage over others for prospective buyers. The kids could, after doing their morning chores, walk a few hundred feet to school. This advantage over other homes and farms in the district surely became reflected in the value of the closer property. Indeed, the site for many a rural school had been donated by a local landowner, who also often got his name attached to the informal designation of the district (Fuller 1982, 62). The donor doubtlessly had both an altruistic and a selfish motive. The selfish advantage was what I would call the proximity effect. It is the differential advantage of being closer to a school. Thus some schoolhouses surely *were* established "for the purpose of enhancing the value of property in the vicinity of the schoolhouse."

The systemic effect of having a desirable school is different from the proximity effect. The systemic value of a better-than-average school accrues to everyone in the district. Having a school that attracted buyers to the district as a whole would be capitalized into the value of all properties in the district, not just those close to the school. This is the effect that most modern studies of school districts find to be capitalized into home values.

The school district boundary, not proximity to the school itself, is the systemic benefit that homebuyers care most about.

It is unlikely that the systemic quality of local schools had much effect on property values in most nineteenth-century one-room districts. Not having any school would be a drawback, of course, but once that relatively low hurdle was overcome and an ungraded one-room school was established, the quality of the school depended almost exclusively on the quality of the instructor. Since one-room school teachers seldom stayed at a single school for more than a year or two, there was almost no way for the district to establish a reputation beyond making the schoolhouse itself a little more pleasant. This may account for why almost all evaluations of rural schools focused exclusively on the physical plant (e.g., Thrun 1933). The teacher who could have made a school district good or bad was usually gone by the time the report was issued.

After age-graded schools became the norm and high school attendance became common, however, rural schools could be evaluated on a systemic level. A school district that had a consolidated age-graded school that channeled its students toward high school or actually provided the high school would have a systemic advantage. Superintendents and principals and much of the teaching staff could stay long enough to establish a reputation. The lack of a consolidated age-graded system put local property owners at a disadvantage when it came to selling their homes and farms to people with children.

3.10 Student Transition from Rural Schools to High School

Children from one-room districts in the twentieth century were usually entitled to attend a nearby high school, but it required adjustments. The one-room school curriculum had to be fitted to the age-graded curriculum to enable its "eighth grade" graduates to go on to high school. Because this fit was almost always imperfect, urban public high schools usually required that the rural applicants take an entrance examination, whose function was usually served by an eighth-grade "graduation" exam (Reese 1995, 143). (Urban students in age-graded schools also were subject to exams, but their preparation was more systematic and geared toward the high school curriculum, and pass rates were correspondingly high.) Many contemporary recollections, such as those collected by Leight and Rinehart (1999), attest that the high school entrance exam was a daunting experience with a high failure rate, the prospect of which surely deterred many rural children from taking the test. There was no guarantee that the applicant would succeed just because he had passed through the one-room school's curricular offerings, even if the school was nominally "age graded."

Avis Carlson (1979, 178–81) recalled the eighth-grade graduation examination, which was necessary to enroll in high school, of her one-room school in Kansas in 1907. "The questions on that examination in that primitive, one-room school taught by a young person who never attended a high school, positively daze me," she wrote. Carlson, who had herself become a distinguished educator, had saved it and offered some examples from the eighty-question test. Among them were "give a brief account of the colleges, printing, and religion in the colonies prior to the American Revolution" and "find the interest on an eight percent note for $900 running 2 years, 2 months, 6 days" and, this being Kansas, "write 200 words on the evil effects of alcoholic beverages."

Intellectual challenges were not the only problem. Educators early in the twentieth century were aware of the problems that rural students had in adjusting to high school. I report one study that addressed this issue with some real data. Calvin O. Davis (1916) was a professor of education administration at the University of Michigan. Several of his previous students had become administrators of small-town high schools in Michigan. Their high schools admitted students who lived within the district confines and also accepted students from rural areas surrounding the town. The rural students had attended one-room schools, whereas the town students had gone through multiclassroom, age-graded elementary schools. Professor Davis enlisted his former university students in a statistical test of the high school accomplishments of the two groups of students.

The statistical test consisted of comparing the course grades of the rural and town-educated students in each school for each of the four years of high school and for various subjects taught in high school. It does not take much reading between the lines to infer that Professor Davis was surprised and perhaps a bit disappointed by the results of this simple exercise. The initial impetus of the test was probably to show that the rural students were disadvantaged by their one-room education once they entered high school. Davis's study may have been undertaken as further ammunition for state programs to consolidate rural school districts.

The results showed that in their first year in high school, the rural students on average did indeed do worse than the town-educated students.

This was consistent with the official line about the drawbacks of the rural one-room schools. But within a year the students from the one-room schools caught up to their town-educated peers, and by the time they graduated, the hicks from the sticks had on average done better than the others. It sounds almost like a hackneyed Hollywood script, with the poor but hard-working rural kid starting with a handicap but eventually beating out the swells from the city.

Professor Davis's statistical methods consisted only of comparing averages, but his disappointing (to him) conclusion actually led him to a statistically sophisticated insight. The problem with the design of the experiment, he concluded, was sample-selection bias. (He did not use those words, but that's what he meant.) High school attendance was optional for both town and rural children, but, as Davis mentioned, the town children only needed to glide along through eight grades to attend the high school.

The rural children who came to high school were a self-selected group of highly motivated students. Having passed the daunting high school entrance exam, they probably had to find their own transportation to and from school. Some may even have boarded in town during the term. When they got there, they had to overcome the strangeness of a new school and deal with fitting in with a new cohort of students who already knew one another and who had been educated in what everyone regarded as the superior, age-graded classrooms of the town schools. Contemporaries were well aware of country boys' and girls' anxieties about attending school in the big city. (I vividly recall my own panicky reaction to the multiclassroom junior high school in Hellertown, Pennsylvania, in 1957 after my six years in a rural township school that had in-room coal stoves and two grades per classroom.)

Professor Davis tried to salvage his Michigan inquiry by focusing on the two subjects, English and history, in which the rural students did not do as well in the end as the town students. His explanations are lame, and he overlooks what I think is the evidence that does show why one-room schools were a drawback. Even after the obvious selection bias in favor of able and motivated students, the rural ninth graders did worse in the first year. Adjusting to high school *was* more difficult for them. The prospect of this adjustment must have deterred a number of rural-school students from continuing their high school education, even if they had passed the qualifying test.

It would be anachronistic to conclude that rural children who did not go to high school were "dropouts." In the 1910–20 period, high school attendance was hardly the norm. But this was the beginning of the period of rapid growth in high school attendance, and a high school education had a big economic payoff. It was no longer reserved for an elite who wanted to go to college or become teachers. Thus the more convincing evidence from Davis's study was what he did not emphasize: the deterrent effect of one-room school attendance on high school enrollment.

Other evidence confirms that there was a systemic disadvantage to one-room schools after 1910 or so. A report on Tennessee schools in the 1920s found that only 6 percent of white students from one-room schools attended high school, compared to 36 percent for the state as a whole (Joe Jenning 1927). It was this systemic disadvantage of one-room schools—the kids could not get into high school as easily—that I believe eventually offset the location and governance advantages of the one-room district and made rural voters vote to consolidate schools. However, I do not have access to property values that would support this claim. My evidence in support of the importance of "demand side" effects is to show that the contrary story about consolidation—that it was imposed from above without regard for local opinion—is not as plausible.

3.11 Top-Down Consolidation and Professor Ellwood P. Cubberley

The dominant "supply side" story about rural school consolidation is that it was forced on unwilling rural districts. Farmers and other rural folk clung to their one-room schools until state legislation forced them to consolidate. Exactly what the "force" was is seldom specified, but the impetus for consolidation and centralization is always traced to the urgings of the education establishment, whose members include state and county superintendents of schools, faculty in education departments and at normal schools, professional teachers, and sundry official commissions set up by philanthropists such as John D. Rockefeller and Andrew Carnegie.

The preeminent academic advocate of consolidation was Ellwood P. Cubberley, the most influential historian of education in the early twentieth century. Cubberley saw the origins of public education in much the same way that I do, as a highly decentralized groundswell. Speaking of early nineteenth-century America, he described with wonder "how completely local the evolution of schools has been with us. Everywhere development has been from the community outward and upward, and not from the State downward" (Cubberley 1919, 155).

Instead of building on the apparently spontaneous order that this evolution might suggest, however, Cubberley regarded it as unfortunate. In his view, it lacked the direction and uniformity necessary for the next phase of development. He admired to the point of triumphalism the development of American public schools in the nineteenth century, but, like many twenty-first-century reformers, he wrung his hands about the future. He could not imagine how institutions might further evolve into a coherent system without a firm, visible hand from the top. Much of the balance of his book was to describe how the situation was to be rectified by educational leaders working from "the State downward."

Indeed, most of Cubberley's teaching and administrative career at Stanford was devoted to the training of these very educational leaders. The primary purpose of the Stanford University School of Education, founded in 1917 with Cubberley as its dean, was not to train teachers. It was to train administrators. Much like the era's burgeoning schools of business and public administration, Stanford and others like it taught modern methods of administration and imparted a sense of mission to its crop of would-be leaders. Bringing order to what they regarded as a chaotically decentralized school system was the grail.

It seems to be something of a rite of passage for modern historians of education to disparage something about Cubberley, who died in 1941. An overview of this scholarship with a slyly disrespectful title is *The Wonderful World of Ellwood Patterson Cubberley* by Lawrence Cremin (1965). Cubberley's triumphalist view of public education's evolution is a favorite target of advocates of private education, religious education, voucher systems, and charter schools. Professional historians gag on his Manichean view of historical struggle and his neglect of education outside of public schooling (Diane Ravitch 2001). His retrograde views about race, eugenics, immigrants, and popular democracy are held up for scorn, leavened only sometimes with the aside that Cubberley was not much different in those respects from other prominent scholars of his day.

My task here is not to defend Cubberley's views about the virtues of American public education in the nineteenth century. That has been done more than adequately by economists Claudia Goldin and Lawrence Katz (2003). Their essay, "The 'Virtues' of the Past: Education in the First Hundred Years of the New Republic," reads, despite the ironic quotes, rather like what Cubberley might have written had he been better at econometrics. I mention Cubberley because a tenet to which both his critics and supporters (though not Goldin and Katz) subscribe is that school consolidation in the twentieth century came about primarily as a result of the efforts of unelected, undemocratic elites. Parents, taxpayers, and the voting public either had no part in the process or were gulled, shamed, browbeaten, or manipulated into compliance with the consolidation movement. Both critics and admirers of centralization regard it as being the product of, depending on their point of view, arrogant elites or enlightened educators.

David Tyack (1974) detailed the bureaucratization and centralization of urban schools in the early twentieth century. Many schools in larger cities had evolved as ward schools, whose organization and pedagogy were much like the one-room schools of the countryside. They received money from the city, which was the ad hoc school district in most cases, often appearing before any state authorization. However, neighborhood and ward officials (such as the city councilman elected from the ward) selected the teachers and pretty much ran the schools (Graham 1974, 150; Teaford 1984, 77). This was sometimes a devolution from centralized beginnings. New York City's schools were initially under the control of a citywide Protestant group, but the growing Catholic population demanded and obtained a more decentralized system in which neighborhoods, or at least ward leaders, could select teachers (Ravitch 1974). Although this did not appease the Catholic hierarchy, who went on to establish parochial schools, the locally controlled ward schools retained the clientele of many Catholic neighborhoods by hiring teachers sympathetic to their faith.

Tyack describes the centralization of control over the urban ward schools in the early twentieth century. He found that education leaders were hardly democratic in their outlook. Many were contemptuous of democratic processes and the hoi polloi of immigrants. Some of the reformers even proposed to disfranchise the poor in order to do good for them (Tyack 1974, 131). Nothing came of such proposals in the North, which was a good thing. As I explain in chapter 5, disfranchisement of blacks in the South was the occasion for creating a vast gulf between schools for whites and blacks. Although Tyack concedes that the voters had to assent to almost every move, he nonetheless, in this work and several others, regards administrative centralization and district consolidation as something done despite the wishes of the electorate (Tyack, Lowe, and Hansot 1984; Tyack and James 1986, 54). (I would point out that Tyack's 1974 history concentrated on the centralization of *management* of city school districts—a reform that was transforming municipal and business governance at the same time—rather than the consolidation of districts, but he also extends his "top-down" conclusions to consolidation.)

Most other modern commentators also hold that rural consolidations were somehow coercive (e.g., Sher and Rosenfeld 1977; Strang 1987). It is something that both the right and the left seem to agree about. Edwin G. West (1967), a conservative who was an early supporter of privatization of education, regarded New York State's attempts to establish rural central school districts in the middle of the nineteenth century as largely the product of bureaucratic machinations at the state level. (As Myer, Tyack, Nagel, and Gordon [1979], point out, however, there were almost no state-level education officials other than the state superintendent anywhere in the nation before 1900.)

On the leftward side of the political spectrum, Michael Katz (1968) examined the disestablishment of high school in Beverly, Massachusetts. Demographic data from an 1860 city referendum in which voters rebelled against the new high school survived to make Beverly famous among quantitative historians. Katz's revisionist education history was premised on the idea that the high school was, as he titled Part I, "reform by imposition" by capitalist and upper-class interests who wanted schools to produce a skilled but docile workforce. He saw the disestablishment vote as a brief rebellion by the common people. (Katz's interpretation is contested by Maris Vinovskis [1985], who found that the opposition to high school was more from residents of remote areas of the town who did not want to pay for a school their children could not conveniently attend. My own reaction to Katz's hypothesis was to wonder what other mischief capitalists were up to when they weren't setting up free high schools.)

Left and right, triumphalist or revisionist, education historians regard the creation of a standardized system of education with consolidated, age-graded, state-certificated schools as having been forced upon a sullen, if not actively unwilling, electorate. To be fair, most of the aforementioned sources do mention at some point that local voters had to approve the change. Beverly residents, for example, voted first to abolish its high school but within a few years voted to reestablish it. But even in these cases, the implication is that the voters were presented with a Hobson's choice, as the state or interest groups set the agenda for centralization of schools that local voters could hardly resist.

3.12 Standards Evolved to Accommodate Teacher
and Student Mobility

My first response to the top-down claim is that the development and accep-
tance of a standard, bureaucratized system of age-graded schools was not
itself invented by a central committee that bent its mind to the task. Most
blue-ribbon committees appointed to examine education issues came
up with recommendations that were ignored or twisted so badly that the
resulting reforms could hardly be said to have evolved from the original
recommendations. For example, a Rockefeller-sponsored committee of
distinguished educators was impaneled in 1923 to study school districts in
Indiana, which seems to have been a magnet for reformers. After much
research and deliberation, the committee recommended that school districts be formed entirely along county lines (James Madison 1984; Barron
1997, 75). The legislature gratefully accepted the report and then simply
ignored it. Indiana's township system of school districts, which actually
was more centralized at the time than that of other midwestern states
(Fuller 1982, chapter 7), is still the basis for school district organization
in the state.

A more successful reform was proposed by another blue-ribbon committee, this time named for Andrew Carnegie. The committee examined
the offerings of the rapidly growing number of high schools and noted the
difficulty in comparing courses from one school to the other, a problem
that was especially vexing for college admissions and teacher compensation. The Carnegie group in 1906 proposed that each course be taught
in periods of fifty minutes per day every day for thirty-two weeks. Each
course was thus assigned a "unit" that consisted of 180 instruction hours,
an hour being in this case fifty minutes plus the ten minutes to move from
classroom to classroom. This pattern came to be known as the "Carnegie
unit," and it was almost universally adopted. A slight variation of it persists to the present day.

The Carnegie unit has been criticized as a kind of straitjacket for instruction. Tyack and Cuban (1995) conclude that it and other standardized
practices formed an inflexible "grammar of schooling" that made progressive experiments such as the Dalton Plan and similar attempts to es-
cape the lockstep of age grading impossible to implement. There are other
schedules by which courses might be taught, such as a month of math, a
month of history, and a month of English, and it is not clear that each subject deserves or should be limited to the hours of a Carnegie unit. But the

advantages of standardization for a system of schools are so pervasive that we tend to overlook such alternatives. Having a uniform Carnegie-unit schedule does allow reasonable comparisons of coverage, if not accomplishment, by students from various schools. It makes it easier to integrate into ongoing courses new students who transfer from another school and simplifies the preparation of teachers who change jobs.

The Carnegie unit, like the Australian ballot and the Prussian age-grading system, is one of those logical standardizations that have a proper name. If it were not for this particular commission, some other organization or committee would have come up with something very similar and straightened out the edges of what was already becoming standard practice. It's kind of like the story about Frank Cyr, "the father of the yellow school bus." His 1939 conference on school transportation established "school bus yellow" as a voluntary national standard for paint, and this standard was widely adopted. It succeeded, most probably, because most school buses were already painted yellow or a similarly bright color to alert motorists and pedestrians in the early morning fog. It was a sensible and simple standard. It is unlikely that many districts had to repaint "midnight black" or "dusky gray" buses to conform to the national standard of yellow. (A national standard also was helpful to school bus manufacturers by reducing choices to a Henry Fordian "any color the customer wants as long as it's yellow.")

Other standard curricular features seem to have come about without a well-known group having promoted them. American literature is almost universally taught in the eleventh grade in the United States. I can think of no pedagogical reason why Twain, Cather, and Hemingway should be taught to students at age seventeen, but the standard does serve a useful function. For students who move from one school to another during high school, it saves having to repeat or entirely forgo American literature if the student stays with his or her new cohort in the school. In a flexible school, the newcomer who had studied American Literature in tenth grade could in a new school take English literature in eleventh grade, but that can make scheduling problematic and is likely to present the student with a set of classroom peers that may be mismatched socially and intellectually. The nearly uniform timing of high school American literature courses has some small benefits and apparently no serious costs.

Another much-debated standard was the frequency of promotion from one grade to the next. Recall that in ungraded, one-room schools, promotion—such as it was—was based on subject mastery. Once the text had been mastered (usually by memorization), the child could move on to the next reader and a more advanced recitation group. Mastery of some but not other subjects did not require that the student repeat an entire grade and wastefully review material already learned and understood.

Proponents of age-graded schools tried various ways to accommodate different learning rates (Rickard 1947; 1948). An early failure was annual promotion by subject: Go to third grade in math, stay in second for history, and go to fourth grade in geography. This did not work, I believe, because it defeated the mobility benefits of age grading. A more moderate approach was to make promotion decisions at the midpoint of the school year, in January as well as in June. But this did not succeed, because transfers of pupils between schools became complicated by fractional accomplishments. By 1900, most larger cities converged on the eight-grade primary system with annual promotions.

As these examples suggest, the standards that were introduced successfully were those that accommodated the mobility of the population. For some, it was useful to have a high-profile commission urging their adoption. This approach made for quicker and more uniform adoptions, but recommendation by a high-profile set of experts was no guarantee of success. Other standards seem to have arisen without much discussion at all. The most prominent one in my mind is the standard school calendar, which I will argue in the next chapter was the product of age-graded education and the need to accommodate the mobility of students and teachers. Regardless of their source, though, standardizations imposed a penalty on districts that did not conform to them. Prospective immigrants would be likely to be put off by an unusual schedule or creative curriculum that did not build on their children's previous experiences in school.

3.13 State Legislatures Were Creatures of Rural Voting Districts

The belief that states simply forced consolidation on local districts may stem from the legal truism that school districts are "creatures of the state." The state's authority to regulate schooling is supposedly derived from state constitutional provisions that are specific about their grant of authority. Local school boards are, in this view, little more than state functionaries, having no more authority to go their own way than the state's road builders could determine the routes of highways without the approval of legislatures and executive agencies in the state capital.

The holes in this story are large. Schools appeared in the Northwest Territories before statehood, as Congress contemplated reserving school sections in newly surveyed townships. The establishment of territorial government was not even a necessary condition. In Wisconsin, Jorgenson (1956, 36–37) found that territorial authority was only sometimes the basis for school district foundation:

> More common, of course, were schools maintained cooperatively by the settlers themselves, even before a school district had been formally organized. . . . The most striking fact about early education in Wisconsin is that the movement for free schools was essentially a local one. Tax-supported schools were not created by territorial legislation; it would be much nearer the truth to say that they developed in spite of such legislation.

The importance of state leadership was likewise a myth in Massachusetts: "Like the colonial grammar schools, higher schools in the nineteenth century appeared only when local leaders perceived sufficient demand and practical need for them" (Reese 1995, 6). Nebraska's 1855 Constitution commanded the establishment of free schools, but they only appeared when local initiative established them (Olson and Naugh 1997, 98). Even Utah, whose Mormon pioneers came from New York and New England but had no special allegiance to its governance forms (they had been made rather unwelcome back East) originally established self-financing, one-room school districts before statehood (Moffitt 1946, 69).

The state constitutional provisions themselves are long on aspirational language—mostly on the order of "knowledge is good"—and short on specific obligations. Tyack and James (1986, 60) indicate that constitutional provisions assumed the continued existence of local financing and local control that had been established before statehood. Indeed, one of the ironies of this story is that several nineteenth-century state constitutions actually forbade public support for education beyond the "common school." Cities that wanted to establish high schools in California sometimes resorted to subterfuge, calling the advanced high school grades mere extensions of the "common schools" rather than separate institutions that were prohibited by state law (Cheney 1888; Tyack, James, and Benavot 1987, 104).

There is no doubt, of course, that local school districts are subservient to state law. This legal status means that courts will seldom intervene to protect districts if the state legislature acts to alter their powers, borders,

apportionment rulings, some states either enshrined a unit of local government as an electoral district (typically the county in the upper house of
the legislature) or had population-based districts that were not reappor-
tioned for many census decades. For example, Chicago was shortchanged
by the Illinois legislature's refusal to reapportion its districts after 1910.
Such prior deviations from the Court's "one man, one vote" principle in
the 1960s usually meant that rural areas received proportionately more
representation than urban areas (David and Eisenberg 1961). A lightly
populated county would get its representative in the state senate alongside
the giant urban county's single senator, as was once the case in California.
Or a rural district that was populous in 1910 might still get a representative who in 1960 was elected by a far smaller number of voters than a city
whose population had greatly increased between 1910 and 1960. (In actu-
ality, it was the suburbs that were most severely underrepresented by this
practice, since that was where most of the urban growth occurred [James
Reichley 1970].)

In either case of malapportionment, it was rural areas, where nearly
all the one-room school districts were located, that had disproportionate
clout in the legislature. Yet they concurred with consolidation legislation
in most cases (Tyack, James, and Benavot 1987, 121). Any applied theory
of the politics of school district consolidation would have to account for
this. If there was any geographic bias in state legislation, it surely would
have favored rural areas (Allard, Burns, and Gamm 1998).

3.14 The "Education Establishment" Lacked Influence

Modern theories of political economy do not simply count votes. Farmers
and other rural residents may have wanted the right to veto school consolidation, but their greater numbers do not necessarily mean that they will get
what they want. Cohesive and well-funded interest groups can often persuade legislators to assist them at the expense of the more numerous members of the public. The typical example that economists give for this process
is, ironically enough, the modern farm lobby. Full-time farmers nowadays
represent only about 1 percent of the population, but state and federal farm
legislation almost invariably favors them over the more numerous consumers of their output.

The implication that rural voters were not getting what they wanted from
consolidation invariably points to the state education establishment as the

interest group that is swaying the legislature. The problem with this story is that this "establishment" had almost no political base. The National Education Association (NEA) did not begin its militant, unionlike phase until the 1960s (Myron Lieberman 1997), after one-room schools had become almost extinct. The early NEA, which typically represented urban school administrators, certainly did support consolidation, but its clout in the state legislature was minuscule compared to that of farmers. State superintendents of schools were either appointed by the governor or elected at large by the population of the entire state. County superintendents were likewise answerable to the voters either by direct election or by selection by locally elected school boards. The average number of staff they commanded was not large. None of these groups had an interest-group constituency that could sway legislation.

The widespread belief that rural consolidation was forced on rural voters is partly the product of the bias in historical sources. The most accessible historical documents about education are reports of state superintendents of schools. Horace Mann was the first state superintendent in Massachusetts (his initial title was Secretary to the State Board of Education, but he ran with that), and from his first report on, he urged consolidation of the district schools. Virtually every state superintendent thereafter echoed these sentiments. In 1861, an Illinois superintendent recommended that the state's ten thousand rural districts be consolidated and reduced to two thousand (Kaestle 1983, 113). If one reads enough of them, one might conclude that they were the source of the consolidation movement. Moreover, their reports constantly complain of local resistance, so that when that resistance is finally overcome, it would seem logical to conclude that it was because of the superintendent's influence rather than assent of the local districts.

This conclusion actually does not seem so logical. It seems more logical to infer from their constant complaints about local resistance that state superintendents were *not* getting their way. The aforementioned Illinois superintendent would have had to wait a century before districts in his state numbered fewer than two thousand. Mann's campaign to consolidate Massachusetts' districts at the town level was a failure. Town districts were established by statewide legislation only in 1883, long after Mann had retired from his position in 1848. Early consolidation legislation in Massachusetts did have a coercive element at one stage, but, in response to local opposition, the next legislature promptly countermanded the rule and returned to a system in which districts could accept or reject a consolidation plan.

Only in 1882, after almost all towns had voted to consolidate their districts, was cleanup legislation passed that forced the remaining holdouts into the townwide system. (This account is drawn from Hal Barron [1997], who makes it clear that legislative deference to local voters was the rule in all of the states he examined, which included New York, Ohio, Indiana, and all of New England.)

3.15 How Consensual Were District Consolidations?

The previous section indicates that school district consolidation was very much in the hands of enfranchised residents of rural school districts. They usually controlled the legislature insofar as it concerned school district structure, and in nearly every instance, local voters had the final say about consolidation. As I proposed in sections 3.4 and 3.5, local voters balanced transport costs and dilution of political control against gains from access to fully age-graded schools and their ticket to high school. Local voters had sound reasons to want to consolidate, and they initiated consolidation or accepted one of the many plans presented when these plans made economic sense to them. A typical example of the feel-your-way, "bottom up" consolidation process was provided by an amateur historian on the Web page of the Bethel Public School (near Shawnee, Oklahoma; http://www.bethel.k12.ok.us/history.htm, March 2009):

> In 1917 a petition to form a Union Graded District encompassing Bethel #25 [and three other districts] was submitted to the County Superintendent, H. M. Fowler, but it did not have the required one-third of the registered voters. It is thought that the measure failed because the consolidation would only produce a larger grade school and would not have included a high school. By February 1919, another petition was presented to the County Superintendent calling for an election to combine Bethel District #25 [and one of the previous districts and two *different* districts] into a consolidated district with a high school. The petition "explicitly stated" that the new school would be located in the "geographical center" of the four districts. All voters except those in Valley Grove approved the measure so the other schools now formed Consolidated District 3.

Because my view here is so contrary to most historians' views about consolidation, I will buttress it with evidence that I found in two extensive reviews of district consolidation that examined it nationwide. *Your School*

District, by the self-designated National Commission on School District Reorganization (National Commission 1948), was a project conceived by the University of Chicago's Rural Education Project and a committee of the National Education Association. Its various authors provide an overview of the consolidation situation in the recent past and then detailed chapters about consolidation in Arkansas, Illinois, Iowa, Kansas, New York, Washington, and West Virginia, as well as thumbnail sketches of ten other states. The other source, *The Relationship of School District Organization to State Aid Distribution Systems*, by Clifford Hooker and Van Mueller (1970), covers all states and concentrates on the period after World War II, but it is sketchier in its descriptions. Both volumes are by authors who think consolidation is a fine thing, but, as people who have been in the trenches of consolidation battles, they are also aware of the nuances of state and local politics and the need to get local voters' consent. (An earlier affirmation of the need to get voters' consent is J. F. Able [1923].)

The picture of consolidation that emerges from these sources might be summarized as "the state proposes, the voter disposes." State education leaders proposed, usually by a commission report, a plan of consolidation for rural districts. It was adopted by the legislature with the proviso that local voters approve it district by district.

3.16 County and Township Boundaries Were Rejected in Favor of "Organic" Districts

In many states, the first attempt to rationalize the process of consolidation was to nominate preexisting political units, such as counties and townships, as the basis for consolidated schools, at least in the rural areas. The ideal was the New England town. New England states had by 1900 largely consolidated their many school districts along township lines. There were still one-room schools in the rural areas, but their budgets and governance were at least nominally in the hands of townwide officials. Even before this time, the subtown districts usually did not cross town boundaries, though there might be "sending" agreements for students in remote areas to attend schools in another town. New England towns had mostly been established as a political unit from the very beginning of European settlement, and so it was natural for school districts to be organized along those lines.

School district consolidators in the early twentieth century tried to reorganize districts in New York along New England lines. Thus New York in 1917 passed a law that attempted to channel consolidations along town boundaries (National Commission 1948, 113). This generated enormous political dissatisfaction, and within two years the law was repealed. New York towns were not settled by groups with strong common interests, and residents in one section of the town often had little social or political contact with residents of the same town living five miles away, across the river or over the mountain. The same problem arose elsewhere. Illinois attempted to create township high school districts in 1905 without much success, even though the township was still the basis for entitlement to revenues from the "school section" provided for by the Land Act of 1785 and its successors. Kansas and Iowa tried both the county and the township as a unit for providing high schools in the late nineteenth century, but local voters did not accept the change (National Commission 1948, 113–14). Wayne Fuller (1982, chapter 7) likewise documents earlier failures to make the township into a functioning school district in the upper Midwest, though he casts local voters' rejections in a more favorable light than the 1948 National Commission did.

Arkansas initially established the township as the school district because of land-grant gifts, but local residents soon opted for smaller districts (National Commission 1948, 114). West Virginia followed a path similar to Arkansas, except that the township-sized "magisterial district" was the basic unit. Again, local school control and financing became fragmented. (West Virginia was the only one of the seven states studied by the National Commission that had adopted the county system, which came about after a statewide tax revolt in the Great Depression decimated local tax bases.) A separate source (Weaver 1944, 20) confirmed the futility of top-down orders. The Illinois state superintendent proposed legislation in 1937 and 1938 to impose consolidation on the state's rural schools but had it derailed both times. Weaver, an ardent proponent of consolidation, ruefully concluded that top-down consolidation was "not within the realm of the politically feasible."

After failing to get voters to approve county or township districts, most state leaders pursued a more subtle approach, which the 1948 National Commission described and endorsed. State legislation set up county commissions to propose consolidation zones. County commissions then undertook studies to see where the "organic" or natural community boundaries might be. These commissions were so dedicated to the concept of organic communities that they often allowed proposed districts to cross county lines. The commissions did sociological studies and held public meetings

to determine the ideal districts. To improve the chances of public accep-
tance, local residents without any ties to the state education department
were put in charge. Once the commissions came up with a plan for consolidation, they sent it up to the state education department for approval.
The reason for this step was to avoid gerrymandering to grab tax-base and
otherwise undesirable geographic configurations. After state approval, the
proposed consolidation was given to local voters to accept or reject.

This orchestrated bottom-up process had been recognized early in the
century. Cubberley (1914) described a Douglas County, Minnesota, plan
that was similar to the commissions commended by the 1948 National Commission. The county superintendent and his local commission sought to
discover the "natural community boundaries" around which local voters
would rally, and the county created about two dozen consolidated schools
as a result. Cubberley only grudgingly approved of this process—he gave
unqualified approval to the South's top-down, countywide consolidation
process—because it resulted in too many districts of irregular shapes: "The
township lines also bore little relationship to the natural community boundaries," the latter being the districts that residents actually chose in his Minnesota example (1914, 248).

In New Jersey and Pennsylvania, it was the township itself that appears
to have been modified to conform to the school district. Townships there
were not laid out along the congressional survey lines (they predated the
United States), so their borders were more often the "organic communities" around which other states later sought to create consolidated school
districts. Pennsylvania in 1834 made townships, cities, and boroughs the
primary units for school districts, and, unlike most other states, townships
were not further subdivided into subdistricts (Wickersham 1886). Instead,
townships themselves apparently split into two or more townships or compact "boroughs" when tastes for schools and other local services were too
heterogeneous, as they often were in multiethnic Pennsylvania. In New
Jersey, the enormous spate of borough formations in the 1890s was said
to have been motivated by a desire to separate urban age-graded districts
from rural one-room school districts (John Snyder 1969, 23).

3.17 Local Voting Rules and Agenda Control

In most states, the local vote required concurrent majorities of every district
in the proposed consolidation. If district A approved by a one hundred-to-

fifty vote but district B disapproved by a thirty-to-twenty vote, the consolidation failed. (Usually more than two districts were involved in a proposed consolidation.) But in other states (or at other times in the same state's history), the total vote of the combined districts would be all that was necessary, and in the foregoing example, the consolidation would prevail. In this latter scenario, district B could complain that the state had forced it to consolidate, and collections of these instances doubtlessly contributed to the overall impression that consolidation was "top down." Purely local autonomy was potentially breached by adopting an at-large count of the votes. But this was rare, and even where such provisions were on the books, they were seldom applied where a district strenuously protested against a proposed consolidation (Link 1986, 143; Barron 1997, 66).

States sometimes adopted a hybrid model that established size or organizational thresholds for giving the districts veto power. A sizeable village that was to be annexed to several small rural districts might be given the right to reject the consolidation, whereas the rural districts would have their votes aggregated as a group. Or extremely small districts that had fewer than a dozen pupils enrolled might not have the power to veto a proposed consolidation. These minuscule enrollment numbers were not fanciful. Many one-room schools in midwestern states in the 1940s and 1950s had fewer than nine students enrolled.

The National Commission that wrote *Your School District* was composed of men whose profession was education, and so they naturally assumed that their activity was so important that only an unreasonable set of voters would oppose them. One gets the impression that they were not too keen on voting, and if voting must be done, they would rather it be done at-large and over a large area rather than district by district. But they were also men of experience. They had seen their plans beaten up in the state legislatures and their subsequent compromise plans defeated by voters. So they became realistic about voting. Without endorsing it, they noted that "it is accepted almost as a principle that school districts ought not to be abolished or altered without the consent of the citizens living in the areas affected" (1948, 45). Even in those few instances (to be discussed below) where legislatures had managed to avoid local votes, the National Commission noted that "the desires of the majority of people affected" play a decisive role in reorganizing the schools.

Elected county superintendents in the "common school" states (roughly the North outside of New England) were often given the authority to alter school district boundaries, but they did so at their peril and "usually only when authorized to do so by popular vote in the territories affected" (National Commission 1948, 65). Local school boards sometimes could authorize consolidations without a plebiscite, as was the case in Pennsylvania in the 1950s. The vast majority of boards, however, were (and continue to be) popularly elected (Berkman and Plutzer 2005, chapter 5). Although the expertise and sophistication of school boards are often disparaged by modern political scientists, infidelity to their constituents is not one of the charges (Berry and Howell 2007). The exceptions to elections were chiefly in the South, where countywide school boards were sometimes appointed in the era of consolidations. County courts would appoint them in Virginia and Tennessee; state legislatures appointed them in North Carolina; hybrids of state-elected and appointed officials appointed county boards in South Carolina and New Mexico; and the governor appointed (and still appoints) most county school boards in Maryland (National Commission 1948, 61–62).

The commission-study process that I mentioned above might suggest to political economists that the state authorities were exercising agenda control. Some degree of agenda control, however, was considered desirable even by local voters. Many were said to realize that uncoordinated consolidations would yield undesirable results. Voters in one district would be harmed if two neighboring districts went their separate ways. But it still remains a question as to whether states may have exercised additional agenda control and proposed more consolidation than local voters wanted.

Agenda control was subject to a serious discipline. The voters could say no to a consolidation proposal and fully expect that in a few years another proposal would be presented. The votes on each consolidation were up or down, but it would have been a naive set of voters who would have thought that a "no" vote would mean that consolidation would never happen. Many districts repeatedly rejected consolidation proposals over a period of decades until an acceptable proposal was brought to them.

3.18 Explaining the Slow Decline in One-Room Schools

This and the following sections address a question left thus far unexamined. I argued that the logic of an age-graded system induced voters to accept consolidation proposals if they conformed to familiar communities.

But if this logic was so compelling, why did it take so long for one-room schools and their districts to disappear? One-room schools persisted in considerable numbers into the 1960s. Although only a small fraction of the nation's students attended them, they were a significant presence in rural areas. And the numbers in figure 3.1 do not count the many rural schools where grades were "doubled up," as they were in the elementary school I attended in Lower Saucon Township, just outside of Bethlehem, Pennsylvania, in the 1950s. The ideal of one classroom and one teacher per grade was long in coming.

Two explanations would seem to compete for the persistence of small schools. One is the story of the obdurate voters. Because they had the final say, it took a long time for voters in one-room school districts to do what should have been obvious wisdom to their parents and grandparents. It is difficult to gainsay this story, but it should be clear that it comes mainly from a quarter that is strongly predisposed to consolidation. Most of the histories of school affairs have as their primary sources school administrators. The contrary story to which I lay claim has two sources, a dissertation and a chart.

My primary source is a Columbia Teachers College dissertation by Verne McGuffey (1929). (He was not, as far as I can tell, related to the famous textbook entrepreneur of the previous century.) His published study, *Differences in the Activities of Teachers in Rural One-Teacher Schools and of Grade Teachers in Cities*, had as its centerpiece the responses to a survey that he undertook. McGuffey managed to get 550 teachers of rural one-room schools and two hundred teachers of urban age-graded schools to fill out a 112-item questionnaire. (His name probably helped the response rate.) The questions were designed to indicate differences between rural and urban schools. Although his sample did represent a wide geographic area of the nation, his method of selecting respondents was hardly random. The oddest respondents were 178 from rural teachers that county superintendents rated "best" and "worst" in their county in response to the author's inquiries. (Because the best and worst responded in almost equal measure, one assumes McGuffey did not tell them all why they were selected.) But it seems likely that the responses to McGuffey's survey were honest and probably not far from what a more scientific survey would have obtained. His results seem broadly consistent with the reminiscences of rural teachers in Iowa in the 1930s recorded by Jeffrey Kaufmann (2000).

McGuffey's results make it clear that even in the mid-1920s, well after age-graded, multiroom schools had become the norm, there were enormous differences between rural one-room schools and urban schools. It was widely known that urban teachers were paid more, but the lower salaries of rural teachers do not tell the whole story. Boarding with the parents of students was not asked about in McGuffey's questionnaire, from which I infer that the custom had died out by the 1920s. Teachers' home accommodations in their one-room districts were nonetheless modest, with 41 percent living in "a home without modern conveniences" such as indoor plumbing. (No urban teachers suffered this privation). Most rural teachers, like their students, walked to school a mile or more, though some either drove a car (19 vs. 6 percent in cities) or rode a horse or a horse-drawn conveyance (18 vs. zero percent). Once at school, the rural division of labor was very limited. Rural teachers "kept all school records" (79 vs. 5 percent in cities) and "supervised playground activities" (79 vs. 19 percent). Less pleasantly, rural teachers would usually "do all the janitor work" (59 vs. zero percent), "start fires in the morning" (55 vs. zero percent), and "actively oversee school toilets" (83 vs. zero percent).

Classroom life was also far different for the rural teachers. Age-graded education was by this time the norm, and rural teachers had to "teach all subjects in eight grades" (73 vs. zero percent in cities). Because this meant that most students did not have the teacher's immediate attention, they had to be able to "keep several groups profitably busy while one is reciting" (82 vs. 13 percent). But the rural teachers enjoyed a great deal of independence. They would "plan and execute work with little or no supervision" (66 vs. 11 percent). (An oral history of Vermont teachers confirmed that teachers most appreciated the independence that one-room schools gave them [Margaret Nelson 1983].) Even though the great majority were females, they were responsive to the interests of the farm community and would "teach agriculture" (65 to zero percent in cities [of course]), and "select materials of instruction from the life of a farm community" (61 vs. 11 percent in cities [surprisingly]).

The difference between rural and urban teachers that was most striking—McGuffey lists it first—was their responsiveness to the local school board and the community at large. Local control was not some abstract matter in rural schools. The rural teachers would regularly "advise school board as to the needs of the school" (78 vs. zero percent in cities) and "meet with the school board" (48 vs. zero percent). School boards were not the only local elements they had to respond to. Rural teachers were far more embedded in their students' community. More than three-quarters (77 percent) of rural teachers would "establish friendly personal relations with all the patrons of the school," but less than one-quarter (23 percent) of urban teachers said they did so. Rural teachers "attended church" (69 vs. 25 percent in cities) and would "conduct entertainments for the community" (59 vs. zero percent), most likely spelling bees and holiday pageants. More ambitiously, though less frequently, rural teachers would "assume active leadership in movement for improvement of community health" (33 vs. zero percent), as well as for a variety of other nonschool activities such as recreation and "economic improvement of the community" (15 vs. zero percent). Some rural teachers may have kept to themselves outside of school hours, but it would not have been easy to do.

McGuffey's survey was probably intended to show how hard life was for teachers in the one-room school, but it actually offers a strong defense of the institution if one looks at it from the point of view of rural *residents*. Rural parents were getting a multipurpose institution that both educated their young and provided important community benefits outside of school. It should not be surprising that rural voters would have decided to keep their one-room schools as long as they were viable. One-room schools adapted to the age-graded norm better than I would have expected (but still imperfectly) and continued to serve their unique role in rural communities. It should be emphasized how much rural communities depended on the schools for social capital. They were often the only nonreligious (and hence nondivisive) meeting place for a neighborhood (Fuller 1982, 7; Reynolds 1999, 26).

Of course, when one-room school districts were finally consolidated, the rural schools did not instantly become as impersonal as urban schools. McGuffey's survey deliberately examined extremes. It is likely that the teachers in the four-room schools that were often the first fruits of consolidation were pretty responsive to their communities, too. But the attention was surely less than before. One does not have to look at one-room schools with rose-colored glasses to see that many voters had sound reasons to hold on to them as long as they could.

3.19 One-Room Schools Persisted Longest in the North

My second possible insight into the reasons for the persistence of one-room schools is simply a chart. A study by the U.S. Office of Education (Walter Gaumnitz 1940) collected what appear to be a reasonably accurate data on the number of one-room schools for each state for 1935. From the

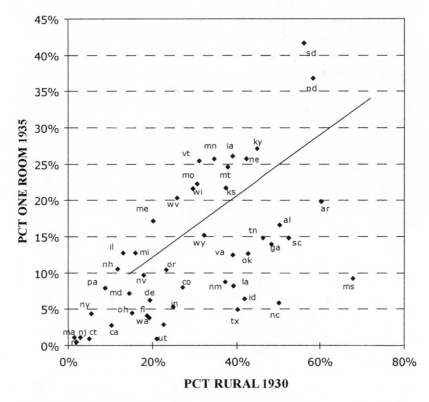

FIGURE 3.2 Percentage of public school children in one-room schools in 1935 versus percentage of state's population that was rural in 1930. Adapted from Gaumnitz (1940); Historical Census Browser of University of Virginia.

U.S. Census, I obtained the 1930 data for the percentage of each state's population that was rural. The resulting graph is shown in figure 3.2. Each state is indicated by its postal code abbreviation on the graph itself.

Figure 3.2 shows two distinct facts about one-room schools. The more obvious is that the most urban states had the smallest percentage of their children in one-room schools. When school technology switched from the tutorial-recitation method to the age-graded method, the early adopters were in cities. In 1935, one-room schools were most prevalent in rural states. (The graph itself exaggerates one-room school attendance nationally, making is look on the order of 15 percent when it was actually only about 5 percent, since the urban states on the lower left—Massachusetts, Rhode

Island, New Jersey, Connecticut, New York, Pennsylvania, and California—had much of the population.)

The other fact about one-room schools is more subtle. The forty-five-
degree line on the graph suggests that there are actually two trends, one
higher than the other. (The forty-five-degree line is discontinuous so as
not to obscure the several states clustered near the origin, which in any
case are not important for this account because they had relatively few
one-room schools.) The upper group (above the forty-five-degree line)
consists largely of northern and north central states. The lower group consists mostly of arid western states and the South. For example, the arid
western states of New Mexico, Idaho, and Wyoming have about the same
percentage (35–40 percent) of their populations in rural areas as the well-
watered, midwestern states of Iowa, Nebraska, and Minnesota. However,
the midwestern states have a larger fraction of their children attending
one-room schools. The lower group also contains most of the South. Only
the southern border states of Kentucky and West Virginia lie above the
line.

As I will demonstrate in chapter 5, the chief variations in modern school
district area across the nation are accounted for by rural population density. Low density in the arid and mountainous West made for large-area
school districts. The reason for this is that creation of multiclassroom, age-
graded schools in arid areas required a large catchment area to get enough
students to make a multigrade school. Pupils had to be transported a long
way in rural Utah to create a multiroom school. By 1915, Utah school
districts had become county based, except for a few preexisting urban
districts (Moffitt 1946, 121). Arid Utah needed a large area to capture
enough students to have age-graded schools and establish regular high
schools. As a result, by 1935, Utah had a lower percentage of pupils in
one-room schools than any other state. (Utah high schools were originally
Mormon parochial schools, but they were converted to public schools in
part to accommodate non-Mormon mining workers from out of state [Ma-
rie Gooderham 1977, 24].)

The other factor that made for large-area school districts was racial segregation. As will also be demonstrated in chapter 5, Southern school districts are large because the population density of whites and blacks taken
separately was low, on the order of the arid West. When Southern whites
sought to establish multiclassroom, age-graded schools, they had to reach
farther into the countryside to get enough white children (bypassing nearby

black pupils) to make an age-graded school. Thus Southern states tend to be below the oblique line in figure 3.2. The South's population was more rural on average—note that Mississippi and Arkansas were even more rural than the Dakotas—but the South had a lower fraction of students in one-room schools than northern states that had similar rural populations.

My reason for illustrating the differences among states is to advance a reason for the persistence of one-room schools even after age grading had become the norm and high-school attendance was widespread. One-room schools offered more flexibility for children whose labor was important to their families. It was easier to attend school part time in a one-room school than in a fully age-graded, multiroom consolidated school. In the consolidated school, students who were absent for many days during the year would usually have to repeat a grade. This was wasteful because of the redundancy of the material, and it was socially humiliating to the student. If this happened too often, the student would be inclined simply to drop out of school.

Dropping out could be done at relatively young ages, since most compulsory attendance laws had exceptions for work on family farms. A 1905 Missouri law, for example, required children to attend school to age fourteen "unless their services were necessary for the support of the family" (Burton 2000, 15). Even if the law made no such exceptions, enforcement was problematic. Tennessee's uncompromising 1912 law had little effect on truancy because "criminalizing the normal behavior of a large group of Tennessee citizens did not cause immediate changes in that behavior" (Keith 1995, 138). It is not difficult to understand why. Truant officers were wary of enforcing attendance laws in remote farming areas. It was easy to swoop down on children who were working in factories, where there were plenty of witnesses. Enforcement of a locally unpopular law on a lonely farmstead was a lot more problematic.

3.20 Age-graded Schools Created an All-or-Nothing Choice in Education

I submit that rural schools' ability to adjust grading for ability and intermittent attendance actually made for *more* overall schooling for low-income children. The most detailed source for this contention is, oddly enough, a study of the history of education in a city, New Haven, Connecticut. Steven

Lassonde (2005) examined how mid-nineteenth century immigrants, particularly those from Italy, fared in the New Haven school system. Up to about 1850, New Haven's schools were ungraded one-room schools located in various neighborhoods. Around 1850, the city began to create an age-graded system with multiroom schools and a standard curriculum. This would ensure that students would receive the benefit of a continuous education and progress uniformly from one grade to the next and perhaps on to high school.

Poorer immigrants experienced problems with this system. They needed their children to help them earn an income. In the one-room schools of the past, they could enroll their children in school and have them attend when money was flush and there wasn't much need for the children to work. When times were hard or when a family business required many hands, the children would be kept at home or at their parent's place of work. After the urgency passed, the children could go back to school again.

In an ungraded school system, this in-and-out attendance was not too troublesome. Children of poorer immigrants might take longer to learn to read, write, and cipher, but they would eventually acquire basic skills by dint of part-time attendance. A fully age-graded school system, however, could not tolerate part-time attendance. Students who dropped back into school after a month's absence upset the schedule. Unless they could catch up, they would have to repeat the grade the next year.

Faced with the discrete choice of attending all the time or not at all, a great many children from poor families simply never showed up at school. Truant officers patrolled the industrial work places to round up children engaged in the formal work sector. As a result, poor children could not take such jobs, so they simply hung around when they were not actually working in the informal sector for their families. For this set of children, age-graded education was a step back for education. Their family circumstances required them to work at least part of the time, and the all-or-nothing choice left them with close to nothing by way of education.

Lassonde (2005, 30) specifically notes that poor children in New Haven were at a disadvantage compared to poor rural children, who could attend ungraded schools on a part-time basis. (Graham [1974, 17] makes the same general point.) The problem of grade repetition was much less significant in one-room schools. A 1910 model curriculum that was intended to get one-room schools in step with their graded counterparts nonetheless advised that in rural schools "children of several different years may

often by taught in the same class" (New Hampshire Department of Public
Instruction 1910, 14). Even as late as the 1930s, one-room school teachers
routinely grouped several grades together. A teacher recalled that back
in the 1930s in her one-room school in New Hampshire, "Because of the
large number of subjects to be covered in the few hours, it was necessary
to group several grades . . ." (Muriel Kendrick 1976, 31). Students in rural
areas during that period may have been better off by having a choice between one-room schools and graded schools.

The advantage of the one-room school for farmers was that distances to
it were not great. By 1935, the standard school year no longer conformed
to the needs of agriculture. The summer term was gone, and school began
before harvest was done and ended after spring planting. But farm children still had daily chores and still were sometimes needed for special
tasks that required multiple hands. If the school could be nearby, that
many more farm chores could be done by children. Reminiscences in
Leight and Rinehart (1999, 28) mention children in the 1920s in a rural
Pennsylvania district who went home at noon to help milk the cows. Norman Frost (1921) describes a similar accommodation to farm life in Tennessee. Thus even for farmers who were conscientious in sending their
children to school, the nearby one-room school had extra value in that it
made more family labor available.

3.21 Gradualism Helped Children in Poor Families

My argument here is about both education and politics. For some rural
children, especially those in poorer areas, the part-time education of the
one-room schools made for *more* education than an insistence that they attend an age-graded school or none at all. Soltow and Steven (1981, 114) attribute the near parity of urban and rural school attendance in 1860 to the
scheduling flexibility of rural schools. Greene and Jacobs (1992) explain
the higher attendance of rural students evident in the census of 1910 as a
manifestation of the greater flexibility of rural one-room schools. A 1935
survey of Michigan one-room schools found that 23 percent of boys and
16 percent of girls in the later grades were "retarded"—the unsympa-
thetic official term for being old for their grade (Maude Smith et al. 1937).
But for the older children, "retardation" may simply have meant that the
school allowed them to complete a single grade in two years instead of one
by dint of part-time attendance.

Angus, Mirel, and Vinovskis (1988, 226) found that rural schools were more relaxed about annual promotions than urban schools, whose administrators were from the beginning of the twentieth century (and continuing into the twenty-first) criticized for "inefficiency" if students did not progress annually on the age-graded treadmill. By offering the possibility of part-time schooling, the persistence of one-room schools to the middle of the twentieth century may have resulted in a more educated population, not less. As Wayne Fuller (1982, 245) points out, the states of the upper Midwest—Hamlin Garland's "middle border"—had the highest percentage of the students enrolled in one-room schools and also was the "most literate part of the nation through the years." It is also possible that the persistence of one-room schools may account for the finding by Christopher Berry and Martin West (2005) that adult wages in 1980 were higher for those who attended school in states with smaller schools during the period 1930–70. In the states with persistent one-room schools—which would make the average school size much smaller—rural children did not have to choose between full-time school and full-time work. (Berry and West also find, however, that larger *districts* were associated with higher wages, though this could reflect the effect of urbanization on wages.)

My political argument is that the presence of a high rural population density allowed state legislators to defer to local sentiment about school consolidation. In the high-density farm area of Iowa, it was possible for several districts to vote to form a consolidated, fully age-graded school system without having to include every district in the township. If the voters in a particular district felt that the flexibility of a one-room school outweighed the advantages of an age-graded system, they could decline to vote for it. State legislators had no need to stir up a local hornets' nest by insisting that all rural districts consolidate. Piecemeal consolidation was still consolidation, and if one district held out for ten years, well, another consolidation opportunity was sure to arise in the next decade.

States with low population densities, however, often required that all the one-room districts in a particular area consolidate. A single holdout district could spoil the entire enterprise. I submit that it was this condition that induced the legislators of several of the western states to forego local consent in many consolidations. In the inventory of school laws compiled by Hooker and Mueller (1970), the states that simply overrode local voting on consolidation matters were disproportionately from the arid West and the South. This was not, I would argue, because New Mexico, Nevada, and Wyoming were less democratic than Wisconsin, Minnesota, and South

Dakota. The legislators from the far-west states were as responsive to local concerns as those from the Midwest. Voters in the far-west states must
have approved of such legislative action because a majority wanted age-
graded schools and knew that they could not get them if some of the local
one-room districts refused to join. What looks like a purely coercive arrangement may have simply been a case of "voluntary coercion," the sort
of collective decision that is made whenever free riders are so pervasive
that the public good cannot be provided without collective force.

The South was subject to the same "low" population density as the arid
West when the universal practice of racial segregation is brought into the
picture (as discussed in chapter 5). The South was more coercive than the
North in the sense of imposing age-graded schools and thus getting rid of
a larger proportion of white one-room schools (Link 1986, 143; Dabney
1936, 2:230). If one just looks at the one-room school percentages and
regards the one-rooms as educationally deficient, the South looks like it
should have had better education (for whites) than the North.

The transition to age-graded schools was more abrupt in the South and
the West, and this was not necessarily a good thing for education. A larger
fraction of students who attended schools in the South did get multiroom,
age-graded schools. But because of the costs of segregation, both transportation and administrative costs per pupil were larger in the South (Horace Bond 1934, 231). These expenses meant less money was available for
classroom expenditures. Moreover, the faster switch to centralized schools
in the South left many whites and blacks in rural areas with the unpleasant
choice of very long commuting to school or dropping out altogether. An
account of consolidated parish (county) schools in Louisiana noted the
long bus rides and disaffection with remote schools for whites (Marion
Smith 1938). The transitional rural schools of the North, which offered
a relatively flexible, partially age-graded curriculum in local one-room
schools was less available in the South. One does not need to be nostalgic
for the old one-room school to see that a gradual transition to the uniformly graded system may have improved the educational opportunities
for many children torn between school and work by family necessity.

The virtues of gradual transition were also recognized by some reformers of urban school systems, who advocated part-time schooling within
the age-graded system. Several Massachusetts factory towns in the 1870s
established separate part-time schools to accommodate the part-time attendance of children who worked in the mills, who otherwise were both dis-

ruptive of and alienated by the new, full-time age-graded schools (Marvin Lazerson 1971, 86). Even James Conant (1959a), whose famous report on American high schools strongly favored larger, more finely age-graded schools and districts, conceded that many students and their families would be better off if students could work for part of the time. The proposed work had a vocational role, but it was not strictly vocational schools that Conant had in mind. In urban New York, they were called "continuation schools," and they accommodated age-graded education with the schedules of working youth (Conant 1959b, 88). The need to supplement family income from part-time work was reason to make some adjustments to the lockstep of grades 1–12.

3.22 Conclusion: The Persuasion of Property

The twentieth-century decline in rural population, better roads and motor vehicles, and the demand for high school education all contributed to the transformation of American education norms. As education moved toward age grading, it became important to coordinate the school experience from one place to another. This coordination came about without much central direction. Education leaders certainly deserve credit for proposing the consolidations and standardizations that a coordinated system required, but local voters almost always had to assent to them.

They assented to them, I believe, because remaining outside the age-graded system was hard on their property values. Families would not move to places that had nonstandard schools. Deborah Fitzgerald (2003, 30) quotes a participant at a U.S. Department of Agriculture conference in the 1920s: "The intelligent man will not go out in an isolated district where his children cannot have educational advantages." Weighing the benefits of a small, one-room district—democratic control, shorter distances, the possibility of part-time schooling—against the costs of remaining outside the system—the less-specialized instruction, the difficulty in accessing high school—almost all voters eventually agreed to the necessary school district consolidations. The holdouts from this system were mainly farmers in remote places who still required some labor from their children. For them, the benefits of school consolidation still did not offset the adaptability of the one-room school and its closer proximity to their farmsteads. Their reluctance to give up their nearby one-room schools made them look obstructionist to education reformers, but the half-a-loaf education of such schools was better than dropping out entirely at an early age.

Finally, I would point out that the account of school district creation in this chapter indicates that the lines drawn were anything but arbitrary "accidents of geography." One-room districts were themselves almost entirely consensual associations, and the one-room districts coalesced into age-graded, multiroom school districts largely by the consent of the governed. Many proposals were rejected, and only when those proposing consolidation identified "organic communities" by on-the-ground research did local voters consent. The school districts we see today are largely produced by the same process, and they deserve more respect than the disdainful "creatures of the state" designation suggests.

CHAPTER FOUR

"Will I See You in September?" Labor Mobility and the Standard School Calendar

This chapter offers evidence that the system of public schooling that evolved in the twentieth century is responsive to migration. Movement of households from one district to another is a serious discipline on the way schools are run. I explore this issue through a seemingly arcane, if not frivolous, topic: why do we have a school calendar that starts at the end of summer and concludes the academic year at the start of the following summer? Everyone I have asked thinks this calendar exists because rural kids once had to work on the farm during the summer, and everyone is wrong. My explanation—that its purpose is coordination of the school year for migratory teachers and families—has convinced most people to whom I've presented it.

I had claimed this idea as my own, but I found that George Huppert (1984, 50) mentioned it in his history of schooling in Renaissance France. Schools in Paris had from 1558 begun on October 8, St. Remy's Day, and this uniform starting date facilitated, as Huppert specifically notes, mobility for both teachers and students within Paris and among other French schools. Despite my own lack of precedence, I will use the school calendar as a portal to explore the importance of migration and property values in the economic evolution of school districts.

Unlike the previous two chapters, the present chapter does not rely on domestic historical evidence to support my claim that labor mobility is a key to understanding school district standardization. The American

historical record reveals almost nothing about the development of a standard calendar. I rely instead on contemporary international experience.
School calendar and related educational standardization actually developed from various historical circumstances, but the need to accommodate
migratory families and teachers has in almost all cases pushed national
school systems toward a more-or-less common calendar. Standardization
has a downside that should be more frankly addressed by reformers. The
mobility-induced uniformity of school calendars and curricula are important constraints on education reforms, and understanding the nature of
these constraints will make for a more intelligent discussion about national school reforms.

4.1 Year-Round Calendars Would Save Money

Economists are apt to look at the ten-week summer vacation of their local
public schools with a Grinchlike eye. Instead of happy kids enjoying an un-
structured holiday, they see a seriously underused stock of public capital. In
districts where enrollments are growing, demand for more classroom space
requires more public funds, which require higher taxes or having to do
without other public projects. Instead of building new schools in response,
many economists (and other reformers) suggest that we use the ones we
have more efficiently by adopting year-round education. School years could
remain at 180 days, but starting and ending dates for various groups would
be staggered so that classrooms would not be empty for long periods.

A school that expected enrollments to rise by 25 percent would not have
to add a single classroom if it switched from a conventional calendar to a
year-round calendar. One plan simply uses staggered nine-month cycles.
The school's population is divided into four tracks, and a new track begins
every three months. Each track gets a three-month vacation, but only one
gets it in summer. With the year-round tracking system, one quarter of
the student population is on vacation at any given time, thus freeing up a
quarter of the space that students would use during a conventional nine-
month calendar.

Although year-round use would increase wear and tear on classrooms
(and teachers would have to get used to a different classroom at the start
of each nine-month school year), the net savings on public facilities would
still be enough to make a difference to taxpayers. If capital costs are 20
percent of a school district's annual budget, a 25 percent savings in capital

costs would reduce overall spending by 5 percent (0.25 times 0.20). Or the savings could be used to raise teacher salaries by 5 percent more than usual, which would presumably raise teacher quality. It isn't the big rock candy mountain, but it isn't chump change, either.

Year-round schooling is an idea that has been around a long time, but it has never gotten very far. About 3 percent of U.S. public school students attend a "year-round" school, according to the National Association for Year-Round Education (NAYRE; http://www.nayre.org/). My examination of the calendars of about a quarter of the schools listed on the site revealed that most "year-round" calendars simply have shorter-than-average summer vacations and longer breaks at other times of the year. Summer typically remains the longest vacation, and the school year usually begins in August. (The rationale is that having more numerous but shorter vacations would reduce students' forgetting of lessons over the long summer [Harris Cooper et al. 1996], but children seem to forget about as much over four, equally spaced three-week vacations—the typical alternative—as over one full summer [Bradley McMillen 2001].) True year-round schools, which have staggered calendars for two or more tracks and thus use the school plant more intensively, are a minority of those listed on the NAYRE Web site. They are situated disproportionately in the Southwest and especially in California, where rapid growth and fiscal constraints give some districts a stronger incentive to conserve on capital facilities.

A different reason for midsummer beginnings is the high-stakes testing mandated by the federal "No Child Left Behind" Act. Since 2001, districts in several states have started school in early August to have more weeks of school before the statewide achievement tests, which are given at a fixed date the following spring (*New York Times*, August 6, 2004, A14). Some districts have tried to conceal their motive for jumping the gun by invoking the supposed benefits of year-round operation. Most states have seen through this ruse and adopted rules against such early-August beginnings, and they are now less common.

4.2 Is the "Agrarian Calendar" the Product of "Path Dependence?"

Given the public's lack of enthusiasm for year-round schools, I have casually asked colleagues why American schools end in June and begin a new school year in September. The answer almost invariably is the farming tradition. Children in a rural society had to work on the farm in the summer, and American schools have simply kept doing it.

Tradition! Otherwise hardheaded economists all sound like Tevye from *Fiddler on the Roof* on this subject. They are surely aware that farmers are a minuscule fraction of the population (about 1 percent in 2000) and have not depended on child labor for several generations. Despite this, economists and virtually everyone else I have asked about this subject (I was something of a cocktail-party bore about this) believe that the twenty-first-century school calendar is the product of nineteenth-century farming schedules.

The "agrarian calendar" account is a version of "path dependence." Path dependence is a fancy term for a historical rut, a practice that cannot be escaped because everyone started to do it that way, and it is too costly to climb out of the rut even after the practice serves no rational end. A now-dubious example of path dependence is the QWERTY keyboard layout. Scholars once believed that it was developed for reasons solely related to mechanical typewriters—the keys would jam less frequently. Once computer-guided typing became widespread, it should have been supplanted by the "Dvorak" keyboard layout, which was purportedly faster, but QWERTY's head start keeps everyone in the historical rut (Paul David 1985).

This account was challenged by Stanley Liebowitz and Stephen Margolis (1990). They found that QWERTY had won many competitions conducted when typewriters were new, and alternative systems have not proven to be superior in the succeeding century. This is partly because an important factor in typing efficiency is balancing the use of hands to avoid overstrain, and several systems do that about equally well. So QWERTY is not necessarily the summit of efficiency. It is just on the same high plateau as several other alternatives (including Professor Dvorak's). In this sense its dominance *is* due to path dependence, but it is a less dire story than was originally told, since little would be gained by switching standards.

One of the reasons for the persistence of QWERTY is that it promotes coordination among users. Many keyboarders use different machines in different places, and it would be enormously inconvenient if each site used a different keyboard layout. Indeed, minor variations on QWERTY are used by most other European languages. Likewise for school calendars. A family leaving New York to take a job in California would usually want their children to finish the school year in New York and start with everyone else in California. Having a standard season for teachers and people with children to change locations helps the schools run more smoothly. Most teachers dread the prospect of a new student arriving in November, even if the child attended a standard school elsewhere. The new student has to be apprised of the particular methods of the classroom and perhaps be brought up to speed on subjects that are taught in a different order within the school year. This takes away from the teacher's time for other students in the class and hinders their education (Hanushek, Kain, and Rivkin 2004). There is a sound educational reason for school districts to want to adopt the same general calendar as everyone else.

One could argue, though, that the school calendar's coordination function could still have originated by historical accident. Maybe the farmers who wanted their kids to work during the summer just happened to have created a system that promoted coordination among districts, and this system just stuck. But even on its own terms, the agrarian-tradition explanation for September beginnings does not work. The nineteenth-century farm work for which extra hands were especially helpful was planting and harvesting. In most temperate regions of the United States, these occur in the spring and the autumn, when the now-standard nine-month school year is in session.

Rural American school districts of the nineteenth century in fact responded to the seasonal rhythms of agriculture. Andrew Gulliford (1991, 47) describes the rural school year succinctly, though he leaves the impression of more uniformity (and longer terms) than actually existed.

> In the mid-19th century, the school year was divided into two terms. The typical summer term extended over five months, from May to August or September. The winter term varied from state to state, depending on local planting and harvesting times; it generally began after harvest in November and continued until just before spring plowing, usually around early April. After 1900 the school year was standardized into one nine-month term, beginning in September and ending in May.

Summer and winter terms were common in every rural region of the United States in the nineteenth century (Kaestle 1983, 15). Soltow and Steven (1981, 114) found that the rural summer term made up much of the difference between rural and urban school enrollments in the decades before the Civil War. Kenneth Gold (1997; 2002) found that the summer term was as well attended as the winter term as recently as 1875 in New

England, New York, Michigan, and Virginia. As late as 1910, many Mississippi rural schools were regularly held during summer as well as winter (Charles Wilson 1947, 50).

The foregoing historical accounts usually mention that the summer term was attended disproportionately by younger children and older girls, in part because winter weather made walking to school difficult for them. Their older brothers would often work on the farm in summer and attend school only in the winter. Thus summer *was* a time for agricultural work for some children. But today's September-to-June school year cannot have emerged from this tradition, since the opportunity cost of school attendance by most youth was higher in fall and spring. The eventual adoption of a nine-month school year that began at the close of summer was actually a blow to farmers, who lost the services of their children at the times they most needed them. (The "agrarian calendar" myth probably arose in the twentieth century when city kids asked the farmers' kids how they spent their summer vacations, and most said they worked on the farm. Of course, most rural kids would also have worked on the farm if vacation were in the spring or fall.)

Another characteristic of nineteenth-century one-room school terms was their irregularity. They were not always held for three months in summer and three months in winter. Sometimes the term would start in spring and go to midsummer; sometimes there would be a fall term; and sometimes the district would miss having any school at all for lack of money or because the teacher departed shortly after the term began and a replacement could not be found. Missing a term certainly was not a good thing, but it was not the catastrophe that we would now think of such a gap. When students finally did get another term of school, they could, under the tutorial-recitation method, simply pick up where they had left off the last time school was held.

4.3 The Standard School Calendar Emerged from Age-Graded Education

My explanation for summer vacation is that it emerged as a coordinating device for mobile families and teachers when age-graded education displaced the one-room schools. Age-graded education expects all students in the same cohort to learn the same lessons at the same time. Once age grading became the national norm, circa 1890–1910, one-room schools had to drop their free-form calendars, which involved instruction during self-contained terms of three or four months in winter and in summer. As rural districts adopted age grading, they had to conform to the eventual standard of nine months of school with summer vacation in between the end and start of a school year. In 1910, the U.S. Census changed its schooling question from the number of months attended to whether the child had been enrolled at any time since the previous September (Day and Jamieson 2003, 1), implying that separate summer and winter terms had become too rare to bother counting and that the new norm assumed continuous attendance starting in September.

The long summer vacation between school years further facilitates labor mobility. The fall-winter-spring school year preserves summer as a low-cost season for families and teachers to move from one part of the country to another after they have finished school in one place. Summer vacation is the longest of the year because it serves as a catchment period to encourage all newcomers with children to assemble at the beginning of the school year and start school at the same time. Its adoption as a national norm around 1900 marked the transition from a nation in which most children attended rural, one-room schools that were ungraded to one in which most students were more-or-less urban and attended multiroom, age-graded schools whose schedules had to be coordinated with one another.

The plausibility of the coordination explanation is enhanced by the likelihood that within the United States and probably most other high-income nations, the summer vacation coordinates age-graded education in a way that keeps total social costs at a minimum. The social costs of a nonstandard starting date for schools include family relocation and job-changing costs (especially for teachers) and the educational disruptions from having new students enter age-graded schools after the term has begun. Being in school when everyone else is in school also facilitates interscholastic activities such as conferences and sports. And no one would deny that summer is in most areas a pleasant time not to be in school, although a summer vacation does not logically require that a new school year begin at its conclusion.

The coordination advantages of summer-and-September, that is, having a summer vacation and beginning school in September, must be weighed against the capital costs of leaving school buildings idle for two months or more. School districts can obtain income from some facilities during vacations, but most of their capital is specialized for age-graded education. The underuse of school buildings, however, is comparable to the underuse of other kinds of capital for which there are schedule-driven demands, such as electric power stations, transportation systems, theaters, and sports stadiums. Their idle capacity is in fact caused by the same reason that schools are underused in summer: the need for civilized people to coordinate their collective endeavors with one another. Summer vacation may get a bit shorter over the years, but a mobile society will very likely find that a longer-than-usual summer vacation period following the end of the school year is a reasonable way to structure educational calendars.

4.4 Other Accounts of Summer and September

As is evident from numerous sources about nineteenth-century rural education, the summer-and-September schedules are not the product of an agrarian tradition. But this does not truly establish that the standard school calendar is not path dependent. It could be that American schools just fell into the September-to-June mode for reasons that are now not relevant. A commonly offered reason for summer vacation in the twentieth century could have been the discomfort of summertime schooling. In the nineteenth century, it was possible to heat buildings in the winter but not to cool them in the summer. Learning in the summer would be less than in the winter, more so because of children's longing to be outdoors in warmer weather. A cost-minimizing approach to education would thus dictate a long summer vacation. (Note, though, that one could logically have a long summer vacation even if the school year began on April 1, as Japan's schools do and whose nonstandard calendar will be discussed presently.)

The climatic explanation is historically refuted by the fact that schools in larger cities in the late nineteenth century were also open in the summer. Many cities had long school years, often twice that of their rural cousins, and had only a few weeks of summer recess (Todd Rakoff 2002). City students did not necessarily attend all year. Although most urban schools were nominally age graded by 1870 or so, they were, like their country cousins, fairly flexible in their curriculum, so that students could come and go without too much disruption in their progress. City schools were often in multiroom buildings, which must have been even hotter during the summer than the one-room schools of the country.

Of the few scholars who actually address this question, all agree that the convergence of rural and city schools on the September-to-June calendar occurred gradually between 1880 and 1920. It was not something that was commanded by the state government. Rural districts were almost entirely governed by local residents. The state might require (sometimes without much effect) a minimum number of days of school, but the local districts had nearly absolute control over when to begin and end school terms. City schools, also largely locally governed, shortened their longer school year by eliminating regular summer classes. Rural districts at the same time lengthened their calendar by eliminating summer term and gradually adding weeks of spring and fall to the winter term, though the resulting term was often still shorter than it was in city schools.

Kenneth Gold (1997), who convincingly demonstrated the importance of summer terms throughout the nineteenth century, offers a highly contingent explanation for the demise of year-round (and hence summer) schooling that existed in many cities in the late nineteenth century. He places it in late nineteenth-century beliefs about children's mental health. Gold cites several sources that argued that children's minds would be harmed by excessive study, and summer vacation was regarded as a necessary respite. Even if such commentators had much influence on public policy, it hardly addresses the question of why *rural* schools gave up their winter and summer terms for a more-or-less continuous September-to-June school year. The continuous year would seem to add more mental stress, and some modern arguments for a more measured school year, one with evenly spaced vacations, commend its reduced stress.

A final explanation for the modern calendar that I will deal with (I am sure there are many others) is imitation of colleges and universities. Although the evidence is sketchy, it appears that institutions of higher learning converged on the now-standard calendar before it was adopted by primary and secondary schools. June graduations were common if not universal in the late nineteenth century, which implies that at least one element of the standard calendar—finishing at the beginning of summer, was a norm. It could be that this norm filtered down to high schools and then to elementary schools. This also reflects a coordination story, but here the source is from higher education rather than from primary and secondary education.

Going to college was so rare at the time of transition from summer terms to the standard calendar that it is difficult to credit this chain of causation. As of 1890, less than 2 percent of the eligible population attended college or university (Church and Sedlak 1976, 294), and most students at elite institutions prepared at private academies, not public high schools. In addition, I encountered a nineteenth-century history of my alma mater, Amherst College, that implied that the college's calendar was actually once governed by the school year of common schools, not vice versa (William Tyler 1895). In the 1830s and 1840s, Amherst deliberately planned long winter vacations so that the (then all-male) college's students could earn money by teaching school during the twelve-week winter term for common schools. (Summer terms were usually taught by women, and the pay was lower.) Amherst College's calendar made up for this long winter vacation by having classes through most of the summer, with commencement occurring near the end of August. At least this college's calendar once adjusted itself to the common-schools' calendar.

4.5 Starting School at the End of Summer Is an International Norm

Adoption of the September-to-June school calendar was apparently so uncontroversial that contemporary participants did not write down an explanation for the change. Until 1880, discussions of education still had plenty of references (always in passing) to summer and winter terms in rural areas, and after 1920 it is difficult to locate a mention of summer schooling except for supplementary or remedial purposes. But no one talked about why it changed. Typical of modern, laconic mentions of this transition is the Fairwater [Wisconsin] Historical Society Newsletter of October 2002, which announced the acquisition of records of a nearby one-room school. It noted without further comment that "until 1911 the school had two annual sessions—a four month winter term and a three month summer term. In 1911, the school year changed to a single October to June term." No one is reported to have talked about the reasons for this change, and the newsletter's author seemed to find it unremarkable. Fortunately, there is another set of sources that illuminate the reasons for the standard calendar: contemporary international experience. It demonstrates that the standard school calendar serves as a coordination device.

Although there is considerable variety in length of school year around the world, as well as their specific vacation schedules, the congruence of beginning and ending dates is striking. A summer vacation whose length exceeds that of any other break followed by the beginning of the school year in mid-August or September (or, in the Southern Hemisphere, around February) is the norm for almost the entire world's population. The variations from the standard calendar—primarily in Japan, some equatorial and South Asian nations, and transequatorial international schools—re-

veal a pattern that is supportive of the worker-and-family mobility function of summer vacation. This and the following section review worldwide
practice by region, starting with North America. (My school-calendar research was done by Web searches and was thus limited to countries with
some Web presence and by my ability to understand the language where
translations were not available.)

Canada's provinces each set their own school year, but all start within a
week of September 1 and end near the last week of June. The school years
of most provinces exceed those of the United States by two or three weeks,
perhaps enough to acquire a politically acceptable competence in French
or English. Several Canadian districts have experimented with year-round
calendars, but they seem no more widespread than in the United States.
Schools in at least the urban parts of Mexico have a calendar similar to
that of the United States.

European nations have greater variety in their school calendars than
the North American nations, but almost all start a new school year within
three weeks of September 1, and most complete the school year in June.
Russia and Middle Eastern nations (e.g., Egypt, Iran, Iraq, and Israel) follow a similar pattern. A few European countries extend the school calendar into July before starting a summer vacation; the maximum appears to
be a region of the Netherlands whose school year ends in the last week of
July. Several countries, most notably Germany and Austria, have different
calendars for different states *(Länder)*, but all begin and end within three
weeks of one another.

The length of Europe's summer vacations varies from six weeks in
Germany and the United Kingdom to twelve weeks in Italy and Portugal.
In all countries, though, summer is the single longest school vacation of
the year. Teachers and families with children and who change jobs within
or between the nations of Europe would have little difficulty starting in
school if they arrive in their new homes in mid-August, though they might
have to hurry some if they left from the Netherlands.

4.6 Japan's April-to-March Calendar Proves the Rule

The school calendar in Japan would give international job changers
with children a major problem. The calendar begins in April, and after a
trimester of work has a six-week summer vacation (half of July through
August), resumes in September, and finishes in March. If you arrive to

enroll your children in August or September, the school year is one-third over. The calendar appears to have little local variation which, along with the centrally determined curriculum, would make it easy for Japanese families to change schools within their country. However, a visiting Japanese business professor assured me that it was rare for any student to change schools. (See also Merry White [1988].) Business executives who are assigned to a company's branch in a different city in Japan would usually leave their families with school-age children behind and expect to return to their original homes within a few years. (The visiting professor had brought his children on his leave year in the United States, but they had to leave Hanover's schools in midterm to restart school in Japan on April 1.)

It is not clear why Japanese schools begin in April. It was the custom in Germany (as will be described in section 4.8) when Japan adopted a national school system in the late nineteenth century and looked to Germany for guidance. Aside from this, spring is said to be the traditional Japanese season for starting new ventures, but that is a notion that would seem to resonate with most nations. More interesting is that one official source (addressed to children: http://web-japan.org/kidsweb/explore/calendar/april/schoolyear.html [July 2008]) admits that it is a barrier to international mobility:

> There are some, though, who want to change the school year so that it starts in September. They say that this will make it easier for students in other countries to come and study here and for Japanese students to attend schools abroad. But because spring is so closely associated with new beginnings, the school year will probably continue to start in April.

A few Japanese universities have a special entrance term in October to accommodate international students, but most of their courses continue on a cycle that also begins in April. A September-to-June school year has been contemplated by the Japanese government, but public opinion does not favor the change. In polls on the subject, what little support was expressed for an "autumn beginning" came from those who were interested in the "internationalization of education," chiefly managers and engineers, who would most commonly go abroad and deal with foreigners working in Japan (Japan Cabinet Office 2001).

Japan's April-to-March school year is not an Asian tradition. Schools in China generally follow a North American/European calendar, starting in

September and ending in early July. South Asian countries often adjust the school year around the summer monsoon, when internal travel (and vacation) are problematic. Only Korea, which was ruled by Japan for much of the early twentieth century, has a calendar and school system like Japan's.

Because I argue that school calendars facilitate migration of students, teachers, and their families within and among high-income nations, Japan's unusual calendar warrants closer examination. The Japanese may feel less need to adjust their school calendar because their uniform national curriculum is so exceptional that it alone retards international families from using Japanese public schools and vice versa. Japanese children attend school 240 days a year, though not all are instructional days (Johnson and Johnson 1996). Many students also attend "cram schools" to help with next-level entrance exams. The uniform national curriculum is geared to learning material that will appear on high-stakes tests, which largely determine students' place in universities and occupations. The most gifted American eleven-year-old who started sixth grade in a Japanese school would find it both academically and socially difficult, even assuming he spoke the language fluently.

Japan's system makes it hard for others to go to Japan, but it also makes it difficult for Japanese students to use other country's public schools. Evidence for this is the existence of several private schools in Japan that specialize in remedial education for Japanese children returning from non-Japanese educational experiences in other countries (White 1988, 57). Japanese children who have learned idiomatic American or British English, for example, often have to unlearn it and adopt instead the unique way of speaking English that is taught by Japanese instructors (Reischauer and Jansen 1995, 438). The exceptional nature of the official Japanese curriculum is also evident in the rules that are applied to international schools in Japan. For example, the English-language Osaka YMCA International School (OYIS), offers a Canadian curriculum (not the aforementioned remedial education) and a calendar that begins in August, not April (http://www.oyis.org/curricularDifferences.html, August 2007). Its Web site warns applicants that

> students graduating from OYIS may find it difficult, if not almost impossible, to continue their studies at Japanese universities. Parents must be reminded that, if a child with Japanese nationality enters the School, it means that the child would be abandoning the "ordinary" Japanese Education set by the Japanese Government. [I would note that the school is not exclusively for North American

visitors. A previous version of the Web site had classroom pictures of children and their names, at least half of which suggest Japanese parentage.]

When Japanese establish expatriate primary and secondary schools in other countries, they do not adopt the calendar of their host country. These are privately run schools, although many receive Japanese government assistance as an inducement for business and government workers to take jobs in other parts of the world (White 1988, 53). All the schools I was able to identify, including those in Kuala Lumpur, Brussels, Atlanta, Chicago, Cincinnati, and Detroit, sedulously follow the April-to-March calendar and, unless they are only Saturday schools for Japanese language and culture, the homeland's curriculum. Perhaps most interesting are the two Japanese-run international schools in Hong Kong. One teaches primarily in English. It is specifically for students of Japanese parentage as well as other nationalities whose families expect to stay in Hong Kong or move on to countries other than Japan. Its school year is mid-August to June, like that of indigenous Hong Kong schools and unlike that of the Hong Kong Japanese-language school, which has Japan's April-to-March academic calendar.

4.7 The Southern Hemisphere Provides a Natural Experiment in School Calendars

The conformity of the expatriate Japanese school calendar to that of the mother country supports the hypothesis that school calendars facilitate employment and educational mobility, but one might question whether the example is too specific to Japan itself. Additional evidence comes from a truly natural experiment. South of the equator, summer begins in December and runs through most of March. Most Southern Hemisphere schools also have summer vacations during at least December and January, and a new school year typically begins in February. Calendars of the Australian states all end and begin within two weeks of one another. New Zealand practice is the same, and it is similar in South America and South Africa and the nations of equatorial and southern Africa for which I could obtain information.

The February-to-December calendar is sufficiently widespread that services involved in international relocations refer to a "Southern Hemisphere calendar" for schools. The term does not always denote location below the equator. Malaysia and Singapore, which are slightly north of the equator, follow the Southern Hemisphere calendar, as do most of the nations of Central America. The most extreme exception is Afghanistan, which follows a Southern Hemisphere calendar, starting school in March and ending in November. Readers of Khaled Hosseini's *The Kite Runner* (2003), a novel set in modern Afghanistan, may recall that kite-fighting contests occurred during the winter vacation between the end and start of the Afghan school year. I have no clue as to why this cold country has a long winter holiday, but the protagonist of the novel speaks of it in the same affectionate way that people from other countries reminisce about summer vacation. Vacation is vacation . . .

The Southern Hemisphere calendar offers indirect but substantial support for the view that summer vacation is a coordinating device. The summer vacation of Australia and New Zealand, most of South America, and sub-Saharan Africa facilitates worker and student mobility within their respective regions. But a Southern Hemisphere calendar *retards* mobility with respect to other high-income countries of the Northern Hemisphere. A Melbourne family arriving in London after school ended in Australia in December would have an eight-month educational hiatus to fill before British schools started their year in September. A Chicago family moving to Cape Town would have a similar gap between the Illinois school's ending in June and the South African school's beginning in February. It is possible that a nation's adoption of a Southern Hemisphere calendar reflects the greater importance of internal and regional mobility rather than international migration.

Here is the critical fact: most private schools for the children of American and European personnel (both corporate and governmental) in the Southern Hemisphere keep *Northern* Hemisphere calendars. (The U.S. State Department lists private international schools and their calendars at http://www.state.gov/m/a/os/c1684.htm. A similar list for European government and business employees is at http://www.cois.org/, October 2007). For example, American "international schools"—a generic designation that does not necessarily mean that its students come from any particular country—in Sydney, Australia; São Paulo, Brazil; Harare, Zimbabwe; and Johannesburg, South Africa, all operate on the Northern Hemisphere calendar of mid-August to June, while the nearby local public schools operate on a calendar that begins in February or March and ends in December. A desire to facilitate family movement to and from North America and Europe apparently dominates the inconveniences that come from not coordinating with the local public school systems. (Inconveniences would include the difficulties of arranging sports and cultural programs with indigenous schools and hiring teachers from a local labor force that runs on a different school calendar.) Some schools are explicit about their reasons. The Buenos Aires Christian Academy listed as one of its advantages: "US Calendar—We recognize that parents like to plan return travel to the United States around the traditional education calendar" (http://www.baica.com/, October 3, 2003).

An especially strong contrast occurs in Singapore, which is on the equator. The *Australian* International School in Singapore operates on the Australian February-to-December calendar, but the Singapore *American* School, located just a few kilometers away, operates on the American September-to-June calendar. (Singapore itself uses the Southern Hemisphere calendar.) The Australians carry their calendar north, too. Their international school in Hong Kong, well north of the equator, operates on Australia's Southern Hemisphere schedule. Hong Kong thus enjoys the distinction of having three separate school year beginnings: the end of January for its Australian school, early April for its Japanese-language school, and August/September for its indigenous and other international schools.

Another example of the school calendar's coordinating function arises among the islands of the Southern Hemisphere. Their calendar variations are consistent with the need for students, government workers, teachers, and business people to be able to transfer to and from the home country at the end of a school year. American Samoa's schools operate on an American (Northern Hemisphere) calendar, which facilitates movement back and forth to the United States, of which American Samoa is a territory. The Falkland Islands follows the school calendar of Britain, eight thousand miles to the north. Tahiti, a French possession in the Southern Hemisphere, operates on the Northern Hemisphere calendar of France. In contrast, Fiji, an independent nation in the South Pacific, operates on a Southern Hemisphere calendar, as does the island nation of Vanuatu.

4.8 School-Calendar Reform in Germany and Switzerland Promoted Labor Mobility

The previous sections suggested that the "standard school calendar" is actually a subtle coordinating device. The reader who agrees with this might nonetheless ask what school calendars have to do with the development of twentieth-century American school districts? One answer is fairly straightforward. The transformation of schooling described in the previous chapter from the one-room district with its tutorial-recitation method of instruction to multiclassroom, age-graded instruction required both a new school year and a new configuration of schools. One-room schools and their districts did not have to coordinate their school terms with other schools and school districts, and the quality of instruction had little effect on neighboring communities.

After the adoption of age-graded instruction, coordination among school districts became important, which transformed the school-year calendar. It also transformed the school district, since age-graded instruction could be undertaken effectively only if there were a large number of students in a single location. School districts had to consolidate with one another to take advantage of the new pedagogy. The move to age-graded instruction also increased the demand for bureaucratic control, because calendars, as well as curriculum, teacher preparation, and instructional materials, had to become more uniform. Thus the coordination of calendars is only one aspect of a total makeover of the method of education that accompanied age-graded education.

The relevance of school calendars to school district evolution raises the question of origins. How did it come about? As I indicated earlier, American sources are silent about the reasons for the transformation of the school calendar. It just happened without much discussion. Since my evidence about school calendars was published in the *Journal of Urban Economics* (Fischel 2006b), I found additional sources from other countries. It turns out that Germans and the Swiss *did* talk some about the reasons that they changed their school calendars to conform to that of their neighbors.

Before World War II, all of Germany started school in the spring, after Easter. As Nazi Germany invaded other nations whose school years began in late summer, its leaders decided the expanded Reich needed a uniform school calendar. Surprisingly, the Nazi occupiers chose to force Germany onto the school calendar of the nations it had conquered, and for a time all of Germany was on the summer-and-September calendar. After the war, however, most of Germany except Bavaria returned to the post-Easter (March or April) start of the school year. The intranational differences now created a problem. As Jørn-Steffan Pischke (2003, 6) describes it:

> This heterogeneity caused frictions, for example, when families moved across state borders and children had to switch schools. Therefore, the prime ministers of the states signed an Agreement on the Unification of the School System in 1964, the so called Hamburg Accord (Hamburger Abkommen). Among other

provisions, the agreement stipulated to move the start of the school year uniformly to summer again, so that the new school year would commence after the summer vacation.

Switzerland had a similar dissonance in school calendars among its fiercely independent cantons (Bernard Dafflon 2003). The cantons in which the local language was French, Italian, or Romansch kept the now-normal calendar of a late-summer start for the school year. But many of the German-speaking cantons, especially those in rural areas, kept a calendar essentially like that of prewar Germany, in which school began in April. The German-Swiss cantons clung to their nonstandard calendar into the 1980s, with the last one, Appenzell, surrendering to the twentieth-century standard only in 1985. (A Danish friend distinctly recalled a similar calendar shift in the 1950s, but I cannot locate any English-language sources that discuss it.)

The more remarkable aspect of the Swiss transformation is that it took a federal constitutional amendment to effect the change. Switzerland may have the only constitution in the world that indicates the dates that public school must begin. Article 65 specifies that each canton must begin the school year between August 15 and September 15. Because the reforms are recent, there is a record of why they were made. The reason comports exactly with my original theory: the changes were made to facilitate labor mobility between cantons (Dafflon 2003, 12). No mystery there.

The mystery is why it took Germany and Switzerland so long to come up with this simple reform, which Americans had arrived at some sixty years before without any national or (as far as I can tell) state legislation. The disparity is especially puzzling because Germany and Switzerland have federal structures like the United States. Education in these countries is largely controlled by lower-level governments, the canton and the *Land*, which are analogous in their powers to the American states. As will be discussed in section 4.12, the difference may be accounted for by the extreme local control enjoyed by American public school districts.

4.9 New Hampshire High Schools Converged on the Standard Calendar

Unlike Switzerland and Germany, American school districts just fell into the end-of-summer calendar without any debate. It seems almost like an example of "spontaneous order." But one could object that the now-standard calendar is so obvious that it is not much of an example. Except for Japan, Korea, and Afghanistan and for equatorial regions where summer is not much different from other seasons, standard schools everywhere start at the end of summer. One could argue that this must have seemed so obvious to American school districts that there was really nothing to converge on. To this objection I offer one state's experience.

The New Hampshire State Board of Education began in 1870 to record the doings of the state's newly born public high schools as well as its mostly one-room common schools. Among the items noted in 1880 was the length of each high school's term, which was almost universally thirty-six weeks, and the date at which various cities and towns commenced the school year. In 1880, nine of the New Hampshire's forty-seven public high schools started their thirty-six-week school years in April or March. Manchester, the state's largest city and school district, started its school year in January (New Hampshire Superintendent 1880, 230). By 1900, however, all the state's high schools had either an August or September starting date. After 1900, the starting dates were no longer recorded, which suggests that there was no diversity to report. By 1920, even the rural one-room schools kept a standard September-to-June calendar (New Hampshire State Board of Education 1920, 77, 240).

Since New Hampshire's were the only state records available to me at Dartmouth, I thought it might be useful to go to Harvard's Guttman Library, whose archives have nearly every states' central education reports. However, a search of ten states whose records looked at least as complete as New Hampshire's failed to come up with any similar mention of the diversity of school years. This is not to say they did not exist, only that the compilers of reports did not find them interesting enough to record. So perhaps the New Hampshire convergence to the September beginning was just a fluke. But I doubt it. A California source (Cheney 1888) indicated in the 1880s that California's common schools commenced in every month of the year. This source did not indicate how the state's graded and high school calendars converged, but there was a remarkable diversity of seasons from which to choose. The end of summer was not so ingrained as a time to begin school that it had to be inevitable.

New Hampshire's experience clearly shows that a move to the nine-month (thirty-six weeks) calendar did not automatically mean that each district would adopt the same starting point. Ten of the forty-seven districts with high schools, which were age graded, did not immediately adopt the August or September beginning. As it happened, one of the 1880 New

Hampshire nonconformists was my hometown of Hanover, and so I dug through local records of the era to see whether the issue was the subject of public discussion. I found that the Hanover Board of Education voted in 1883 to end the school year in the last week of June, presumably giving up its former April starting date. Alas, there was no reported discussion of why the board decided to change the school calendar.

So let me speculate about why Hanover changed from starting high school in April and ending it in January or February. Here would be Hanover's problem. Most of the early teachers in the village school (where the high school was located) were local women, though the principal was usually a man. (He was formally the "principal teacher" and taught as well as presided over the school; only after their duties became purely administrative in the twentieth century were they called simply "principals" [Kaestle 1983, 125].) As high school education became attractive for local students, more specialized teachers would be demanded. These teachers were making it a career rather than a placeholder prior to marriage or some other occupation, and many would have had normal-school training. (David Reynolds [1999, 63] mentions that Iowa's early normal schools trained exclusively for graded schools.)

High school teachers with a career in mind would want to be able to have continuous employment, and at least some knew that they would be teaching in other districts. To take a job in Hanover in April would be complicated. For newly minted graduates from normal schools, it would mean a nine-month wait from their June graduation to their first pay check. For teachers currently employed in other high schools with the now-standard calendar, it would require their leaving their jobs two months before the end of the school year. Even if Hanover's April beginning was not a problem for a new teacher, she or he would surely realize that getting another job elsewhere would be difficult, since the end of Hanover's school year would be several months before the beginning of a fall term in more than three-quarters of the high schools of the state. The new teacher would suspect that her ability to negotiate better salary or working conditions with Hanover's school board would be compromised by her immobility, and she might shy away from the Hanover job from the outset, heading instead for nearby Lebanon, New Hampshire, whose high school had a September-to-June calendar like the majority of other districts.

Similar problems would attend to Hanover high school students. It should be kept in mind that the "high school division" in Hanover was, as in most other places at the time, a small and not necessarily separate appendage of common school in the town's main village, where Dartmouth College is located. Starting in April would not be so much of a problem, especially since April was typically the end of the common-school winter term. (Many students would in 1870 still have come from ungraded one-room schools in outlying areas that held terms in summer and winter.) Graduating from high school much earlier than June, however, would be a problem. If students were preparing for college, it would be a long time until September, when most colleges by then began their terms. If they were planning to teach in age-graded schools, for which a high school education was increasingly required by that time, they would find that it would also be a long time before their first paycheck in most other districts. Graduates who sought jobs in the business world could begin at any time, but as the standard fiscal year of July to June took hold, job openings would be more plentiful during the summer months. (It is possible that the traditional fiscal year actually follows the school year; Japan's nonstandard April-to-March school year is the same as the business and government's fiscal calendar.)

4.10 Interurban Job Mobility Made Standardization Desirable

Age-graded schools and increased attendance at high schools in the late nineteenth century clearly warranted a single beginning date for all students in the same school district. But why should that same time of year be early September, and why should it be preceded by ten weeks of vacation? And how did these dates become a national standard? I submit that the standard calendar became universal in the 1880–1920 period because of mobility among the growing ranks of urban workers. Their interests made summer vacation with a September beginning the inevitable choice all over the nation.

Economic historians have found that intermetropolitan wage differentials among workers were persistent up to about 1880, and a national labor market did not truly appear until about 1915 (Joshua Rosenbloom 1996). Regional wage differentials for similar occupations are normally interpreted to mean that out-migration was not sufficiently rapid to boost wages in low wage areas and in-migration was not so rapid as to depress wages in high wage areas. By the end of the nineteenth century, however, wages for labor with similar skills were fairly similar within most regions, which implies considerable mobility by workers at least among nearby cities.

Furthermore, between 1880 and 1920, the fraction of the labor force employed in agriculture fell from 50 percent to 27 percent, and after 1920, employment in agriculture began its long and steady decline in absolute numbers (U.S. Bureau of the Census 1976, 138). During the period that the September-to-June school year was being adopted, urban workers were becoming a majority of the population, and they were able to move to new opportunities anywhere in the country. Being able to enroll their children in schools would have been an important consideration in such moves.

In age-graded schools, children learn best if they all begin at the same time. Schools within a given city or region had to settle on a single starting date because families often changed locations within the city. A standardized, age-specific curriculum reduced the redundancy of education in a child's new school (Church and Sedlak 1976, 187). But within-district standardization actually made it easier to move during the school year. A February move from one school to another was not too disruptive if the school the child entered was closely following the annual curriculum of the school he or she had left.

When new students and their families were coming from outside the district, however, urban school districts needed to allow sufficient time for newcomers to arrive and get settled. So both parties (new and existing families) have an incentive to want to begin with everyone in the class at the same time. A long vacation between the end of the school year and the beginning of the next served as a catchment for new students.

September was most likely the preferred time to start the school year because transportation of people and household goods was least likely to be disrupted by inclement weather in June, July, and August. Snowdrifts and windstorms and washouts were common problems for both rail and over-the-road carriers in the early twentieth century. Summer was thus the logical season for families to move and for age-graded schools to be closed. By the beginning of the twentieth century, interurban job changers must have found that it paid to leave in summer so that they could move to another area and start their children in an age-graded school in September. The elements are less of a problem for twenty-first century movers, but they are still a consideration. Summer remains the prime season for households to move, especially if they have children (John Goodman 1993).

A modern example that confirms the importance of schools in determining the relocation season, rather than vice versa, comes from the province of Quebec. Like several American cities (notably New York and Chicago), Montreal and other Quebec cities had adopted, by law or custom, April 30 as the day when residential rental leases expired. May 1 was thus the traditional "moving day" for tenants, and this allowed the stock of apartments to be more efficiently used (though it did create congestion in the moving industry). By the middle of the twentieth century, this tradition had died out in the United States (without much commentary as to why), but it persisted in Quebec until 1971. At that time, the provincial government changed the official moving date to July 1. The reason for the change was that, under the May 1 tradition, "the headache of a move was only exacerbated by the fact that kids were being yanked out of classes before their school year was up" (*CBC Online News*, June 28, 2005). A summer move allowed children to finish school at their old home and begin the next school year in their new neighborhood.

4.11 Property Markets Promote Calendar Coordination

Interurban migration and age-graded schooling make it *rational* for school districts throughout the nation to adopt a September starting date and give new teachers and students and their families sufficient time to arrive. But as far as I can tell, no state or national politician or school official noticed this fact and urged a uniform law to enforce it. By almost all (sketchy) accounts, it just happened. For example, Gary Courchesne (1979) noted that Holyoke, Massachusetts, established age-graded schools in 1872, the same year that summer term was abolished there. James Leloudis (1996, chapter 1) likewise noted the simultaneous adoption of an age-graded school and a fall-winter-spring calendar in Wilson, North Carolina, in 1881. But neither historian connected the two events, most likely because there was no discussion of it at the time.

There is some circumstantial evidence of a connection between age grading and the uniform calendar. Myer et al. (1979) calculated the average number of school days per year by state between 1870 and 1930, when the summer term went from a common condition to nearly nonexistent. The average number of days rose from 117 in 1870 to 170 in 1930. By the start of the Depression, the school year had nearly reached the now-standard 180 days. This increase was accompanied by a reduction in the variance. Myer et al. calculated the standard deviation (a measure of how much districts within each state deviated from the state's average days of school per year) for those figures over the same period. The standard deviation declined steadily, which suggests that age grading brought more regularity among academic calendars, as well as a longer school year.

An exception to the general inattention to the origins of the academic calendar was an article by Joel Weiss and Robert Brown (2003). They described how the administrators of Ontario's more centralized school system haltingly commanded that summer vacation become the province's norm between 1877 and 1913. As in the United States, rural Ontario schools had winter and summer terms, whereas urban Toronto and some other cities had almost year-round schooling. Rural interests were resistant to the central directive to have a minimum-length summer vacation, most likely, I suspect, because summer was an ideal time for younger children to attend and use otherwise empty buildings. But central control of schools, which was more accepted in Canada than in the United States, did not help convert Ontario's schools to the now-standard calendar any faster. Weiss and Brown did not, however, suggest that summer vacation and September beginnings were a coordinating device for age-graded schools, nor did they propose a reason for the change.

I propose that a decentralized mechanism, the property market, provided American school districts with the necessary information and incentive to adopt what became a national norm. American household mobility has always been high, with about one in five changing residence every year (Fischer 2002). As mentioned at the beginning of chapter 2, numerous studies show that housing prices are influenced by families with children, who pay a premium for homes in better school districts. To maintain or improve the value of their largest financial asset, homeowners, even those without children, insist that local school boards keep their school systems attractive to potential homebuyers. Most of the scholarship concerning this link has focused on school spending, taxes, and test scores, but it is reasonable to suppose that features like the friendliness of the school calendar enter into it.

School districts that deviated substantially from the summer-and-September norm would have found themselves at a disadvantage in that their education systems were more costly or less effective and thus less attractive to potential residents with children. As my speculation in section 4.9 about Hanover's initially nonstandard school calendar suggested, it would be more difficult to hire teachers and place graduates in teaching jobs. In modern districts, interscholastic activities such as athletics, debate teams, and professional conferences would be more complicated to arrange. A nonstandard school calendar makes it not only harder for a family to move into the district but also more complicated to leave it for a destination with a standard school year. Both prospects would be unattractive to potential homebuyers. By trial and error, districts would learn that substantial deviations from the September-to-June norm were costly, and political feedback from employers and property owners would induce local officials to conform to the national standard.

The problem with an empirical inquiry along this line is that nonstandard school years do not last long. An advocate of year-round education described pre–World War II experiments in year-round schools, all of which quickly reverted to the standard calendar once enrollment pressure ceased or new buildings could be built (Don Glines 1995). The anti–year-round school Web site (http://www.SummerMatters.com, February 2004) had an extensive list of schools that have dropped their year-round schedules. Another anti–year-round school Web site displayed letters from a Texas realtor claiming that a particular district with a year-round school calendar was less attractive to homebuyers.

The voices that question the benefit of summer vacation and lobby instead for year-round schools are typically those of people who are not moving from one school district to another. Local school governance is undertaken by established residents. But the majority of students change school districts at some time during their thirteen years of public schooling, and many change more often (Skandera and Sousa 2002). The parents of these students had no voice, before their arrival, in local debates about year-round schools. But they did have the option of selecting school districts when they were planning to move. By voting with their feet not to buy or rent homes in nonstandard districts, nonresidents may have enforced the summer-vacation norm as effectively as any established resident.

4.12 Decentralized Decisions Converge More Quickly

If property markets promoted coordination of calendars, why did Germany and Switzerland require conscious and long-delayed national decisions, as described in section 4.8, to coordinate their calendars with the rest of Europe? Here I borrow an important point made by Claudia

Goldin and Lawrence Katz (2008, chapter 5), who examined the causes of America's rapid increase in high school attendance between 1900 and 1950. American high school attendance grew much more rapidly than that of Europe. Goldin and Katz attribute this to the more decentralized governance of American public schools, which did not initially require that every district in the state offer a high school education.

Consider, for example, Kalamazoo, Michigan. (My example, not theirs.) The city was the defendant in a famous court case, *Stuart v. Kalamazoo*, 30 Mich. 69 (1874), that swept away constitutional challenges to taxation for local high schools. (Some scholars attribute the rise of high school to this decision, but Justice Cooley's opinion made it clear that the court was merely endorsing what voters had already established, not breaking new ground.) The city could decide by a majority of its local voters to offer free public high school as early as 1860. Rural schools and other cities in Michigan did not have to offer high school at the same time. The funds for high school were largely locally generated at that time, so one city's decision did not affect the taxes of another.

However, Kalamazoo surely did affect other districts' decisions about high school. Once it became evident that having a high school attracted more families to a locale, other cities decided they had to do it as well. Writing of the piecemeal process of district consolidation (which was necessary to undertake a high school education) in the early 1900s, Cubberley (1914, 241–43) described how "progressive communities do not have to wait for years for unprogressive communities to experience conversion." After the success of the early adoptions, "others follow with more ease, and before long most of the progressive portions of a county can be induced to form unions for the maintenance of such consolidated schools." Maris Vinovskis (1985, 64) mentions that similar emulation motivated towns in Massachusetts in the 1800s.

Thus a "race to the top" for consolidated and high school districts ensued. Almost every locality of any size, and many without much size at all, sought to have a high school. Cubberley complained that the process left some remote locales out of the consolidated districts (he was writing before motorized buses became widespread), but Goldin and Katz's main point is that if the entire state of Michigan (for example) had to decide whether to finance high school for every location simultaneously, it would have taken much longer to do so. Most Michiganders in 1860 did not want to pay for high school education, and their children had little use for more than the traditional common-school curriculum.

Only by 1920 did high school become a widespread norm, and it became a norm not because educators persuaded voters of its merits but because so many cities and towns had already adopted it and sent high school graduates on to successful careers. Towns without high schools felt they were being left behind both educationally and in the race to attract potential residents and businesses. Indeed, many commentators thought that too many small towns were trying to stretch their resources to build a high school (Reynolds 1999, 64). Europe lagged behind, according to Goldin and Katz, because their centralized governance systems required a national or statewide majority that was willing to pay for high schools. And the secondary schools that European nations initially established were largely geared toward training a technical elite that would serve the state. The mass education high school that became the norm in the United States before World War II was not common in Europe until the 1960s.

The school calendar story seems similar. The schools of each German *Land* were run by the state as a whole. (Goldin and Katz [2008, 403] note that Prussia's schools were centrally financed by the late nineteenth century, as were those of the rest of Europe.) Changes in the calendar had to be made for all schools, just as offering high school had to be made for all. The transition from one school calendar to another has costs in an age-graded system of education. When Germany did it in the 1960s, it caused a large number of students to have shortened school years. This cut into their education for some time, though most eventually made up for it (Pischke 2003). Teachers likewise had a shorter year, and either the state had to pay them when they were not working or their annual incomes declined for the year. Either prospect would seem uninviting for state authorities.

These state authorities would probably have been less connected by the electoral process to local voters or employers who might want to attract workers from other places in Germany. This is not to say that education was not subject to political debate. The difference was the level of the government at which the debate would take place. In the United States, the debate was almost totally local, and local property owners had the strongest voice. American teachers and administrators were transient or lived elsewhere and had little influence on local decisions. At the higher-government level at which Germany and Switzerland made their school decisions, interest groups besides property owners had more power.

This analysis, of course, reverses the view that is widely held in American sources in education history. The standard view is that the school districts themselves were resistant to change, and only the persistent effort of the state education establishment was able to overcome this resistance. The German and Swiss account belies this, just as the evidence about school consolidation presented in chapter 3 belies the top-down story. The education establishments of German *Länder* and Swiss cantons had the authority that American schoolmen longed for, but the Germans and the Swiss were for decades unable to make a simple adjustment to the school year so that teachers and pupils and their families could move easily from one region to another.

4.13 The Tyranny of Interchangeable Schools

So far I have presented an upbeat view of the creation of a standardized system. Now it is time to look at some drawbacks. The economic appeal of a uniform, age-graded system of education is its interchangeability. The standard school calendar allows parents and teachers to move from one place to another and still begin school with everyone else. The standard curriculum (in the loose sense in which I use "standard") means that new-comers from other districts will not have to be brought up to speed with costly diversions of instructional time, nor will most newcomers have to cool their heels while other children are taught things they already know. But this same virtue comes at a cost. Consider just two good ideas that were tried but failed to take hold: (1) Phonetic alphabets for reading in-struction and (2) instructional methods that permit students to learn at their own pace, such as Montessori, Waldorf, and Dalton, and "open class-room" instruction.

The school district of Bethlehem, Pennsylvania (my childhood address, though not my school district), at one time seriously experimented with teaching students to read with a special phonetic alphabet. I was a child who was unsuccessfully taught with the "look and say" method in first grade, and I still remember the epiphany of learning to read phonetically in the second grade. (Thank you, Miss Long.) When I heard about Beth-lehem's experimental system in the 1960s, I regarded it with unalloyed approval.

The main barrier to truly phonetic reading instruction is that English words are often—to put it mildly—not spelled the way they sound. The creators of the "initial teaching alphabet" (ITA) have overcome that drawback by inventing and promulgating a special phonetic alphabet. Letters in ITA are Roman characters except where it is necessary to distinguish different sounds made by the same letter, such as the two "g" sounds in "garage." Young students learn this alphabet and quickly learn to read with it. After that, they gradually make the transition from the ITA to "traditional orthography." Learning to read this way and then transitioning to the standard alphabet is faster than starting with the standard alphabet. The evidence from the Bethlehem experiment in the 1960s confirmed that the ITA method enabled students to read in less time than the non-ITA method (Albert Mazurkiewicz 1965).

Why has this method not taken the nation by storm? The problem is that it usually can not be entirely accomplished within a single school year, and turnover of students between districts greatly complicated the task of learning to read. A child who had but one year of ITA instruction would move to another district because her parents took a new job elsewhere. She would have a problem. Back in Bethlehem, she would not have transitioned very far into the standard alphabet in her reading materials, and her new school could not permit her to continue along a track by herself. She would now be behind instead of ahead of her cohort and might have to repeat a whole grade.

Students moving to Bethlehem after first grade—which was fairly common—usually had no experience with the ITA method. They had begun with traditional orthography, and the new letters and method of reading would be a mystery to them. Newcomers would have to be given special tutoring to get them up to speed in the phonetic alphabet, or they would have to repeat first grade. Neither prospect would have been attractive to the new family or to the Bethlehem School District. (Similar problems would arise for new elementary school teachers, who would have to learn how to teach with ITA.)

The same problem arises with the more humane, "child-centered" methods of learning that are undertaken in Waldorf, Montessori, and Dalton plan schools, which are reviewed in David Tyack and Larry Cuban's *Tinkering Toward Utopia* (1995). The common element of these educational reforms is to avoid imposing the lockstep of age-graded education on children. Children learn at their own pace and often according to their own interests rather than following a teacher-imposed curriculum. By the end of their school experience, they will have learned as much or more than children in standard schools, but at any given moment there is no reason to suppose that one eight-year-old in one of these progressive schools will be studying the same thing as any other eight-year-old in the same school, let alone in the public schools.

The problems again are mobility and transition. Most of these alternative schools are private, so they can insist that newcomers begin at the beginning. But one of their most serious constraints is the transition from the Waldorf, Montessori, or Dalton method school to a traditional public or private school when parents relocate or otherwise have to take their children out of the school. The alternative schools that have retained elements of these educational philosophies have to implement them within a single-year context. Children can undertake self-directed or object-oriented learning during a single year, but their teachers must nudge them along to be prepared to advance to the next grade at the end of the year.

4.14 The Problem with School Reform: Low Variance Trumps High Mean

Suppose the new school superintendent in your district proposes a system by which all students can learn one-third faster than in any other district. Thus students who have completed the first year of schooling in their schools will have completed the equivalent of grade one and one-third of grade two. In their second year, students complete two-thirds of grade two and two-thirds of grade three. In their third year, kids complete the rest of grade three and all of grade four. Thus at the beginning of their fourth year in school, they will be entering what to the rest of the country would be grade five.

It is a bit tedious to follow this in text, so I offer the following chart to compare what I will call the "Accelerated System" to the standard system, along with the age ranges in table 4.1. It is evident from the chart that family mobility among school districts would greatly complicate life in this school district. You move to this great district in July with your fifteen-year-old, who has just completed ninth grade in his previous school district and is ready to start tenth grade. However, all the other fifteen-year-olds in his new hometown are done with high school and are going off to college. (And won't they have fun there, being three years younger than the other freshmen.) Your fifteen-year-old will have to join either the local twelve-year-olds, who will be starting grade nine (as measured by the traditional

TABLE 4.1 **Accelerated versus standard grades**

Age of child at end of school year	Standard school (grade completed)	Accelerated school (grade completed)
7	First	One-third of Second
8	Second	Two-thirds of Third
9	Third	Fourth
10	Fourth	One-third of Sixth
11	Fifth	Two-thirds of Seventh
12	Sixth	Eighth
13	Seventh	One-third of Tenth
14	Eighth	Two-thirds of Eleventh
15	Ninth	Twelfth
16	Tenth	
17	Eleventh	
18	Twelfth	

method), and be bored for most of the year until he gets to the tenth-grade curriculum, or join the local thirteen-year-olds, who will be starting at grade "tenth and one-third," and have to scramble to catch up with them. Either way, he is going to be the oldest kid in the class by at least a year.

Suppose, on the other hand, your ten-year-old daughter had started in the Accelerated System from first grade. Now you move to a different school district and enroll her in the local standard school system. At age ten, she has completed one-third of sixth grade in the previous Accelerated District. Should she start sixth grade all over again with the twelve-year-olds, or should she rush into seventh grade with the thirteen-year-olds? Or perhaps she should stay with her age contemporaries and start fifth grade all over, being bored for a whole year but at least not the youngest in her class by a year or two.

Aside from the batching problem created by the fact that the Accelerated System puts most students a fraction of a grade ahead in most years, what is the matter with being either a couple of years older or younger than your contemporaries if you move into or out of the Accelerated School District? After all, there are successful people who skipped grades in standard schools, and some children are deliberately held back before starting school in order to be a few months older than their classmates. This is helpful to them and maybe even to the cohort as a whole, as research by Bedard and Dhuey (2008) suggests.

But these examples of precociousness are not relevant to the thought experiment I describe here. The students in the Accelerated School District are not brighter than those in a standard school district. The school superintendent found a way of teaching one-third more material per school year; she did not find a way for children to learn more per hour of school. Ordinary children—as opposed to the preternaturally intelligent or precocious—who are visibly older or younger (especially younger) than their school peers will have a difficult time socially and maybe intellectually. Even the unusually bright students who skip grades in standard schools often have social and personal adjustment problems, and they are the students who are mentally better equipped.

The reader may be impatient with a riff about a teaching method that is steadily one-third better than standard schools. What is to be learned from a magical system? But it is not magic. The Accelerated District simply has a school year that is 240 days long, which is one-third longer than the standard 180-day school year. Teachers in that school system work sixty days (two and a half school months) longer than regular teachers. They are paid one-third more for their efforts. (Because children get through public school one-third faster, there is no added fiscal burden to taxpayers.) Children in the Accelerated School attend classes for essentially the same work year as their fully employed parents. They start school on August 1 and end school on July 15. They get two weeks of summer vacation in July, standard weekends with no school, and eight days for miscellaneous holidays. True, they won't go to summer camp, but they graduate from high school three years early and can go to college and graduate four years later at age nineteen. Don't we want the best for our kids?

The point of this exercise is not to promote the 240-day school year. That it might be possible to do it—the Japanese come close to it by attending on many Saturdays—does not make it a good idea. One problem with the very short break between 240-day school years is that students who fail a subject cannot make it up with summer school. They would have to stay back for a whole year or do what the Japanese do, enroll in a "cram school" at night to catch up with their peers. (This pressure may have something to do with the "school refusal" problem in Japan, in which otherwise able students become stay-at-home truants [Iwamoto and Yoshida 1997]. It has even been suggested that South Korea's similarly exacting system may have something to do with the nation's very low birth rate [*New York Times*, June 8, 2008].)

As my snide aside about very young college students may have revealed, I personally think it is a dreadful idea to push children so rapidly through childhood. In a society in which people can expect to live twenty years longer than they did a century ago, we should accept that childhood is being lengthened, not abbreviated. In any case, my point here is that the current 180-day school year and the standard curriculum that it facilitates actually puts a *ceiling* on how much better a school can be.

Some real schools are better than others. They have better teachers, more savvy administrators, a sensible school board, plenty of funds, and parents and community members who are supportive. But better school districts do not accelerate their students in the way I described in the hypothetical example. They don't do more than one grade in one year. They typically, at least below the high school level, offer "enrichment programs" for the quicker students. They study Chinese art or write local histories or make robotic vehicles—any subject that is not an essential part of the next grade's curriculum.

More importantly, "good schools" see to it that the slower learners are brought along so that they can stay at their age-appropriate grade level. Think about the state and national tests for successful schools. Schools are judged mainly by the percentage of students who are below some standard, not by the mean or median score. If a school has 20 percent of its students reading below grade level, that figure is not offset by the school having a different 20 percent of students reading above grade level. In fact, a school that has no students reading (or doing arithmetic or whatever) below grade level and none above grade level is considered more successful than a school that has 10 percent of its students below grade level even if another 30 percent are above grade level.

Success in public education generally means achieving the correct mean—everyone on grade level—and low (ideally, zero) variance. As an old study of age-graded schools in Michigan put it (in typically redundant phrasing), "The theoretical goal is to have zero per cent of under-ageness and over-ageness, zero per cent of retardation and acceleration, and 100 percent of normal-ageness and normal progress" (Maude Smith et al. 1937, 343). The modern, upbeat way of saying this is "no child left behind," but that is the same as having all children march in lockstep, to which the Michigan folks aspired. If some children march faster, then some others must be proceeding more slowly and will at any given moment be "left behind." Regardless of how it is framed, upside variation creates almost as much of a problem as downside variation. That's why transformative school reforms are so difficult to do. (I consider the difficulties of two such reforms, school-finance equalization through the courts and vouchers, in more detail in chapter 6.)

4.15 Pretty Good Schools Facilitate Labor Mobility and Productivity

A major theme of this book has been that school districts respond to American mobility. Families can move from one part of the nation to another and put their kids in schools that will be reasonable extensions of those they left. This facilitates labor mobility, and the mobility of American labor is a considerable strength. The more intensively trained high school graduates of Germany or Russia or Japan, whose education systems Americans have anxiously envied during the previous century—at least when those nations were thought to be in some way ahead of us—are not especially productive if they cannot move to the jobs that take advantage of their skills. American high school graduates may make up for their middling educations by being able to easily move to jobs in Houston or Spokane or Tampa that match the skills they acquired in Minneapolis.

The mobility that American schools facilitate may help resolve a paradox that many scholars have noticed. American high school students are only about average in test-based comparisons with other high-income countries (National Center for Education Statistics 2004). Yet productivity of American workers in high-tech industries has grown in the last decade more rapidly than in countries where schools are more rigorous (Susan Houseman 2007, 62). The usual explanation for this is that technological advantages of American industry offset the modest training of American workers. But that seems doubtful. Technology is itself highly mobile, so it should be as readily available in all countries that do not block trade. If other countries can adopt the same technologies, they should be able to take even greater advantage of it with their well-educated workers.

The mobility of American workers offers a resolution to this paradox. As van Ark, O'Mahony, and Timmer (2008) point out, the greater mobility of American workers seems to account for the more rapid adoption of new technologies of the knowledge economy. It may be the very looseness of American education that makes its workers more mobile. They can move from one part of the nation to the other with their families in tow and take jobs that match their skills. Mobile workers will fit into their communities both because their kids can easily fit into the relatively unspecialized, loose-jointed education system and because adults will easily get to know other adults by way of their schools and the social capital they provide their communities. (I discuss the social capital issue in chapter 6.) In other nations, workers with children are less mobile because their children's education is more specialized and because adults have less in common with strangers in communities to which they might move. (That specialization in education retards mobility is suggested by the greater reluctance of American families to move when their children are in high school, a time when many students' education becomes more specialized and oriented toward college preparation.)

These strong points about American education necessarily imply that it is difficult to change the system in a short period of time. Public education *has* improved over time. Classes have gotten smaller in elementary schools, music and art are mainstream subjects, and many college-level subjects are offered in high school. Within recent decades, American scores on national exams such as the National Assessment of Educational Progress (NAEP) and on standardized international tests have crept steadily upward, though similar progress by other nations has kept the United States near the middle of the high-income nations (Hanushek 1998). But such improvements are increments measured by decades, not academic years or even Presidential terms. They come about by gradual emulation of successful ideas, much like the adoption of the "standard" school calendar and of the norm of high school early in the twentieth century. Rapid adoption of sweeping reforms is always complicated by the need to coordinate one's schools with those of the rest of the country, and sometimes the rest of the world.

This is not to downplay the importance of having a system that teaches useful skills. Eric Hanushek and his coauthors have shown that the quality, not just the quantity of education, has an important effect on economic outcomes around the world (Hanushek and Kim 1995; Hanushek and Woessmann 2007). Closer to home, Goldin and Katz (2008) show convincingly that America's broad-based high school movement was one of the most important engines of economic growth in the twentieth century.

The rapid spread of broad-based education was also, Goldin and Katz argue, an important source of income equality in first three-quarters of the twentieth century. With so many high school graduates and, later in the century, college graduates flooding the labor market, competition for low-skilled jobs was more limited. Workers without educational advantages could command higher wages than otherwise because there were so many well-educated workers competing for the more skilled positions. (The argument always reminds me of the "gospel of wealth" preacher whose motto was, "The best thing you can do for the poor is not be one of them.") Goldin and Katz conversely attribute America's rising wage inequality since the 1970s to the stagnation in rates of attendance in colleges and universities, which now are to high school what high school once was to elementary school.

This book is about school districts, not education reform in general. But school districts are a durable component of the reform picture, and their virtues and drawbacks must be taken into account in reform issues. Given the constraints that mobility imposes on drastic changes in schooling, education reforms might more profitably facilitate a *longer* period of education. One approach is to start earlier. Preschool education is becoming a norm, and substantial research by Flavio Cunha and James Heckman (2007), among many others, supports the idea that systematic attention to disadvantaged students at a young age helps level the playing field.

The other side of this coin is to keep going longer. The problem identified by Goldin and Katz is not with public schools per se, but with access to postsecondary education. As Cascio, Clark, and Gordon (2008) point out, America's standing in international education comparisons is much better for young adults in their twenties. They attribute this to the less specialized secondary-school curriculum and the greater access to college in the United States, so that people in their twenties in the United States are more likely to have a university degree. As it did with high school in the 1960s, the rest of the high-income world (chiefly Europe) has recently gained in university education, largely by imitating the American approach. The United States is no longer alone at the top in university education, though why economists, raised on a diet of mutual gains from international trade, should find this worrisome is something of a mystery. In any case, making university education more generally available and keeping the cost within the means of a larger fraction of the population are obvious ways to deal with the (comparative) American educational slowdown. There is no reason to believe that public school districts cannot accommodate such a policy, just as they did early in the previous century, when universal access to high school became a goal.

We should not expect a longer span of education to overhaul the K–12 years. Education reforms that work on the foregoing extensive margins make more sense than those that attempt to create a more intensive use of the school year. Cramming more into the school year or making the school day or term longer may be more costly than extending the period we think of as childhood farther into the twenties. Our children and grandchildren will live longer than we expect to live, and they will be healthier for a longer period (Robert Fogel 2005). Delaying a serious commitment to the workforce to ages twenty-five or thirty is not much of a disability if one can work productively past age seventy. (For the same reason, anxieties about the slight increase in the age at which children usually enter first grade seem misplaced.) Education reformers might be better advised to stop wringing their hands about the mild expectations of public school—a mildness that may facilitate a desirable interchangeability of all schools— and look instead at our extended lifetimes and try to facilitate learning over a longer period of time.

4.16 Conclusion: Calendar-Bound Reform

The standard school calendar, in which classes begin near the end of summer and end near the beginning of the next summer, is a worldwide standard. Its adoption and persistence have little to do with agriculture. Its purpose is to allow teachers and families with children to end school in one place, use a cost-minimizing season to move to another place, and begin the school year along with the preexisting students and teachers in their new home. The transition from irregular calendars to the standard system was occasioned by the widespread adoption of age-graded schooling. America's ungraded one-room schools had little reason to adopt a standard calendar, but urbanization by about 1900 required that all schools get with the age-graded norm and adopt the standard calendar.

I argue beyond this point that American schools adapted to the new norm more easily than several other nations because of its decentralized school system. The impetus for conformity to the new calendar was property values. Districts that would not conform to the system would have repelled buyers of farms and homes and made it more costly to hire teachers, which would have reduced property values. Homeowners, farmers, and business owners all had a stake in joining the standardized system, and they did so without much debate about it.

The further, and perhaps more hazardous, generalizations from this theme concern the nature of education reform. Here the message is not as upbeat. The need to respond to mobility puts a ceiling on the extent of reforms that can be adopted in a short period of time. A school district that quickly adopts some apparently desirable reforms would find political resistance from parties interested in moving to or from the area. Even if the district stuck to its guns and persisted in radical reform efforts, the benefits would be difficult to sustain. The advantages achieved would be eroded as emigrants had to fit into other school systems and immigrants had to be brought up to speed in the reformed system. Age-graded education has a grim logic to it that makes it difficult to undertake rapid reforms. As a result, efforts that work on either end of K–12 education—preschool and postsecondary education—are the more viable candidates for restoring American preeminence in education.

CHAPTER FIVE

The Economic Geography of School Districts

So far I have treated school districts in a largely nonspatial way. My description of the pedagogical transformation from the ungraded one-room schools of the nineteenth century to the age-graded, multiroom schools of the twentieth century did not systematically examine differences in regions of the nation or differences among urban, suburban, and rural districts. Almost all education researchers are acquainted with some of these differences. We know that most of the older big cities have large-enrollment districts. It is widely assumed that suburban districts are numerous and relatively small. Everyone knows that the South is different, often having countywide districts. And many, if not most, observers know that school districts do not always line up perfectly with municipal or county boundaries. What few people know is the extent of these variations and explanations for them. Why are big-city districts so large? How fragmented are suburban districts? Why does the South have county districts? And how much divergence is there between municipal and district boundaries?

Answers to these questions required original research. Studies of school district structure at the national level are scant. Economists interested in school district competition have examined national data about structure, but they have typically excluded areas not considered to be germane to their hypotheses. I have encountered no previous study that has attempted to explain the structure of school districts in the United States as a whole.

My focus will first be to explain the differences in the geographic size of school districts by region of the country, especially why the South's school districts are so much larger in area. Race has a lot to do with it, but not always in ways that one would expect. Then I examine the metropolitan structure of school districts to examine the parameters of "Tiebout competition," in which households choose among different school districts to buy their homes (Tiebout 1956). There is a lot of competition, but, more surprisingly, the variation in the competitive structure of urban districts is largely the product of previous rural conditions. Finally, I will present evidence that, despite their differing functions, legal status, and governance, school districts and municipal governments are not strangers to one another.

5.1 Variation is More by Region than by State

The size distribution of America's 15,000 school districts is, like many other geographic aggregates, skewed toward the largest. As of 2005, the largest district, New York City, had about 987,000 primary and secondary students, more than the total population (not just students) of Montana or Vermont or four other small states. But as enormous as the New York school district is—it corresponds to the boundaries of the nation's largest municipality—it nonetheless accounts for only 2 percent of all public school enrollments. (There were 54 million K–12 school-age children in 2000, 90 percent of whom were in public schools.) By contrast, the New York Consolidated Metropolitan Statistical Area—the city and its many suburbs—contains almost eight percent of the United States population. The three largest districts in the United States, New York, Los Angeles and Chicago, together enroll over two million students, but that is still only a little more than 4 percent of all students in the continental United States. After the big three, there is a considerable decrease in size. It takes the next ten largest districts (five are Florida counties) to equal the enrollment of the big three. And the tail of the distribution is long. Almost half of public school children in the United States attend school in a district with fewer than 10,000 students. (The enrollment numbers are from the National Center for Education Statistics [NCES] assembled by Garofano and Sable [2008]. I excluded Hawaii and Puerto Rico from the NCES totals because they have no local school districts: the state or territorial government runs the schools directly.)

The more interesting aspect of American school districts is their geographic variation. The map of the United States in figure 5.1 shows all the unified and high school districts in the contiguous forty-eight states, circa 2000. "Unified" districts control schools for all grade levels—from kindergarten through high school—in their territory. Such districts account for the vast majority of both districts and students. However, several states still have some territory in which elementary districts educate grades one through (usually) eight, and then send their children off to a high school that is governed by another district whose territory usually includes several elementary school districts. This arrangement used to be fairly common, and most "unifications" have wedded a high school district with its component elementary school districts. Thus a reasonable national comparison of school district density is to count (and display in figure 5.1) only the unified and high school districts, leaving out the boundaries of the elementary-only districts.

I should add that the areas denoted on the map as having "no district" are not actually without schools. They usually have only elementary schools, and their eighth-grade graduates choose one or more nearby high schools, with the elementary district paying the out-of-district "tuition." In some cases, there is no designated high school to which tuition is earmarked, and these rural students can shop for a high school in essentially the same way that voucher proposals envision, except that choices are usually limited to public schools. (Chapter 6 discusses vouchers in more detail. I would point out that the system described here is mainly used in very rural areas, and students' choices are thus limited by the considerable distance to the nearest high school.)

The map of school districts in figure 5.1 suggests that regions of the nation rather than state boundaries are what matter for the geographic size of school districts. In the Northeast and North Central states, the boundaries between states would actually be difficult to locate if they were not included on the maps because their school districts are so generically similar in size and shapes. As I will show presently, the regional variables that matter are rural population density, which is primarily determined by rainfall and mountainous terrain, and whether all the states' school districts had racially segregated schools after World War II. It is obvious from the map that the South is different from the rest of the country. Southern school districts are much larger in land area than in the North and often

U.S. Secondary and Unified School Districts

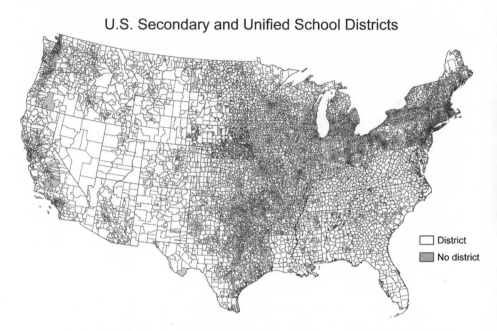

FIGURE 5.1 Boundaries of unified and secondary school districts in the contiguous forty-eight states, circa 2000. Adapted from U.S. Census Bureau Topologically Integrated Geographic Encoding and Referencing (TIGER) by Sarah Battersby.

correspond to county lines. I will argue presently that segregation created a strong diseconomy of scale that required a large-area school district to run separate schools for whites and blacks.

If one squints hard enough, it is also apparent from the large-scale U.S. map that most large metropolitan areas have numerous school districts. The northern-state metropolitan areas of Boston, New York, Philadelphia, Cleveland, Detroit, Chicago, Minneapolis, and St. Louis are easily identified because of the large number of districts jammed together so that their borders merge into a mass of black pixels. This is evident to a lesser extent in western metropolitan areas such as Los Angeles, San Francisco, Phoenix, and Seattle. But it hardly applies at all in the South. It would be difficult to pick out the large metropolitan areas of Florida (Miami, Tampa, and Orlando) from this map, since Florida school districts are organized entirely by county. The same is true for Washington, DC, Baltimore, and New Orleans, and approximately so for Atlanta and Charlotte. Only the western part of the South—Texas, Oklahoma, and Arkansas—

have relatively small districts in both urban and rural areas. Thus one can vaguely make out the location of Dallas and Oklahoma City from the U.S. map.

The reason for highlighting the regional geographic regularities is to exempt myself from too much state-by-state recitations of school district lore. School districts are shaped by state laws, and the differences in state policies do provide useful variation for social scientists. But states within the same region are actually pretty similar to one another in the general structure of their school districts. The greater variation, as we shall see, is among schools within urban areas, but these, too, were influenced by rural patterns that existed when the high school revolution took the nation by storm in the 1910–50 period. For this reason, it is important to examine the overall trend in school districts in the twentieth century.

5.2 School Districts Often Cross County Lines

The county has traditionally been the geographical unit that serves as the arm of state government. Courts and property records and other vital registrations that are the state's business are typically located in the county seat. County boundaries are the basis for the distribution of many state programs, and schools are no exception. When one consults state sources for lists of school districts, they are usually arrayed by county.

But maps of school districts by state tell a different story. In the great majority of states outside the South, school districts often cut across county boundaries. The maps of Iowa's districts (figure 5.2) and its counties (figure 5.3) show this clearly. The regularly rectangular shapes of Iowa's ninety-nine counties contrast with the entirely irregular jigsaw-puzzle shapes of Iowa's school districts. There is in fact not a single county in Iowa that contains all the territory of all its school districts. Districts leak over county boundaries almost as if counties did not exist.

The Iowa pattern is dominant in most of the rest of the North and the West. In the sparsely populated areas of the West, counties are sometimes the basis for school districts simply because there are not enough people in the county to maintain more than one district. (The land areas of counties of the rural West are usually large for the same reason.) But where rural population densities are higher, as in California west of the Sierra and in the wet, western portions of Washington and Oregon, the Iowa-style jigsaw-puzzle pattern reappears, and county boundaries are not sacrosanct.

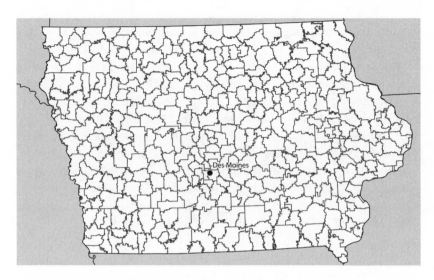

FIGURE 5.2 Iowa school districts in year 2000. *Source*: National Center for Education Statistics Map Viewer, adapted by Sarah Battersby.

The map of Washington State (figure 5.4) offers a useful example. In the Puget Sound area, where most of the state's residents live, there are numerous school districts, and several of them cross county boundaries. (The county boundaries are not shown.) In the Cascade Mountains and in the dry territory to the east, Washington's school districts are larger and seldom cross county boundaries. This is not so much because of county supremacy as because counties are so large that there are fewer lines to cross. The two major western exceptions are Nevada, which merged all its school districts into county units in 1956 (Hooker and Mueller 1970), and Utah, which merged most of its districts into counties early in the twentieth century (Moffit 1946), though there are a handful of subcounty, independent districts in the more populous Salt Lake and Provo area.

County lines also are seldom crossed by school districts in the Northeast, including New England. This is not because of the importance of counties in this region—New England counties are their least important unit of local government—but because school districts in these states are usually arrayed along city, town, and township lines. Municipal lines in these states (and in most others) seldom cross county boundaries.

The irregular shapes of school districts with respect to county boundaries would seem trivial except that it confirms the continuing power of local voters. My discussion of school district consolidation in the mid-twentieth century in chapter 3 emphasized how local voters shaped the process. State officials in many states (including Iowa) wanted to consolidate schools along county lines. The voters would have none of it. They agreed to consolidations only when the boundaries of the new district conformed to what local voters regarded as a socially and economically sensible unit. Such units often crossed preexisting county lines and created a jigsaw puzzle of districts covering the state. The persistence of this pattern to the twenty-first century suggests that the "organic communities" around which districts coalesced are persistent entities. The "social capital" that glues these communities together will in the next chapter be the basis for my explanation of the resistance of voters to reform schemes that would reduce the role of school districts in providing public education.

The disrespect of school district lines for county boundaries might be thought to stop at the state line, but even that is not necessarily true. Along the border between Vermont and New Hampshire, for example, students from one state often attend a high school in a town across the border (the Connecticut River) that is more convenient to their homes. In most

FIGURE 5.3 Iowa counties in year 2000. *Source*: National Center for Education Statistics Map Viewer, adapted by Sarah Battersby.

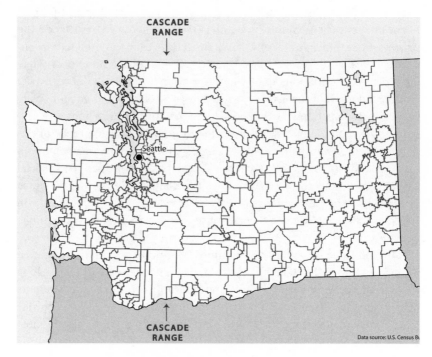

FIGURE 5.4 School districts in Washington State in year 2000. *Source*: National Center for Education Statistics Map Viewer, adapted by Sarah Battersby.

cases, the sending district, which usually has an elementary but not a high school, simply pays tuition for the out-of-district students. True interstate districts, which share governance as well as students, are rare and require Congressional approval under the "interstate compacts" clause of the U.S. Constitution (art. I, sec. 10, cl. 3). One of the handful to have done so is my hometown's high school district, which in 1963 established a common governing board elected by residents of Hanover, New Hampshire, and Norwich, Vermont. The high school for the "Dresden School District" is in Hanover, and the district can be dissolved by vote of either town.

A more concrete approach was taken by the residents of College Corner, Ohio, and its conjoined twin, West College Corner, Indiana. It created a single interstate school district in 1893. To cement their interstate bonds, the two College Corners in 1893 built (and rebuilt in 1926) their high school straddling the border of Indiana and Ohio. As if to advertise its union, the half-court line of the basketball court is on the state line, which allowed for interstate and, at one time, inter–time-zone scoring opportunities (*New York Times*, August 23, 1988). Maureen McDonough, the principal of the school, confirmed in a phone interview in July 2007 that the state-line location made it more difficult—as was intended—for either state to break up the district in subsequent years. College Corner did lose its high school in the 1970s after student population declined, as described in *College Corner v. Walker*, 68 Ohio App.3d 63 (1990), but the building still serves as an interstate elementary school for the two towns.

The region where the county lines are sacrosanct is the South. Louisiana, Florida, West Virginia, and Maryland have county-only districts (Kenny and Schmidt 1994). There are no subdivisions of districts within the county. (The city of Baltimore is considered a county in Maryland and is distinct

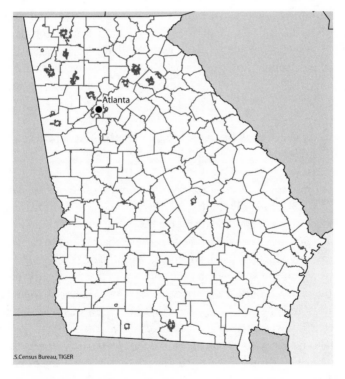

FIGURE 5.5 School districts in Georgia in year 2000. *Source*: National Center for Education Statistics Map Viewer, adapted by Sarah Battersby.

from adjacent, suburban "Baltimore County"; each is a separate school district.) Virginia school districts also are county based, but the state has dozens of "independent cities" (in the sense of Baltimore) that are their own school district. Thus, the independent city of Fairfax, Virginia, has a school district separate from that of Fairfax County.

The map of Georgia (figure 5.5) is representative of most of the rest of the South, at least the states east of the Mississippi River and south of the Ohio River. The boundary lines of all but a handful of Georgia's city districts—the Rorschach blots mostly in the northern part of the state—correspond to a county boundary. The city districts seldom cross county boundaries. Atlanta, whose school district conforms to city lines and occupies parts of Fulton and DeKalb counties, is the main exception.

It is perhaps notable that counties in Georgia and the other seaboard states of the South are irregularly shaped, unlike the gridiron pattern of Iowa and much of the Midwest. The Southern counties are often bounded by natural features such as rivers and mountain ridges, which make them somewhat more natural territories to serve as school districts. But this is unlikely to be the reason for county organization. Most of the original states of the Northeast also have counties with the irregular shapes dictated by rivers and mountains (though somewhat less than in the South), but none have countywide school districts except in their most remote regions.

5.3 Climate Accounts for East-West Variation in Rural School Districts

There are three regional variations in the land-area size of modern school districts: (1) The relatively small-area districts in the North; (2) the irregularly large districts of the West; and (3) the large, usually countywide districts of the South. The regions discussed here correspond to the tripartite divisions of the U.S. Census, in which the West includes the states entirely within the Mountain and Pacific time zones, and the North and South are divided by Pennsylvania's southern boundary (the Mason-Dixon line), the Ohio River, and the northern boundaries of Arkansas and Oklahoma. (The westernmost states of the U.S. Census South—Texas, Arkansas, and Oklahoma—actually look more like the North with respect to school districts, but I will for convenience adhere to the U.S. Census classifications unless specifically indicated.) The discussion focuses initially on rural districts rather than the far more populous districts of metropolitan areas for two reasons: the rural-area variations are easy to see on maps, and the rural districts turn out to be the mothers of the suburban districts. Much to my surprise, metropolitan-area variation in school district size and competitiveness is largely explained by the history and geography of *rural* school districts.

The basic explanation for the regional variations stems from consolidation of rural, one-room schools into multiroom school districts, as described in chapter 3. The small, independent rural school district with its one-room school at one time was spread all across rural America. It was not just in the North and Midwest. The South in the early twentieth century also was covered with small, one-room schools, many of which had some degree of fiscal autonomy necessary to classify them as districts rather than as attendance zones (Walter Gaumnitz 1940). (Attendance zones will be discussed—and largely dismissed—in chapter 6.) Given rural voters' concern about maintaining local control, I believe that they were willing to accept a consolidation no larger than that needed to have an age-graded school that would support a high school (or feed into one). Voters typically rejected larger-area districts unless subsequent rural population decline required further consolidation. Achieving the minimum size meant combining the areas of anywhere from four to twelve one-room school districts. Where one-room school districts were thick on the ground, as they would be in rural areas with relatively small farms packed close together, the resulting consolidated school district would be relatively compact. Thus, in the well-settled rural areas of the North—roughly speaking, east of the hundredth meridian (which vertically bisects the Dakotas)—the minimum land area for a consolidated school district was modest.

In the arid West it took much more territory to round up the minimum number of students needed to make a comprehensive, age-graded school district. (This was the basis for my explanation in section 3.21 for the more rapid disappearance of one-room schools in the West.) An arid climate dictated land-extensive agriculture such as ranching. The number of school-age children per square mile on ranches was less than half of that in well-watered regions, where small farms were economically viable. Utah and Nevada's rural school districts are huge in area for the perfectly sound reason that they needed entire counties in many cases to assemble enough students to run age-graded schools that would lead to high school. This is also true in the wilderness parts of the East and upper Midwest, such as the northern sections of Maine and Minnesota. That climate and terrain rather than state-specific variation are the cause is confirmed from

modern maps of those parts of the West that are not as arid or mountainous as the inland territory. In the areas close to the Pacific Ocean, such as
Washington's Puget Sound area (shown in figure 5.4) and California's Central Valley, where rainfall or low-cost irrigation made it possible to have
many modest-sized farms placed close together, rural school districts are
much smaller in area.

5.4 Low Rural Density Was Imprinted on Urban Districts in the West

Modern school district patterns seem to support the idea that climate determined the land area of districts. It would be more convincing if the trend
could be spotted earlier in the history of consolidation. I could not locate
any systematic source on school district size during the formative period
of consolidation, but I did encounter one contemporary source that seems
generally to support my claim. Professor Macy Campbell of Northern
Iowa University was, like almost all other professional educators, an advocate of consolidated schools. His *Rural Life at the Crossroads* (1927) was
a work of persuasion that described thirteen newly consolidated schools
from Virginia to Utah.

Salted among Campbell's glowing descriptions were some hard facts
about the new districts, all of which had been formed from preexisting one-
room schools. Among the facts was the land area of the rural districts. Arrayed from east to west, the general trend was for district land area to become larger as the surrounding climate grew dryer or more mountainous
and the rural population density declined. The largest-area districts outside
of the South were two in the mountainous West (Del Norte and Center,
Colorado), arid Jordan, Utah, and Holcombe, Kansas, in the low-rainfall,
western part of the state. Each of the western districts encompassed an
area of more than one-hundred square miles. All but one of the districts
in the flatter and rainier states to the east were less than fifty square miles.
(The exception was Tipton, Iowa, which had an area of seventy-five square
miles, and those of the South. The Southern districts' larger sizes were the
result of racial segregation and are discussed in the following sections.)
Each of the districts Campbell described is still in existence, though most
have undergone further consolidation with their neighbors as their rural
population declined.

My explanation for the distribution of modern school district size depends on three behavioral assumptions. One is that resident-voters in one-room schools consented to consolidation, as I demonstrated in chapter 3. It was not forced on them by state officials. Second, I believe that the great majority of these voters preferred the smallest district they could have and still run a K–12 school. (In some states, there was an option to run a K–8 school and join several other elementary districts to feed into a separate high school district.) As I will discuss in chapter 6, smaller school districts in the modern world are preferred by homebuyers to large districts. Voters in both the past and the present are less concerned about scale economies than about governance, which, as modern evidence confirms, was more responsive to voters in small districts (Rose and Sonstelie 2004). The third assumption is that it is next to impossible to break up an age-graded district into smaller components when its population grows. Population decline induces smaller districts to consolidate (usually by having the entire district join with another), but population growth within an established school district almost always made for a district with more pupils, not subdivision into several districts.

These three assumptions offer an explanation for the geographical diversity of school district land area across the North and the West. Voters in one-room districts were generally willing to consolidate up to, but not far beyond, the minimum student population necessary to form a district that could support a high school or an elementary district that was fully age graded. In sparsely populated areas, this required a larger land area; therefore, newly consolidated districts had to be larger in land area than was necessary in more densely settled rural areas of the country.

The rural pattern was imprinted on subsequently urbanized districts in the West, since districts seldom break up. An example of how a small-population, large-area school district in the arid West became a local behemoth is the Meridian School District, adjacent to Boise, Idaho. (A dissertation by Douglas Rutan [1996] provided one of the few thorough histories of a single school district.) The town of Meridian—a principal meridian runs through it—had been a small farm and ranch center with little connection with Boise, ten miles to the east. In 1894, the town consolidated several one-room districts into a four-room school, which allowed it to offer a more efficient, age-graded education. Meridian expanded its four-room school to an eight-room school in 1904 and established a rural high school in 1913, which served the area as the only high school until the 1950s.

Like many other states, Idaho in the 1940s began a statewide consolidation effort to create in all rural areas the multiroom, age-graded schools that would stream students to high school. Southern Idaho is a near desert, getting only about ten inches of precipitation per year (Minneapolis gets about twenty-nine), and its rural population density was far lower than in the Midwest. Ada County outside of Boise did not have sufficient population to support more than two or three high schools in the small towns of the valleys of the Boise and Snake Rivers. In 1950, Ada County voters rejected a single-district proposal and consented instead to the creation of two rural consolidated districts, Meridian and Kuna, in addition to the already established urban district of Boise.

The consolidation brought more than two dozen one-room school districts into what is now the Meridian School District. However, in the 1950s, growth of the city of Boise caused Meridian to become a suburban district. The urban area of Boise (and parts of the city of Boise) spilled into the Meridian School District. From 1950 to 1995, its student population grew by nearly a factor of ten, and it had to build several additional schools. (There was discussion of dividing the district during this time, but nothing came of it [Rutan 1996, 114].) Growth has continued since 1995. According to its 2008 Web site, the district now has twenty-eight elementary schools, eight middle schools, and seven high schools that serve 32,000 students. Its student population is the largest in Idaho. Had Meridian been in a higher-density rural area, consolidation of one-room districts earlier in the century would have been able to support more high schools, and the number of districts in the county would surely have been much greater.

5.5 Slavery and Segregation Shaped the School Geography of the South

The biggest exception to the climate theory of school district size is the South. For this reason, I will limn the exceptional (and still somewhat murky) history of Southern public schooling before addressing modern geographic issues. Before the Civil War, education in the South was different from the rest of the United States in several respects, all of which were related to the system of slavery. One difference was that black slaves received no education. Indeed, after slave revolts in the 1830s touched off fears about slaves communicating with one another by writing, teaching slaves to read and write was made a criminal offense in most of the South. Another difference was that the plantation system created great disparities in income and wealth among Southern whites. Now, this disparity could have had beneficial consequences for public education. When wealth is unequally distributed, local property taxes for schools would be paid by a relatively few plantation owners. This reduced the "tax price"—the amount a voter would have to pay for a dollar's worth of public expenditure—well below one dollar for the great majority of voters.

Plantation owners anticipated that they would end up paying for public expenditures that would not do them much good but cost a lot in local taxes. To guard against this, plantation owners and allied interests in the South made sure that local taxation for schools would be greatly constrained by state law (Henry Bullock 1967). Instead of sending their children to local public schools, wealthy Southerners before the Civil War educated their children at home or in private academies. They had to pay for it themselves, of course, but they did not also have to pay for the education of other children.

Another aspect of slavery also worked against establishment of local public schools. As Gavin Wright (2006, chapter 3) has demonstrated, the white population density of the rural South before the Civil War was unusually low compared to that of the North. Wright attributes this to the displacement of white farmers by large plantation owners and their slaves. It was not simply that the plantation owners bought the best land and (as emphasized by Robert Fogel 1989) used large-scale "gang labor" of slaves to produce more than free farmers could. Wright emphasizes that slavery was a portable institution, and plantation owners were more inclined to invest in their slaves rather than in local institutions such as education. In North Carolina, for example, "Political power rested in the hands of eastern slave owners who held the great bulk of their wealth in the form of human rather than real property. Unlike land, that investment was movable, and its value bore little relation to local development. As a result, North Carolina's governing elite gave scant attention to improving the countryside" (Leloudis 1996, 3).

In contrast to the slave-owning settlers in the South, land speculators in the North could make money by attracting residents, and, as I noted in chapter 2, local schools were part of the bait. Moreover, having a larger number of free settlers created agglomeration economies that made pioneering easier. Noncash labor exchanges were an important part of pioneering farmland development in the Old Northwest (Faragher 1986). Southern plantation owners who pioneered new farmland relied on slaves to develop their agricultural infrastructure. The presence of schools would not enhance the value of the property in which plantation owners were most heavily invested, their slaves. As a result, slave owners were indifferent to attracting white yeomen farmers, and farmers without slaves were in many cases economically repelled by the establishment of plantations (Wright 2006, 75).

The resulting low density of white population in rural areas of the South worked against the establishment of a district school system and other local governments. Poor whites in many places were so spread out that not enough children could walk regularly to the few one-room schools that were established. It is not surprising that most white immigrants would find the nonslave territories more congenial.

After the Civil War, Southern wealth at all levels was greatly reduced both by the exertions of the war and the physical ruin of much of the countryside. Emancipation of the slaves by itself did not reduce the South's aggregate wealth, since blacks now owned the rights to their own labor. The end of slavery also ended the deterrent to rural settlement by whites, and the population density of the rural South—counting, of course, both blacks and whites per square mile—soon exceeded that of the rural North (Wright 2006, 79). With higher population densities, it became more feasible to establish rural one-room schools.

During the Reconstruction period (1865–77), the occupation of the South by the Union army enforced the voting rights of blacks. In this period, local schools were established for blacks and whites, generally along the lines of the inevitable one-room district system prevalent in the rest of the rural United States at the time (Edgar Knight 1913, 43; Link 1992, 5). Schools were separated by race except in rare instances, but the level of inequality among them was not especially large during this period (Bullock 1967, 85).

The widening gap in school spending between schools for whites and blacks in the South is usually attributed to the end of Reconstruction. In 1877, Union troops were withdrawn from the South, and the federal hand that had empowered black voters was withdrawn. Black political office-holding quickly declined, and the enforcement of national civil rights laws became largely hortatory, not a real constraint on white southern politicians. After the 1877 "Redemption" restored white control of Southern legislatures, independent local funding of schools, which had begun under Reconstruction, was disallowed or severely curtailed by state law (Horace Bond 1932).

Because the county distributed state education funds, selection of county officials had to be more carefully controlled in Southern states to assure that blacks would not gain control over the schools. V. O. Key (1949, 541) observed that after 1877, local self-government was "radically subverted" by having governors appoint local officials to assure white supremacy in black-majority counties. Local school boards in the South also were usually appointed by state officials rather than locally elected (John Richardson 1984, 185). The South's undermining of all local government also had an indirect political effect later in the twentieth century. The local political forces that in the North resisted efforts to consolidate schools beyond local boundaries were less robust in the South (Link 1986, 143).

5.6 Disfranchisement Enabled the South to Progress Separately and Unequally

There is a problem, however, with attributing the fiscal disparity between white and black schools to the "Redemption" of white political power. For at least a decade after Reconstruction ended, black and white school expenditures stayed relatively close on average (Robert Margo 1990, 21). This was most likely because it is actually difficult to spend a lot more money on one-room schools. White schools were undoubtedly better appointed than those of blacks, and white teachers were paid more, but the differences on a per-pupil basis were not especially large. It was only after 1900 (give or take ten years for state effects) that average spending per pupil for whites greatly exceeded that for blacks (Tyack, James, and Benavot 1987, 151; Bond 1934, 153). Instead of spending differences measured in terms of 5, 10, or 20 percent, by 1920 the per pupil spending differences between black and white schools were denoted in terms of 100, 200, and 300 percent. It was notable that absolute spending on black schools seldom declined during this period, and often it grew considerably. The dramatic difference was caused by a true acceleration in spending on white schools (Margo 1990, 28).

The occasion for this growing gap was high school. By 1900, Southern politicians realized that in order for the South to reconstruct itself economically, it would have to become more educated. Northern states were by this time well into the transition from ungraded, one-room schools to an age-graded system, which funneled growing numbers of students to high school. The South wanted to do that, too. Even if some of its leaders did not fully appreciate the benefits of high school education, they knew that prospective migrants to their cities from other parts of the country valued the new education (Graham 1974, 124). These potential immigrants would be reluctant to set up shop in the South if they could not enroll their children in modern, age-graded schools that would prepare them to continue to high school.

As in the North, cities were the early adopters of a more systematic public education. At an Atlanta meeting in 1870, an English visitor reported: "One of the speakers, a mechanic, said that he and others would leave the town and seek a home in the West unless their children could be better and more cheaply educated" (quoted in Racine 1990, 39). By 1900, business leaders in Southern cities were as eager "boosters" as their compatriots in the North, and they saw better public education as an important attraction.

The new education system was more costly than the old one-room schools that both blacks and whites (separately) attended. State funds were inadequate to the task of financing such increases. It was not just that the South was poorer than the North. The South's political problem was that not every location within the state had the same demand for an age-graded education system. State funds in largely black counties were actually more than enough to fund improvements in *white* schools. This was because state funds were allocated to counties on a per student basis, counting whites and blacks equally. White school officials in counties with a larger fraction of blacks could thus divert more state funds for white schools (Harlan 1958, 19). A large black population was thus a fiscal bonus to whites, though, of course, it denied blacks an education in those areas.

Whites in largely white counties had to rely on their own resources to expand education spending, and the only way they could get them was to restore some measure of local fiscal autonomy so they could tax local property. But raising funds through a locally elected school board would in many areas of the South have allowed blacks some control over school spending. To forestall any risk of this, most states in the South changed their constitutions and adopted other stratagems to disfranchise blacks (Margo 1990, 34).

Even before the adoption of disfranchising institutions, such as the poll tax, literacy requirements, grandfather clauses, and the white primary, black voters participated far less than whites. Some of this was due to local laws, some to intimidation, and some to indifference and alienation. But the right to vote was still there, and even if participation was usually low, blacks could be roused by one white faction or another to become the swing vote in a close election. It was probably this latent turnout that accounted for the rough equality of school expenditures between blacks and whites in the 1877–1900 era. "So long as blacks could vote . . . it was politically dangerous to tamper too much with the educational system" (Tyack, James, and Benavot 1987, 150).

Disfranchisement was specifically embraced so that schools could be *locally* controlled by whites (Harlan 1958, 40; Margo 1990, 36). In much of the South, the combination of disfranchisement and local taxation to expand educational opportunities for whites was regarded as a progressive idea (Link 1992, 125). Once the possibility that blacks could swing local funds toward themselves was eliminated, white constitution makers felt confident enough to permit localities to tax themselves for schools. As historian William Link (1992, 131) summarized the situation, "If the county superintendent could 'devise some plan for leaving the negro out,' the community was eager to proceed."

And leave them out they did. Without the vote, blacks could not effectively protest when local whites established high schools for themselves while relegating blacks to the traditional one-room schools (Davison Douglas 1995, 13). By 1935, it appears that most one-room schools in the Deep South were for blacks. According to a survey reported in Gaumnitz (1940, 8), one-room schools for blacks in 1935 accounted for a disproportionate fraction of one-room schools in states of the Deep South: North Carolina (70 percent), South Carolina (78 percent), Georgia (74 percent), Florida (57 percent), Alabama (65 percent), Mississippi (84 percent), and Louisiana (76 percent). (Reporting in the survey seems to have been spotty, so these figures should be taken as illustrative rather than definitive.) Whites were increasingly attending multiroom, age-graded schools. Disfranchised Southern blacks, more or less abandoned by the federal government and the courts, were stuck with the education technology of the nineteenth century (Charles Bolton 2000, 787). In Mississippi in 1935, the school term for blacks in most counties was no more than five months, whereas whites attended for at least eight months (Wilson 1947, 50). In his epic study *An American Dilemma*, Gunnar Myrdahl (1944, 947) noted that Southern rural blacks—that is, most blacks—were still relegated to one-room schools, whereas whites in the same areas were transported by school bus to consolidated elementary and high schools.

The fact that blacks were provided with any schools at all after disfranchisement was probably due to some minimal level of court supervision of state funds and, as Robert Margo (1991) has argued, by white employers' need to attract and retain black workers. For example, employers in Forest County, Mississippi, urged officials to fund black schools "to persuade the black population that had only recently moved to the area to work in the timber industry not to leave" (Bolton 2000, 788). Putting it more broadly, Booker T. Washington warned in a public speech in 1903, "Destroy the schools in the country districts and the negro will vacate your farm lands and come to the cities, where he is sure of finding a school in session eight or nine months of the year" (quoted in Harlan 1958, 229).

Disfranchisement efforts also kept a large portion of poor whites from voting (Margo 1990, 34). With a thinner voter base than ever before, the county became the paramount local unit for school funding. Local white elites were thus in charge of raising and distributing local funds at the county level. Considering Alabama's experience, William Link (1992, 234) concluded: "By the 1920s, local financial authority in district-based systems was sharply curtailed."

5.7 Segregation Made the South More Like the Arid West

The previous section indicates a vacillating attitude toward local school districts in the South. At some times they were attractive as a way to improve education for whites, and at other times more centralized controls were sought to limit the potential influence of black voters. By 1910, though, most of the Deep South had "resolved" that conflict: local control and local taxation were made "safe" for white voters by the expedient of thoroughly disfranchising almost all black voters. This should have allowed for the district system that was prevalent in the North. Why, then, did the county become the dominant organization for Southern school districts? My answer will require a closer examination of the geography of the South.

Many historians note that the county was always a more important unit of government in the South and attribute its county-based school districts to that tradition (Tyack, James, and Benavot 1987, 60). This begs the question of what made the South more reliant on counties; all states were divided into counties early in their history. A related claim is that the Anglican Church imprinted its ecclesiastical organization—the parish—on the schools in the South (Roald Campbell et al. 1990, 111), although it is not clear why this would have resulted in county organization: Congregational parishes in early New England made up towns, not counties. In any case, the strength of a tradition is demonstrated by its portability, and the county tradition was not. Southerners who moved to northern and western states did not transplant county governance of schools. When Wisconsin attracted a large number of Southerners to its southern tier of counties, schools were originally organized as counties. But it did not last. All of them opted to switch to township-and-district schools, like the rest of the state, after statehood was established (Rosenberry 1909, 238; Jorgenson 1956, 41). North Carolina's history also challenges the county-tradition claim. Unlike other Southern states, it adopted a Northern-style system of local school districts early in the twentieth century, but it ended up with the same county-district pattern as the rest of the South by the 1950s (Douglas 1995). Tradition does not account for much of the story.

The rural population density of the South was, during the transition from one-room schools to age-graded districts (the early twentieth century), at least as great as most of the North. The difference was that the rural population of the South consisted of a substantial fraction of blacks. Moreover, blacks and whites were residentially integrated in the rural South, simply because transportation was not very good, and blacks and whites had to work in proximity to one another (Harlan 1958, 15).

Modern Americans are accustomed to thinking of African Americans as a minority group, yet, blacks were a majority in many counties of the South. In the early part of the twentieth century, blacks outnumbered whites in two states, South Carolina and Mississippi. In 1910, black majorities existed in 262 Southern counties, about a quarter of the total number of counties in the former Confederate states (T. Lynn Smith 1966, 172). In Alabama, which is representative of the Deep South, blacks accounted for more than three-quarters of the population of eleven counties in 1910. In large areas of the South, local control of school districts with even limited enfranchisement of blacks would have resulted in black governance of some school systems, a result whites could not tolerate.

As I described in the previous section, the route to making local control "safe" for whites was statewide disfranchisement of blacks. Blacks and whites remained in the same local jurisdictions, but only (some) whites could vote. Even when liberated by disfranchisement from having to pay much for black education, the creation of age-graded school districts was more costly for Southern whites than those of the North. In order to create a school district large enough to run a fully graded white school system, whites in small towns had to reach farther into the rural hinterland to get enough students to create the necessary minimum student population.

Taken by themselves, whites, especially in the counties of the "black belt" that swept from South Carolina through Georgia, Alabama, and Mississippi, had to encompass more territory than similarly situated whites in the rural parts of the North.

The South's lower population density of white and black families, taken separately, is evident in table 5.1, which shows family-population densities of the states in 1930, when age-graded schools and district consolidations were reaching into the countryside. To exclude the unpopulated mountainous and desert areas of the West, the land area for computing density in table 5.1 is "land in farms," which includes livestock ranches as well as farms growing row crops. "Rural" population includes both farmers and nonfarming residents who are not in "urban places" with a population of 2,500 or more. The states of the South (as designated by the U.S. Census) are listed in small caps.

Rural population density in 1930 was (and still is) clearly lowest in the driest and most mountainous of the western states at the top of table 5.1. Wyoming, New Mexico, Montana, the Dakotas, Nevada, Colorado, and Arizona had fewer than three rural families per square mile of farmland. (Farmland in these states was mostly grazing land for cattle ranches.) The South, by contrast, had total rural population densities more like the well-watered North. But the *white* population density in the Deep South states of (by order of increasing white population density) Mississippi, South Carolina, Georgia, Alabama, North Carolina, Arkansas, Virginia, and Louisiana was on the same order (six to ten families per square mile of farmland) as the lower-density western and upper midwestern states of Utah, Minnesota, Oklahoma, Iowa, California, Washington, and Wisconsin. This meant that all-white school districts in the Deep South would have to have land areas that were larger than those of the Northern states east of the Mississippi River. This force would be especially strong in the black-majority counties of the Deep South, where density of rural whites would be far below the state's average.

But the South's geographic problem of creating an all-white, rural school district does not fully explain the countywide districts of the South. Southern white population density was lower than in the eastern part of the North, but not much lower (and sometimes higher) than the states of the upper Midwest, all of which ended up with relatively small, subcounty school districts. And although the history is sketchy, it appears that several Southern states did not adopt countywide districts until the middle of the twentieth century. The influence of the county as a disburser of state

TABLE 5.1 **State rural population density in 1930, by increasing order of total rural families per square mile of farmland**

State in 1930	Total density	Black density	White density
Wyoming	0.99	0.00	0.99
New Mexico	1.16	0.01	1.16
Montana	1.23	0.00	1.23
North Dakota	1.94	0.00	1.94
South Dakota	2.17	0.00	2.17
Nevada	2.19	0.01	2.18
Colorado	2.61	0.01	2.60
Arizona	2.68	0.07	2.60
Nebraska	3.09	0.00	3.09
TEXAS[a]	3.64	0.62	3.02
Kansas	3.91	0.04	3.86
Oregon	4.83	0.00	4.83
Idaho	5.04	0.00	5.04
Utah	5.74	0.01	5.73
Minnesota	6.14	0.00	6.14
OKLAHOMA[a]	6.38	0.43	5.95
Iowa	7.02	0.01	7.01
California	7.57	0.05	7.52
Washington	8.28	0.01	8.26
Missouri	8.48	0.26	8.23
Wisconsin	9.34	0.00	9.34
Vermont	9.75	0.01	9.74
Illinois	10.45	0.12	10.33
Indiana	12.08	0.06	12.02
GEORGIA[a]	12.43	4.74	7.69
KENTUCKY[a]	12.91	0.84	12.06
VIRGINIA[a]	13.07	3.29	9.78
TENNESSEE[a]	13.34	1.85	11.50
ARKANSAS[a]	13.53	3.89	9.64
Michigan[a]	14.17	0.07	14.09
Mississippi[a]	14.17	7.79	6.38
ALABAMA[a]	14.91	5.48	9.43
Ohio	15.98	0.25	15.74
NORTH CAROLINA[a]	16.33	4.35	11.98
Maine	16.46	0.01	16.45
New Hampshire	16.93	0.01	16.92
SOUTH CAROLINA[a]	17.05	8.10	8.95
WEST VIRGINIA[a]	18.69	1.39	17.31
NEW YORK	18.80	0.15	18.64
LOUISIANA	19.15	8.31	10.84
DELAWARE[a]	20.67	2.70	17.96
MARYLAND[a]	21.81	3.43	18.38
FLORIDA[a]	22.17	7.13	15.04
Pennsylvania	29.19	0.52	28.67
Rhode Island	30.78	0.40	30.37
Massachusetts	32.90	0.40	32.50
Connecticut	49.39	0.40	48.98
New Jersey	63.34	2.64	60.70
U.S. (48 states)	7.99	0.96	7.04

Source: Minnesota Population Center, National Historical Geographic Information
System: prerelease Version 0.1 (Minneapolis: University of Minnesota, 2004). Available at http://www.nhgis.org.
Note: "Total rural families" includes the categories "white" and "Negro" in the 1930 census. Other racial classifications such as Asian and American Indian are omitted.
[a]States considered part of the South, as designated by the U.S. Census, are in small caps.

funds was always greater in the South. Subcounty districts did exist in the 1920s, though Cubberley (1914, 245) mentions that in the South "district authorities have no functions of any importance" and those in Mississippi in 1920 were little more than segregated attendance zones for which county authorities made the fiscal decisions (Wilson 1947, 40). Florida and Georgia nonetheless did not formally move to county-based districts until the 1940s, and Georgia allowed some exceptions and, like several other southern states, still has a few city-based school districts (Hooker and Mueller 1970; Boex and Martinez-Vasquez 1998).

5.8 Legal Pressure on Segregation Furthered County Consolidation

The next impetus for Southern school district consolidation at the county level arose in the 1930s. As a result of litigation by the NAACP, blacks began to win the right to attend graded schools and high schools. Many blacks did not initially oppose segregated schools for fear that integration would reduce white support for all public education or, if successful, result in loss of black control over the schools that they had established for themselves with some help from Northern philanthropies (Michael Homel 1990, 239). The NAACP had opposed segregated schools from its beginning in 1909, but its initial strategy was not to attack it head-on. Its legal campaign was first to hammer on deviations from the "equal" part of the "separate but equal" doctrine of *Plessey v. Ferguson*, 163 U.S. 537 (1896).

By the 1930s, the NAACP was making some headway along these lines. After the U.S. Supreme Court's decision in *Gaines v. Canada*, 305 U.S. 337 (1938), which held that Missouri had to provide an equal, in-state law school for qualified blacks (Missouri had previously paid the tuition for black applicants in other states' universities), the Southern states realized that the days of separate and unequal schools were numbered. They responded with efforts to upgrade black schools so that they would at least appear to be equal to those of whites (Bolton 2000), and some progress was made in this direction (Donohue, Heckman, and Todd 2002).

Because rural blacks were not residentially segregated, it was not possible to create separate school districts for blacks and whites. Several states attempted to create racial taxing districts—blacks taxed for their schools, neighboring whites for theirs. Curiously enough, both state and federal courts were hostile to such laws and invariably struck them down (Harlan

1958, 265; Tyack, James, and Benavot 1987, 152). Courts in that era would accept the most extreme forms of social discrimination, but property was property, and black and white owners were required to be taxed equally. Go figure.

A single school district thus had to manage both white and black schools. Running two parallel, if not exactly equal, school systems over the same territory meant that school districts had to be bigger. Historian Louis Harlan (1958, 11) wrote that

> each community by maintaining two schools made districts too large, except in urban areas, and schools too small . . . . And it was in the country districts that both the financial and social costs of the dual school system were heaviest. In the cities Negro and white school districts were coterminous with areas of residential segregation, whereas in rural areas children of the two races were scattered out side by side.

The Southern effort to respond to the NAACP's legal victories made the *black* population density the relevant constraint in deciding how big school districts should be. As table 5.1 indicates, the average rural density of the white population in the South resembled that of the upper Midwest. But the rural black population density of the South was more like the overall population density of the arid, low-density states of the West. Where statewide segregation was most relevant (i.e., not including the western wing of the South—Texas, Oklahoma, and Arkansas—where blacks were concentrated in the eastern regions and few counties had black majorities), rural black families per square mile of farmland ranged from 1.85 per square mile in Tennessee to 7.79 in Mississippi, with the median state (North Carolina) being 4.35. Running a separate school district for blacks—which had to be coterminous with that of whites—was much the same as organizing rural schools for whites in the sparsely populated states of Nevada, Colorado, Nebraska, Kansas, Oregon, Idaho, and Utah, whose overall rural densities ranged from 2.19 to 5.74 per square mile of farmland.

It is also worth noting that Southern rural counties were steadily depopulating early in the century as both whites and blacks—but especially blacks—migrated to urban areas with better job and educational prospects. There was little reason for Southern officials to expect enrollment increases to fill up rural districts. Moreover, racial segregation itself confounded most economies of scale: it required not just separate schools, but separate teaching staffs, separate transportation systems, even separate buildings for storing textbooks. As a result, rural Southern school districts by the mid-twentieth century had to be very large in order to collect black and white students and keep them in separate schools. Once blacks had to be included in the age-graded school systems in the South, the county became the logical, perhaps even the inevitable, unit with which to organize rural education.

Once age-graded school districts are formed, it is always difficult to break them up. When suburbanization of Southern cities grew after segregation's demise in the 1950s and 1960s, the previously established rural districts were well entrenched. Occasional efforts to carve out smaller districts in the South had a special disability. The Voting Rights Act of 1965 required federal administrative and judicial review of boundary changes that might alter the racial makeup of a jurisdiction (Hiroshi Motomura 1983). Most Southern states continue to be subject to this review, and the courts and the U.S. Department of Justice have consistently ruled against any subdivision of the South's large-area school districts that might create a fragmented pattern like that of the North.

The foregoing explanation of school district structure is not the entire story of racial segregation. It was practiced in an ad hoc way in the North, especially after the "great migration" of blacks to northern cities after 1915 (Homel 1990). Black immigration also seems to have influenced the school district patterns. In the North, the unstated strategy seems to have been to *avoid* consolidation. Alesina, Baqir, and Hoxby (2004) found by dint of painstaking econometric investigation that northern metropolitan areas with more blacks created a more fragmented school district structure by the middle part of the twentieth century. This should be thought of as "reluctance to consolidate," since the initial degree of fragmentation of one-room districts was extreme everywhere, and secession from an already age-graded district was very rare. Separate school districts, rather than separate schools within the same district, contributed to racial segregation in the North. (See also Martinez-Vazquez, Rider, and Walker [1997] and Davison Douglas [2005, 208].)

I would point out, however, that this effect is statistically significant but not geographically large. As explained in the following sections, the national pattern of urban and suburban fragmentation can be largely accounted for by rural population density (proxied by rainfall) and the aforementioned history of segregation in the South. The dramatic differences between the east-of-the-Mississippi North and the South—obvious even on the national map in figure 5.1—swamp the differences detected by

Alesina, Baqir, and Hoxby. I would also question why racial exclusion required many *small* suburban districts rather than large suburban districts (such as the counties that surround Virginia's "independent cities") that could fend off consolidation with a racially diverse central-city district.

The modern irony is that the South's oversize school districts, which were created to assure white control of black schools, now make it difficult for Southern whites to avoid desegregation by moving to the suburbs with independent school districts. Many of the largest cities in the South are within unified city-county school districts, such as Miami-Dade, Florida, Charlotte-Mecklenburg, North Carolina, and Nashville-Davidson, Tennessee, from which a "flight to the suburbs" is a long trip indeed. The modern view that fragmented suburbs contribute to segregation presupposes that a larger unit of government—say, the county—would be dedicated to school integration. This supposition was not valid in the South until federal legislation in the 1960s effectively enforced desegregation orders and also reenfranchised blacks (Gerald Rosenberg 1991; Sass and Mehay 1995).

But there is a second irony in this. Because Southern blacks emigrated to the cities (North and South) more rapidly than Southern whites, most rural counties in the South now have a majority of whites. In 1910, there were 262 Southern counties with black majorities; by 1960, the number was down to 134 (T. Lynn Smith 1966), and the 2000 U.S. Census found only 95 black-majority counties (Jesse McKinnon 2001). Meier, Stewart, and England (1989) found that Southern school board elections in the 1980s closely replicated the racial makeup of their districts, in large part because of the Voting Rights Act of 1965. Thus, most county school boards in the South have some black directors, but the majority are typically white. (Meier et al. suggest that this works to the disadvantage of blacks because of local implementation of "ability tracking" systems.) It is mainly in the fragmented school districts of Northern cities, where blacks sometimes form a majority of the population, that a black majority actually governs.

5.9 Scale and Governance Influenced the Competitive Structure of Urban Districts

In this and the following sections, I will focus on the geographic structure of urban school districts. It is not easy to see variations in school district size on national or even state maps. In general, school districts in urban areas are smaller in area than rural districts, but urban areas contain the great majority of the U.S. population. It is often unappreciated how little land area is actually occupied by any sort of urban development. The fraction of land taken up by nonagricultural development of any kind—houses, offices, factories, airports, railroads, roads, highways, airports, golf courses, urban parks, shopping centers, parking lots—is only about 4 percent of the contiguous forty-eight states. The fraction taken up by truly urban areas is even less, only about 2 percent (Marcy Burchfield et al. 2006). Because we cannot easily see urban boundaries on a map, I shall revert to statistical measures. (Some of the following was written with Sarah Battersby [Battersby and Fischel 2007], who is the second person of the "we" in these sections.)

Until 1990, no national source produced comprehensive maps of school districts in all states. This made it difficult to provide geographic measures of the structure of school districts across states. Researchers in the Tiebout (1956) tradition who have been concerned with school district competition have had to develop their own measures. Almost all these measures have used the number of districts within a county (e.g., Blair Zanzig 1997; Alesina, Baqir, and Hoxby 2004) or a Metropolitan Statistical Area (MSA) (Caroline Hoxby 2000) as the unit of analysis. The MSAs outside of New England are aggregations of counties around cities of fifty thousand or more, so the county has for all practical purposes been the unit of account in measuring school districts' market structure. Counties are extremely useful in this regard because the entire country is blanketed by counties. There are no "dead spots" that are not subject to county government or the "county equivalents," such as Louisiana Parishes, Alaska Boroughs, and the independent cities of Virginia. For comprehensiveness, counties are good.

Counties are less good for measuring school district competitiveness because the urban population in almost all metropolitan counties occupies only a small fraction of the land area of the county. Nationwide, MSA counties occupied about 24 percent of the land area of the forty-eight states in the year 2000, whereas the "Urbanized Areas" (a U.S. Census term designating the built-up land within an MSA) within these MSAs occupied only about 2.4 percent of the territory of the forty-eight states. Since 80 percent of the population of MSAs is within their Urbanized Areas, it follows that the population density of non–Urbanized Area parts of MSAs is not much greater than most rural (non-MSA) counties.

The foregoing facts warrant a more geographically nuanced approach to measuring school district competition. The rural school districts within

an entire metropolitan county might be numerous but actually offer no realistic alternative for the mostly urban homebuyers in the MSA. Focus on
the Urbanized Area eliminates the potentially misleading count of school
districts in outlying, rural parts of metropolitan counties. It is important to
establish a consistent *land-area* base for comparing school districts because
school district choice is largely spatial. Most parents want their children to
live at home while they attend elementary and high school, so their homes
must be within reasonable distance of a school. Public schools no longer
have to be within walking distance of homes because of the school bus, but
parents and children regard the time riding school buses as a cost.

There are undoubtedly some scale economies in school districts. Multi-
school districts can spread the costs of administration and specialized
services (e.g., speech therapists) over more schools and taxpayers. The
literature on district scale economies is not clear about the point at which
scale economies cease. Most of the evidence comes from examining the
consolidation of very small rural districts (Duncombe and Yinger 2007),
and a study of larger districts that consolidated in Georgia does not point
to dramatic cost saving (Boex and Martinez-Vasquez 1998).

The limiting factor on school district scale, however, is not administrative cost but political governance. Very large school districts are governed
with less input from the voters (Romer, Rosenthal, and Munley 1992), and
research has suggested that the largest districts respond more to the political demands of teacher unions than is the case in smaller districts (Rose
and Sonstelie 2004; Terry Moe 2006). Voters are probably aware of this,
and if they are not, there is ample opportunity for them to learn it during
the special election that must precede most school district consolidations.
Voter reluctance to consolidate districts most likely stems from their view
that consolidation will reduce their role in governance, which would not
be offset by the gains in administrative scale economies.

Reluctance to consolidate means that urban school districts will be more
numerous within urban areas of a given land area. Because of higher population density, the urban district can locate its schools closer to its students and also achieve administrative scale economies. Hence we would
expect urban school districts to be smaller in *land area* than rural school
districts. They can achieve the desired scale economies (balanced against
governance diseconomies) over a smaller land area.

The smaller land area of urban school districts provides new families with
more school choice. For any given job location in an Urbanized Area, there
are usually several school districts within reasonable commuting distance.

As mentioned above, the rural parts of the MSA county are not realistic choices for most urban households. Hence we want a count of the choices of school districts that are located within Urbanized Areas, where most people live.

If voters are reluctant to consolidate to create larger districts, and small districts are better, why are there any big districts? The short answer is that school district consolidation is subject to a ratchet effect; easy to go up, hard to go down. (More evidence for this is in chapter 6.) A large-area district that was once an ideal size for a rural township may experience substantial population growth because of suburbanization of a nearby city. The schools thus become larger and more numerous, and the seemingly ideal size can only be obtained by creating another district from the existing territory. This hardly ever happens. A school district is an atom that can join with others to make a new molecule when necessary, but the resulting consolidation can be split only by the greatest force.

5.10 The Four-District Concentration Ratios for Large Urban Areas

The basic statistic that we develop to measure competitive structure is the percentage of Urbanized Area land area occupied by the largest school districts. The idea is borrowed from the literature on industrial organization, which considers an industry more concentrated (and thus less competitive) if a few of the largest firms dominate some measure of industry activity, such as sales or employment. (This method is the same that Fischel [1981] used to measure municipal competition.) Since it is land area over which districts compete, our measure of "activity" is the land area of the district within the Urbanized Area.

To illustrate the process, consider the Urbanized Area of Portland, Oregon, in the year 2000, in table 5.2. The largest district in the Urbanized Area is the central-city district, Portland. It occupies 18 percent of the Urbanized Area. However, only about half of the Portland School District is within the Urbanized Area. Many "urban" districts include some rural (not in an Urbanized Area) area. The lightly populated rural area of the Portland School District would not be counted in the 18 percent calculation. The second largest district within the Urbanized Area is the westside suburban district, Beaverton, which occupies 11 percent of the Portland Urbanized Area. The third largest school district area within the Port-

TABLE 5.2 **Four largest school districts within Portland, Oregon, Urbanized Area (UA), and percentage of UA land area they occupy**

School district	UA land occupied by school district (percent)
Portland	18
Beaverton	11
Vancouver (Washington State)	8
North Clackamas	8
Four-district concentration ratio	45

land Urbanized Area is that of Vancouver, Washington, with 8 percent of the area. (Urbanized Areas can cross state lines, just as MSA boundaries do.) The fourth largest is North Clackamas, which is the suburb south of Portland.

The general measure of "competitiveness" that is adopted here is the "four-district concentration ratio." This is the sum of the percentages within the Urbanized Area of the four largest districts. For Portland, the four-district concentration ratio is 45 percent, which is about in the middle of the range of concentration ratios of the Urbanized Areas with populations over half a million. The other 55 percent of the Portland Urbanized Area is occupied by twenty-four other school districts or parts of those districts.

The number *four* is not by itself important as the sum of concentration ratios, but it is useful for two reasons. One is that the four-firm concentration ratio is a common measure for industry concentration. Industries are not usually measured for spatial concentration (though the unit of space within which to count them can be critical), but there is a common norm among economists that a four-firm ratio of less than 40 percent is competitive, and above 80 percent is not competitive. The other use of the four-district ratio is that some previous studies suggest that the benefits of interdistrict competition kick in at four districts (Blair and Staley 1995; Zanzig 1997). Thus knowing something about the four largest districts gives some parameters for judging the competitiveness of school districts in an Urbanized Area and offers a reasonable basis for national comparisons. The relatively intuitive interpretation of the four-district concentration ratio is why we prefer the four-district ratio to the more sophisticated Herfindahl index of competition.

The data presented in table 5.3 are measures of the competitiveness of local school districts in the U.S. Urbanized Areas that had a population of at least 500,000 in the 2000 U.S. Census. The seventy Urbanized Areas within this category are sorted by their four-district concentration ratios, with the lowest concentration (most competitive structure) at the top. The first numerical column is the total number of school districts of any size that are within or partly within the Urbanized Area. Because school districts are listed as consisting of three types—elementary (typically K–8), high school (grades 9–12), and unified (K–12)—it was necessary to weight the various districts.

It is not obvious what weighting system is ideal. Caroline Hoxby (2000) cuts through this by not weighting districts at all—an elementary district counts the same as a high school district, and each is equivalent to a unified district. We nonetheless believe that weighting is important. A high school district that contains two elementary districts that feed into it (as is typical) presents parents with more school choice than a single unified district. But it does not present *three times* as much choice, as an unweighted count would imply. Residents can choose between two elementary schools but only one high school. Indeed, if there were only a single elementary school feeding into a single high school, it would be the equivalent of choosing a unified district.

The weighting we use is based simply on years of attendance, assuming kindergarten is counted as half a year. Thus a high school district is weighted as $4/12.5$ (=32%) of a unified district, and elementary districts are weighted as $8.5/12.5$ (=68%) of a unified district. In most places, two or more elementary schools feed into a single high school district. Thus if there are two elementary districts that feed into one high school district, the combined elementary and high school districts count for $2 \times 68\%$ + $1 \times 32\% = 1.68$ unified district rather than three districts. (Elementary districts were never by themselves one of the four largest districts; they entered our calculation only in combination with high school districts.)

The second numerical column of table 5.3 gives the four-district concentration ratio of the Urbanized Area, based on the weighted district counts and using the method described in the previous paragraphs. Thus the New York Urbanized Area (ranked second on the list) has a four-district concentration ratio of 13 percent, while the ratio of Los Angeles (ranked twenty-fourth) is 40.4 percent, indicating by our measure that Los Angeles has a less competitive structure than New York.

Table 5.3 also lists two alternative measures of competition. The third column shows the percent of the Urbanized Area land area occupied by the largest *single* district, which is usually the central-city school district. This could be called the "one-district concentration ratio." It is given because sometimes the largest district is much larger than the next three (as

TABLE 5.3 **Measures of school district competition for the seventy largest Urbanized Areas**

Urbanized area (four-district ratio rank)	No. of school districts (weighted)	Four-district ratio (percent)	One-district ratio (percent)	Kids/district
Boston, MA (1)	157.7	8.50	2.70	4,290
New York, NY (2)	417.9	13.00	7.10	7,575
Pittsburgh, PA (3)	86	17.10	6.40	3,366
Chicago, IL (4)	198.2	19.40	10.60	8,133
Philadelphia, PA (5)	152.7	19.70	7.50	6,632
Providence, RI (6)	49	22.30	7.10	4,206
Hartford, CT (7)	47.4	22.70	5.90	3,235
Detroit, MI (8)	85	23.00	10.90	8,898
Cleveland, OH (9)	58	25.40	12.10	5,732
Bridgeport, CT (10)	35.4	26.10	7.30	4,536
St. Louis, MO (11)	62.2	26.50	7.40	6,502
Seattle, WA (12)	37	27.00	8.80	12,856
Minneapolis, MN (13)	45	28.80	11.70	10,057
Buffalo, NY (14)	30	31.10	11.20	5,891
Springfield, MA (15)	34.4	32.30	10.50	3,091
Cincinnati, OH (16)	55	33.90	13.10	5,282
New Haven, CT (17)	28.7	34.70	9.80	3,255
Indianapolis, IN (18)	33	35.40	14.20	7,068
Albany, NY (19)	32	36.20	12.00	3,003
Akron, OH (20)	30	38.00	17.40	3,396
Allentown, PA (21)	30.1	38.50	11.50	3,415
Dayton, OH (22)	28	39.00	14.30	4,577
Milwaukee, WI (23)	40.4	40.20	19.30	6,269
Los Angeles, CA (24)[a]	91	40.40	30.10	26,026
Dallas, TX (25)[b]	48	41.30	18.10	17,196
Kansas City, MO (26)	27	41.90	12.80	9,562
Rochester, NY (27)	24	42.50	12.00	5,510
Portland, OR (28)	31	44.80	18.00	9,140
Houston, TX (29)[b]	32	46.10	22.00	25,058
Grand Rapids, MI (30)	23	46.50	16.30	4,699
Riverside, CA (31)[a]	20.4	46.70	15.80	18,254
San Francisco, CA (32)[a]	35.2	48.20	14.90	13,177
Phoenix, AZ (33)[a]	30.9	48.80	17.00	17,811
Atlanta, GA (34)[b]	23	54.00	16.10	28,961
Columbus, OH (35)	23	54.00	29.90	8,966
McAllen, TX (36)[a,b]	15	55.50	19.00	8,671
Toledo, OH (37)	16	60.20	29.50	6,135
Sacramento, CA (38)[a]	21.5	60.50	20.60	13,224
Virginia Beach, VA (39)[b]	12	63.10	27.00	22,524
San Diego, CA (40)[a]	23.6	64.90	22.40	21,110
San Jose, CA (41)[a]	23.6	66.80	29.20	11,443
Oklahoma City, OK (42)[b]	15	68.80	29.80	9,309
Denver, CO (43)[a]	14	69.80	30.10	26,247
Omaha, NE (44)	12	74.50	43.90	10,282
San Antonio, TX (45)[b]	18	76.00	26.00	15,099
Tulsa, OK (46)	12	77.10	39.80	8,742
Washington, DC (47)[b]	16	80.60	28.50	43,835
Austin, TX (48)[b]	11	85.20	48.50	14,182
Birmingham, AL (49)[b]	11	85.30	38.70	11,076
Richmond, VA (50)[b]	10	86.50	36.20	15,266

TABLE 5.3 *(continued)*

Urbanized area (four-district ratio rank)	No. of school districts (weighted)	Four-district ratio (percent)	One-district ratio (percent)	Kids/district
Tucson, AZ (51)	9	87.10	52.70	14,436
El Paso, TX (52),[a,b]	9	87.90	42.30	17,493
Louisville, KY (53)[b]	9	90.00	65.80	17,069
Concord, CA (54)[a]	12.7	90.40	29.00	7,837
Nashville, TN (55)[b]	7	92.70	63.30	18,139
Baltimore, MD (56)[b]	7	96.90	38.20	54,128
Fresno, CA (57)[a]	9.7	96.90	53.60	13,396
Memphis, TN (58)[b]	7	98.40	54.30	28,751
New Orleans, LA (59)[b]	5	98.60	50.00	38,898
Charlotte, NC (60)[b]	7	99.40	80.60	19,576
Mission Viejo, CA (61)[a]	6	99.90	62.70	16,504
Miami, FL (62)[b]	4	100.00	33.60	212,883
Sarasota, FL (63)[b]	4	100.00	48.40	18,281
Salt Lake City, UT (64)[a]	4	100.00	49.80	47,838
Tampa, FL (65)[b]	3	100.00	52.50	111,666
Orlando, FL (66)[b]	3	100.00	66.80	71,458
Jacksonville, FL (67)[b]	3	100.00	80.90	56,985
Albuquerque, NM (68)[a]	4	100.00	84.40	27,880
Raleigh, NC (69)[b]	4	100.00	99.80	23,854
Las Vegas, NV (70)[a]	1	100.00	100.00	238,408

[a] Arid states (<20 inches of precipitation/year) are in italics.
[b] States considered part of the South, as designated by the U.S. Census, are in small caps.

is the case in Los Angeles) and thus might be expected to exert even more monopoly power. The simple correlation between the single-largest and the four-district concentration ratios is 0.87, which suggests that one could get a pretty good idea of competitiveness just by calculating the area of the biggest district in the Urbanized Area to the total Urbanized Area. This high correlation also suggests that the more sophisticated measure of competition, the Herfindahl index, would not add much to the four-district ratio. (The Herfindahl squares the percentage market share of the districts and so would give greater weight to the largest than to the next smaller districts.)

The last column of table 5.3, kids/district is the Urbanized Area population of children between ages five and eighteen divided by the weighted number of districts. (School-age children were used because, in some smaller Urbanized Areas, large universities skew the age distribution.) This gives a measure of the average district size according to potential student enrollment, though it must be kept in mind that children outside the Urbanized Area are not counted in any of these data. The average enrollment of a district does not seem to be a good measure of concentration. The simple correlation between kids/district and the four-district ratio is only 0.47, which indicates that it would account for less than a quarter of the variation in size between the two measures (0.47 squared is 0.22). This is important for economic research because many if not most empirical studies have used average district size or some variant as their measure of competition among school districts. Average district enrollment tends to make smaller Urbanized Areas appear more competitive. It would seem to be more productive to use a measure of competition that is meaningful on its own terms, and the four-district concentration ratio looks most appropriate for that purpose.

5.11 Climate, Size, and Segregation Account for Urban District Competitiveness

The array of Urbanized Areas in table 5.3 strongly suggests that regional variation in school district size is accounted for by two historical factors: climate (which determined rural population densities) and a history of racial segregation. The districts listed in small caps are in Urbanized Areas in the South; italics denotes districts in areas with *less than twenty inches* of precipitation per year. Table 5.3 suggests two regularities in the competitiveness of school districts: (1) The South has the least competition because so many of its districts are organized by county. (2) Arid areas, chiefly in the West, have larger and less-competitive district structure.

More systematic evidence is presented in table 5.4, which summarizes a linear regression using as data the seventy cities in table 5.3. The dependent variable is the four-district concentration ratio. The independent variables are a dummy variable for Urbanized Areas located in the South (those Urbanized Areas in small caps in table 5.3), which is positive and clearly statistically significant. Positive in this case means less competitive structure, since the concentration ratio rises as there are fewer school districts.

The variable RAINFALL in table 5.4 is the average annual precipitation (in inches) in the main city of the Urbanized Area from 1961 to 1990. (Precipitation averages do not change much, so the modern figures are reasonable proxies for earlier times of settlement.) Wetter cities are likely to have had higher rural densities in the early 1900s, when age-graded districts were formed. The higher rural densities were the result of smaller average farm size. Besides this, the suburbs of dry-area cities were more likely to have

TABLE 5.4 **OLS regression explaining variation in district concentration ratios**

(higher values mean less competition)

Regression statistics			
R square	0.591		
Adjusted R square	0.572		
Observations	70		

	Coefficients	Standard error	*t* Stat
Intercept	0.8300	0.063540	13.06
SOUTH	0.4709	0.054907	8.58
RAINFALL	−0.0096	0.001877	−5.10
CHILD POPULATION	−1.569E−07	4.68E−08	−3.36

been dependent on central-city water, which would make them more likely to consolidate with the city than remain independent. RAINFALL is clearly negative and statistically significant, indicating more school district competition in wetter areas outside of the South. (The South itself is among the highest rainfall areas in the nation, which supports the idea that racial segregation was the driving force behind larger district size.)

A dry climate is not the only reason for a low rural population density. Mountainous regions and other places remote from transportation were (and are) sparsely populated. But no sizable cities developed in such places, while some large cities did develop in arid places. One might ask why local population density in 1910 or thereabouts would not be a better variable, since the hypothesis is predicated on rural density itself. The problem is that one could make a case for reverse causation: population density was higher where there were more school districts. Since rainfall was not something people could do anything about, it is an ideal exogenous variable.

The last variable in table 5.4 is simply the number of children between ages five and nineteen within the Urbanized Area. CHILD POPULATION is negative, indicating that the larger Urbanized Areas are more competitive in their school district structure than smaller Urbanized Areas. It should be noted that the minimum-size Urbanized Area in the sample is half a million people (not just children), so "smaller" is not tiny. It is often noted in the Tiebout literature that smaller cities and rural areas have fewer jurisdictions simply because there are usually some minimum sizes in area and population for establishing a modern school district. Indeed, many smaller (say, less than one hundred thousand total population) Urbanized

Areas have fewer than four districts in total, so that their "four-district ratio" is hardly meaningful. Of the Urbanized Areas listed in table 5.3, only four have fewer than four districts: Las Vegas (1 district), Tampa (3), Orlando (3), and Jacksonville (3). Note also that the bottom of table 5.3 lists five Urbanized Areas that have exactly four districts—all in the South or arid West.

The positive effect of total Urbanized Area population (as represented by CHILD POPULATION in table 5.4) on competition, independent of climate and segregation, might suggest some limitations on the measure of competition adopted here. One objection might be that it is obvious that a larger Urbanized Area would have more school districts, so that district population should not itself be an independent variable. But other countries often have school administrative units that encompass the entire metropolitan area. As the area expands, the center's school administrative lines are moved outward. So it is not "obvious" in a technical or comparative sense that larger American Urbanized Areas should necessarily have more districts, and there is actually considerable variation.

A different objection to population size as an explanatory variable relates to commuting distances between home jurisdiction (which is where the school district is defined) and work jurisdiction. The New York Urbanized Area is the second most competitive in the nation by the metric adopted here, but the area's immense geographic size—stretching more than 120 miles from eastern Long Island to Pennsylvania—surely limits the choices of an in-moving family. Columbus, Ohio, has a 54 percent concentration ratio, but its twenty-three school districts are realistic choices for a family with employment somewhere in Columbus. But this bias is less critical if one keeps in mind that average commuting distance is greater in larger urban areas. Someone with a job in Manhattan and an inclination to live in the suburbs really can choose among a large number of suburban districts on Long Island, Westchester County, southwest Connecticut, and northern New Jersey. The agglomeration economies of larger cities are manifested in the number of school districts, as well as in the variety of employment and recreational opportunities.

5.12 Proxies for School District Size: Rivers or Rainfall?

The primary contribution of our study to the literature on school district competition is to generate a national, urban-centered measure of school district competition. Our measure is based on land area rather than population, but within Urbanized Areas, the two measures should not differ greatly. Urbanized Areas do not include the low-density areas of MSAs (which is our point in using Urbanized Areas), and the population densities of central cities and the close-in suburbs that make up the Urbanized Area have almost converged by the census of 2000 for all but the largest cities. We have made no effort to determine the effects of school district competitiveness on student achievement, though most evidence indicates that competition does help (Blair and Staley 1995; Hoxby 2000). Our empirical contribution to the substantive issues has only been to show that there is (1) a lot of competition among public school districts in many large urbanized areas and (2) a great deal of variation in competition among regions of the country.

It may be worth comparing our explanation for school district variation with a well-known measure for competition among school districts that was developed first by Hoxby (2000) and later incorporated into several other papers. To avoid the econometric biases created by simply counting the number and size of school districts to measure competition, Hoxby created an indirect ("instrumental variable") measure of competitiveness. Her story is that districts in urban areas are influenced by a preexisting geography. Cities that were divided by numerous rivers and streams and other physical barriers (though in practice rivers were the important one) would be likely to have more school districts.

The reason is that streams are costly to bridge. Using rivers as boundaries for school districts that had to transport children to a few schools would minimize transportation costs. An Oklahoma historian (Oscar Davison 1950, 76) described how one newly formed county in his state first established its school districts (circa 1900). (This process looks "top down," but it was only the first cut in a political process.) The county superintendent "drew an imaginary line in any direction which presented the least resistance. If he found the line tending to cross an unbridged stream, he drew it in and started downstream. That was cheaper than building a bridge and safer than swimming school children across swollen streams in time of high water." (The "swimming" was not facetious; it referred to how horse-drawn school wagons—the predecessors of school buses—forded streams in high water.)

Our account of school district variation outside the South is related to Hoxby's. High rainfall makes for better growing conditions and thus higher rural population densities. In high-rainfall places, this rural pattern had relatively small-area districts because farms could be small and thus population density could be higher than in low-rainfall areas. But of course high-rainfall areas also have more streams and rivers, which would have formed the logical school district boundaries for many rural areas. Arid areas have fewer rivers, and the "imaginary line" that the Oklahoma official drew could have gone on for a longer distance without hitting a stream. Indeed, he would have had to go farther in order to round up enough children to make a viable school district. In one sense our explanation is complementary to and thus difficult to distinguish from Hoxby's. Those who established school district boundaries in well-watered areas did not have to include too much territory in order to get an adequate-sized district, so turning the boundary line aside at a natural barrier such as a local stream was a cost-minimizing strategy.

One advantage of our account is that it can explain the countywide districts that characterize much of the South. (Alesina, Baqir, and Hoxby [2004] do not explicitly exclude the South, but because they focus on district variations within counties, they effectively delete the countywide districts that are most common there.) The South is a well-watered region with many streams and rivers, so on both our and Hoxby's account, the South ought to have competitive districts. Our account, though, offers an economies-of-scale–based reason for the South's larger districts and less competitive structure. By insisting on racially segregated schools, the South made itself like an arid area. In most of the South, the density of total population was similar to that of the rural North. But the density of the white population, taken by itself, and (especially) the black population, taken by itself, made each potential school district more like those of the arid West.

Thus when a Southern official who drew up school districts ran the "imaginary line" from a central point, and the line ran into a stream, he could not easily stop and follow the "line of least resistance" paralleling the river. If he did, he would not have a population large enough to create a black and a white school district. Once white politicians decided they had to provide age-graded schools and high schools for both blacks and whites, Southern school districts had to be twice as large as their Northern counterparts to operate with the same economies of scale. (In defense of Hoxby's measure for the South, I would note that Southern counties are often bordered by sizable rivers, making them more natural boundaries for the school districts as well.)

5.13 The Advantage of Aligning School Districts and Municipalities

This and the following sections step aside from the question of competitive structure of school districts and ask how closely school districts and municipalities are related to one another. In one sense, we should not expect much overlap among municipalities and school districts. Municipalities can be a lot different from one another because they do not have to offer interchangeable services. Some can have city-provided water and sewer services, and others can require on-site wells and septic systems. Some can offer golf courses and riding trails, and others can provide beaches and softball diamonds. But school districts cannot, in a world of family mobility, offer substantial variations on the K–12 curriculum. Moreover, the norms of American education require that school districts have to be everywhere. We don't get upset if some city decides not to have sidewalks or bicycle paths, but most people would regard it as intolerable for any residential area not to offer public schools.

The formal separation of city and school district early in the twentieth century is said by many to be the product of "progressive ideology" (David Menefee-Libey et al. 1997). A more practical explanation is the need to coordinate age-graded education with other districts. Cities could not afford to have their schools be much different than those in other places, and maintaining a standardized, nonpolitical approach was more compelling for education than for, say, police and fire protection. Most cities had established age-graded and high schools as arms of the city government. Those that still run them this way are called "dependent" districts. But "dependence" was formal rather than practical. Glaab and Brown (1967, 175) emphasize that from the "early nineteenth century," city-run school committees were kept "outside of politics." School construction contracts might be political plums, but school operations were controlled by nonpartisan committees. This continued into the twentieth century. Thomas Reed (1926, 324) affirmed that the "school department" of the city government was run independently of other city departments, and voters paid more attention to the schools than other city affairs. By the 1930s, school district governance was becoming almost entirely independent of city government (Henry and Kerwin 1938).

There are, however, important advantages to having a school district and city boundaries match up that have long been recognized. Cities that are congruent with their school district can more easily transfer city resources to "their" school district. The city library can supplement the school district's libraries. Recreation facilities, civic auditoriums, and meeting places can be shared more easily. Coordination of city services that affect the school district is also simpler if city and district match up pretty closely. A safety program aimed at young people is more easily implemented, and the benefits of crime-control efforts directed at high school students are more fully internalized by a city that is congruent with its school district. City elections and school district elections can be held in the same time and places with less cost, and school board membership becomes a more attractive first step into the political arena if the voters in the district are mostly the same as the voters in the city.

Zoning decisions by the city can make a great deal of difference for the school district. If a city matches up with the district, it has an incentive to consider the consequences of its zoning decisions, since the same set of voters—city and school district—will be affected. Indeed, the economic theory of "fiscal zoning" was developed with school districts in mind (Bruce Hamilton 1975). When the city does not match with a particular district whose land it controls, it may be happy to rezone to a higher density and get more property tax revenues, although the district may suffer overcrowded schools and higher taxes. A city that is congruent with its school district also has a stronger incentive to earmark the exactions and impact fees that it collects from housing developers to benefit its schools.

I do not examine the congruence of county boundaries with school districts because counties are different from municipalities. They are entirely created by the state; there is no "bottom-up" process for county incorporation as there is for municipalities (Fischel 2001, chapter 2). Counties are also static in number and area. Since the spread of the automobile, circa 1920, which made a visit to the county seat a matter of hours rather than days, almost no new counties have been created anywhere in the United States (Edward Stephan 1995). The number of municipalities, by contrast, has continued to grow as new suburbs are carved out of county territory (Gary Miller 1981). Counties sometimes do provide municipal services, and in the South they often line up with school districts. But even in the South, counties are seldom the exclusive provider of municipal services in urban areas. The county-based school districts of Florida are dotted with many municipalities within their borders, and it is municipal congruence that is examined here.

The official word since at least the 1960s is that school districts and cities really have nothing to do with one another any more (Campbell et al.

1990, 112). The question I want to pose is whether the official word and the real world actually mesh. I knew that school districts and municipal boundaries almost always matched up in only one section of the country, the six New England states and the state of New Jersey. This does not mean that these states lack multijurisdictional school districts. Rural places in all these states often have consolidated school districts or joint regional high schools. But what distinguishes these states from others is that school district consolidations almost always involve the entire municipality. Consolidations almost never involve half of the town's area joining one school district and the other half joining a separate district. When the town of Canaan, New Hampshire, joined with its neighboring towns to form Mascoma Regional School District, there was no thought given to the possibility that some of the town's residents might actually be more conveniently merged with some other district. It's the whole town (or city or, in New Jersey, borough or township) that joins the new district, or none of the town. (The same is true to a lesser degree for the townships of Pennsylvania and Indiana, the difference being that the boundaries of the townships are more easily compromised by expanding cities.)

This is distinctly different from the rule in most of the rest of the country, where school districts can run wild over the countryside without respect for municipal boundaries. But the real question is, how wild do they actually run? The answer to this question, which has puzzled me for some time, has been difficult to find because of the lack of maps that match school district and city boundaries. One can find maps of districts and maps of municipal boundaries, but there seems to have been a strong aversion to juxtaposing one over the other. At least there was until Google Earth came to my attention in the summer of 2006.

5.14 Eyeballing City and School District Overlap Using Google Earth

Google Earth allows one to view aerial photographs of any location in the United States. The photos can be adjusted to see the boundaries of both cities and school districts, and viewers can zoom in to examine the land use within any part of the district. Municipal boundaries can thus be juxtaposed on school district boundaries to get a good qualitative judgment of the extent of school district and municipal overlap. Unified, elementary, and secondary districts can be shown separately. (What is "unified" about a unified district are age grades K–12, not the city and the school district.)

Google Earth's boundary markings depend on geographic information provided by the U.S. Census Bureau, and indeed the census TIGER maps can be accessed to produce the same juxtaposition of boundaries. (TIGER stands for Topologically Integrated Geographic Encoding and Referencing.) The big advantage of Google Earth over the census mappings, aside from being faster and more easily manipulated, is that Google Earth allows viewers to see what is actually on the ground from the aerial photos. This allows an additional degree of judgment about district overlap that cannot easily be obtained from most maps.

For example, most school districts in the western United States have land areas that are greater than those of the municipality. From just the outlines of municipality and school district, one would assume that there was little congruence of interest between the voters of the city and the voters of the district. But from Google Earth one can often see that most of the excess territory of the school district is uninhabited desert or mountainous terrain and that the inhabited part of the school district is actually quite closely aligned with the inhabited area of the municipality. Alternatively, one might see on an outline map that some part of the municipal boundaries extends beyond the otherwise congruent school district. Based on just the census boundary maps, the outlying part of the city might make you conclude that the city is really distinct from the school district. But on Google Earth, the observer can get close enough to see whether the outlying section is a neighborhood (and hence is isolated from the district) or is an airport, parkland, or oil refinery that the city annexed to serve its needs or add to its tax base.

After some experimentation, I decided to examine the Google Earth maps of all American cities whose population exceeded fifty thousand in the census of 2000. I excluded Alaska and Hawaii because their unique history and geography make their urban and school district experience much different from the first forty-eight states. I did not include Urban Places that were exclusively "Census Designated Places," which meant that their area did not correspond to a municipality. I did include towns, townships, and villages, which in other contexts the census (and, unfortunately, Google Earth) does not consider a municipal government. These county subdivisions are often important units of urban municipal governments in New England, New Jersey, Pennsylvania, New York, Michigan, Indiana, and Illinois. I did my best to infer their boundaries from Web-based sources and TIGER maps in conjunction with what was shown in Google Earth.

The 661 municipal governments that met these criteria were supplemented by a stratified sample (as described in the next section) of 106 local governments whose population exceeded twenty-five thousand but was less than fifty thousand. The smaller sample was used to determine whether smaller cities followed the same general pattern as larger cities, and in fact they did.

The more subjective criterion was the degree of congruence between the city and school districts. Keep in mind that I selected a group of cities, not a group of school districts, since the issue I want to examine is whether the city can transfer resources from itself to "the city's" school district. (As limited-purpose municipal corporations, school districts can seldom transfer resources to other entities.) I ended up with six categories, which I have further merged to three for summary purposes. The basis for the six categories was a simple question: What configuration of city and school district would make it *politically* easy to transfer resources from the city to the school district? The main consideration is the extent to which populations overlap one another, but it is possible to consider the distribution of population and other geographic features. This main consideration led to examining each city in order to put in one of the following six categories, which are visually summarized in figure 5.6:

1. "Virtually coterminous" was the classification when the city and a single school district share the same boundaries, as they invariably did in larger New England and the Virginia cities and in all but one case in New Jersey (the exception being a joint high school district in Glouster). The advantage of examining the Google Earth maps was important here, because there are many cities outside of New England that do not have the formal congruence of New England towns and their districts but do correspond so closely that they belong in this classification. The close calls in this category involved minor deviations involving airports and parks that the city had annexed but the school district had not. In addition, if a discrete community with less than 5 percent of the larger city's population happened to be included in the larger city's district, or if a similarly small neighborhood of a city was outside the city's school district, it was included in this category. Thus Cleveland is in this category despite a tiny part of the city being in the Shaker Heights School District (where Cleveland's mayor once resided

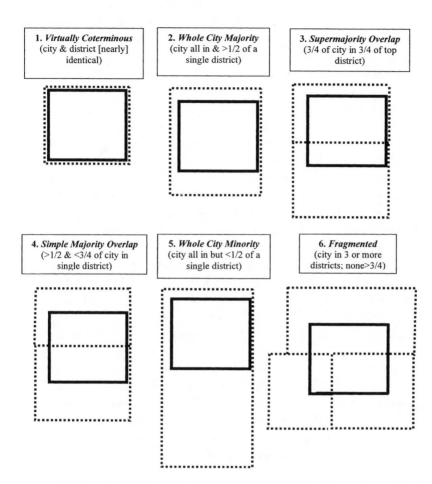

FIGURE 5.6. Categories of city and school district overlap. Solid lines denote the municipal boundary, and dotted lines the school districts.

and sent her kids to the suburban school district, not without controversy), and Pittsburgh is included despite the city's school district encompassing also the Borough of Mount Oliver, which has a population of 3970.

2. "Whole city majority" indicates that the city lay entirely within a single district for which the city's population was a clear majority. In this situation, the city's residents all have the same incentives with regard to a single district, but some of the transfers they might make to the district will go to noncity residents. I originally had several subdivisions of this category depending on the size of the city's majority over the rest of the district, but I concluded it was not especially useful.

3. "Supermajority overlap" is for cities that had a substantial but not exclusive overlap with a single district. This category does not have neat boundary lines. The city's boundaries might wander outside the main district's to one or two other districts. Or a single district might be entirely encompassed by the city, so that outer parts of the city would be in different districts. The key for membership in this category is that at least three-quarters of the city's populated area is in a single district, and that population comprises at least three-quarters of the populated area of the district. The minimum population for membership is three-quarters rather than 50 percent (as in category 2) because the political transaction costs are higher when even some of the voters in the city belong to separate school districts. Not only do these sets of voters interact less with one another (because their kids go to different schools), but their interest in transferring resources to their respective districts may vary. One part of the city might want to supplement the safety program for its school district, and the other might be more interested in supplementing its schools' playgrounds. I assume that such disputes would be less of a political barrier if a large majority of the city were in the same district. On the other side, this majority would need to have a bigger payoff from the transfer of resources than a 100 percent majority would (as in category 2), so it seems reasonable that a larger part (at least three-quarters) of the district also be in the city.

4. "Simple majority overlap" was basically the same as category 3 but with less than a three-quarters' majority in either the city or the district. This involved some close calls visually, and it is here that hard numbers might prove to be helpful in resolving them. But I actually don't think hard data would change many cities from category 4 to category 3 or vice versa, in part because there weren't that many close category 4 cases.

5. "Whole city minority" consisted of cities that were entirely within a single district but were a minority (less than 50 percent) of the district's total population. In other words, everyone in the city had an interest in the same school district, but transfers to the district would mostly benefit nonresidents (and nonvoters) of the city. Many of the members of this category were medium-size cities in the South, especially Florida. Besides these, several cities have separate elementary and high school districts, especially cities in California and Illinois. This necessitated some compromise judgments, the most common being classification of a city whose elementary schools were "whole city majority," whereas the high school was "whole city minority" as a "supermajority overlap" (category 3 above).

6. "Fragmented" describes those cities that are divided into three or more districts and lack a three-quarters' supermajority in any district. It should be noted that

a number of cities in this class have a district with their names on it, but a substantial part of the city's population resides in another district or districts. It is not my contention that such cities cannot transfer resources to schools within their boundaries and so benefit their residents. It is just that they will have a more difficult time obtaining the cooperation of district officials. They will have to go to at least three sets of school officials, and they will have to explain to them why they are doing something for one set of schools in the school district and neglecting others. This is not an impossible sell, but it is surely more difficult to do than in instances where the city and the school district match up more closely, as in categories 1, 2, and 3 above.

For readers who can look at Google Earth (the download is free) and want to check my judgments, the San Francisco Bay Area offers the full range of categories for cities with populations over 50,000. Here is how the cities were classified, largest city first in each category:

1. Virtually coterminous: San Francisco, Oakland, Fremont, Vallejo, Berkeley, and Alameda. (The Bay Area is unusual in California for having this many.)
2. Whole city majority: Concord, Livermore, Napa, Union City, Pleasanton, Milpitas, and Palo Alto.
3. Supermajority overlap: Santa Rosa, Hayward, San Mateo, Antioch, Vacaville, South San Francisco, Pittsburg, San Rafael, and Santa Cruz.
4. Simple majority overlap: Fairfield, San Leandro, and Redwood City.
5. Whole city minority: Santa Clara, Richmond, and Cupertino.
6. Fragmented: San Jose, Sunnyvale, Daly City, Mountain View, Walnut Creek, and Petaluma.

5.15 Cities and School Districts Are Not Strangers

For all 661 municipalities in the United States with a population greater than fifty thousand in the census of 2000, table 5.5 shows how they were classified. (The three largest cities of each category are in parentheses.) The first column counts cities by population weight, so that a city of one million counts ten times as much as a city of one-hundred thousand residents. The second column is the unweighted percentage, in which New York City and Albany, for instance, each count the same. Where the first-column number greatly exceeds the second-column number, the city-school district overlap

TABLE 5.5 **Congruence of U.S. cities with a population over fifty thousand with their school districts in the census of 2000**

Classification category	Population weighted (percent)	Unweighted (percent)
1. Virtually coterminous	35	24
(New York, Chicago, Philadelphia . . .)		
2. Whole city majority	16 (Σ51)	21 (Σ45)
(Los Angeles, Nashville, Charlotte . . .)		
3. Supermajority overlap	14 (Σ64)	16 (Σ61)
(San Diego, Dallas, Columbus [OH] . . .)		
4. Simple majority overlap	12 (Σ76)	11 (Σ72)
(Houston, Indianapolis, Austin...)		
5. Whole city minority	9 (Σ85)	15 (Σ87)
(Las Vegas, Miami, Arlington [TX]...)		
6. Fragmented	15 (Σ100)	13 (Σ100)
(Phoenix, San Antonio, San Jose...)		

Note: Three largest cities of each category are in parentheses. The first column counts cities by population weight, so that a city of one million counts ten times as much as a city of one hundred thousand residents. The second column is the unweighted percentage. The Σ indicates the cumulative percentage of the category and those above it.

is greater for large cities than for small. The Σ indicates the cumulative percentage of the category and those above it.

Table 5.6 reduces the foregoing categories into two statistics. The left-hand column shows the percentage of cities in the state or region that fall into category one, in which city boundary and a single school district are "virtually coterminous." The right-hand column shows the *cumulative* percentage of cities that were classified as one, two, or three, which are labeled "substantial overlap." I would maintain that for cities in the "substantial overlap" group, a stranger who asked a local city official about the "city's schools" would find the conversation directed to a single district.

The primary discovery from this table is how much city and school districts do overlap. About one-third (35 percent) of the population living in cities with a population greater than fifty thousand live in a city that is "virtually coterminous" with their school district. This seems small if one expected cities to exactly overlap, as quite a few social-science discussions of school districts do. For the disappointed social scientist, I offer the comfort of the second-column number, which shows that 64 percent of all large-city dwellers (and 61 percent of all large cities) have a "substantial overlap" with a single school district. As a social-science generalization, merging the interests of a city and a single school district is not grossly inaccurate. This is a conservative generalization, because one could make a case of more-than-random overlap between cities and school districts

THE ECONOMIC GEOGRAPHY OF SCHOOL DISTRICTS 205

from categories 4 (simple majority overlap) and five (whole city minority). The cities with no apparent overlap with their school districts (category 6) account for less than 15 percent of the urban population (table 5.5).

The regional subdivisions in table 5.7 follow the major U.S. Census divisions of regions of the country. The pattern that emerges from these three regional tables is that city-school district overlap is strongest in the North by any measure of overlap. The population-weighted numbers for the "virtually coterminous" group are skewed by the presence of New York and Chicago in the North, but some skewness is evident for other regions, too. For reasons discussed in the next section, older big cities are more likely to have their own school district than other cities.

Table 5.8 summarizes congruence for the 106 smaller cities that I sampled to get a sense of whether smaller places repeated the pattern of larger cities. I calculated the proportion of the U.S. population in each state in 2000 and assigned cities in whole numbers to each state. Thus California got twelve cities, New York and Texas seven each, Florida six, and so forth. I added one city each to the states (but did not count any in Alaska and Hawaii) that were too small to have a whole number, which is why the sample is 106 instead of one hundred. Then for each state I selected the city or cities with a population closest to twenty-five thousand and, if more than one city was to be counted in that state, added the next largest city, and so forth. Mean city size was thus about thirty thousand, and none was larger than forty thousand. Nevada and South Dakota were omitted because they had no cities larger than twenty-five thousand and less than fifty thousand. I did not include incorporated boroughs, villages, or towns in this sample—they were included in the previous tables—because it was too difficult to locate their boundaries, so this table may slightly understate the degree of municipal school district congruence.

Table 5.8 for this sample has data that suggest that the pattern for the larger (fifty thousand or more; shown in table 5.6.) cities is nearly identical to those in the range of twenty-five to forty thousand. The unweighted

TABLE 5.6 **Summary congruence of 661 U.S. cities with population over fifty thousand with their school districts**

U.S. 48 states	Virtually coterminous (percent)	Substantial overlap (percent)
Population weighted	35	64
Unweighted	24	61

TABLE 5.7 **Regional congruence of U.S. cities with a population over fifty thousand with their school districts**

Region	Virtually coterminous (percent)	Substantial overlap (percent)
North (267 cities)		
Population weighted	59	80
Unweighted	42	74
South (176 cities)		
Population weighted	26	53
Unweighted	18	49
West (218 cities)		
Population weighted	11	53
Unweighted	8	54

TABLE 5.8 **Congruence of school districts in 106 U.S. smaller cities (25,000–40,000 population)**

106 Smaller cities	Virtually coterminous (percent)	Substantial overlap (percent)
Population weighted	19	61
Unweighted	19	61

group of "substantial overlap" cities is exactly the same (61 percent) for both groups. (Because the small-city sample was chosen within a narrow range, weighted and unweighted percentages are the same in this table.)

To check whether there was a geographic bias toward larger or smaller cities, in the foregoing exercises, I selected the city whose year-2000 population was closest to one-hundred thousand in each of the forty-eight contiguous states. Examples were Waterbury, Connecticut, population 107,271; Athens, Georgia, 100,266; and Billings, Montana, 89,847. Thirty-one of these cities (65 percent of the lower forty eight) had a "substantial overlap" with its school district, with the overlap being most common in the North and least common in the South. This supports my conclusion that a majority of cities have their "own" school district."

5.16 Big-City Districts Are Vestiges of their Former Monopoly on High School

The final pattern to be explained is the existence of very large districts that are coterminous (or nearly so) with the boundaries of large cities. The explanation is purely historical. The large city districts that are "virtually coterminous" with their school districts all reached their status as very large cities early in the twentieth century. Urban districts were the first to adopt multigrade elementary schools, which began in the mid-nineteenth century, and also the first to start public high schools. Cubberley (1919, 237) used Buffalo, Detroit, and Chicago as examples of cities that took control of their numerous one-room "ward schools" and by 1860 consolidated them into age-graded schools that enabled the city to offer high school education.

As in most aspects of public education, state governments were seldom leaders in developing high schools (Tyack, James, and Benavot 1987, 104). High population density and a wealthier citizenry made it possible for cities to fund high schools for those few students who could continue beyond the "common-school" (we would now say "elementary") education. Their large amount of commercial and industrial property also made public schools attractively inexpensive to voters. City voters had a lower "tax price" for education: they could view taxation of business property as taxes paid by someone else. Like voters in modern districts, they might worry that excessive taxes might cause the businesses to move away (Helen Ladd 1975), but usually natural advantages such as a port or urban agglomeration economies would keep nonresidential real estate relatively immobile. Farmers, on the other hand, lived on and owned their own business property, and so most rural voters perceived the full cost of local taxation: if they wanted a dollar extra in school spending (per household), they had to pay a dollar more in taxes. (Modern concern that high-income residents might move away is probably why voters prefer local taxes on property rather than income [John Spry 2005].)

After 1900, popular demand for high school education increased dramatically in response to the demand for a more educated work force (Claudia Goldin 1998). The fraction of the eligible population attending high school approximately doubled every decade up to 1950. Rural school districts nearest the city often were willing to join with the urban district rather than form their own high schools. One of the attractions of becoming annexed by a city was joining its school district and getting local children on the highway to high school. Up to about 1920, cities could easily annex their suburbs, even if the suburbs were incorporated, and there was usually little suburban resistance (Jon Teaford 1979, chapter 3).

By the 1920s, however, high school began to be a norm in all districts. Consolidated rural districts started their own high schools—that was usually the reason for rural consolidation. If the rural district was the beneficiary of population gains from the suburban growth of a nearby city, its high schools could begin to match the sophistication of city schools. Being annexed by the city for municipal purposes no longer required that the city's school district boundaries also had to be adjusted. Perhaps not coincidentally, the 1920s were also the turning point in central-city annexation of suburbs (Teaford 1979, chapter 5). Suburban towns began to resist the city's offer of annexation, in part because a new institution, zoning, allowed them to control the rate of urban development (Fischel 2004a). Even when central cities did annex their suburban territory, the rapid growth of "independent" school districts—those not run as departments of the city government—meant that the newly annexed suburban territory did not necessarily have to merge with the old city's school district.

Evidence for this can be seen by comparing the largest American cities in 1920 and 2000. In 1920, the twelve municipalities with more than 500,000 people were mainly "old" cities of the North plus California. By population rank they were New York, Chicago, Philadelphia, Detroit, Cleveland, St. Louis, Boston, Baltimore, Pittsburgh, Los Angeles, Buffalo, and San Francisco. Most had annexed suburban territory until early in the twentieth century. Every one of them in the year 2000 was still "virtually coterminous" (as defined in section 5.14) with its school district except Los Angeles. They had become large cities in the days when city school districts were attractive to suburbs because of their superior high school system. (Some still-independent suburbs of Los Angeles, such as South Gate, joined its school district during the Depression [Becky Nicolaides 2002], and Glendale and Beverly Hills managed to withdraw around the same time, but the city of Los Angeles remains by far the largest component of the Los Angeles Unified School District.)

The growing megacities of the latter part of the twentieth century did not follow the pattern of having the city coterminous with its school district. Twenty-one municipalities joined the half-a-million club by 2000. (Some of the 1920 members dropped out, but that is not at issue here.) All but three are in the South and West. Only six of twenty-one new megacities were, like the 1920 list, "virtually coterminous" with their school district in 2000: Jacksonville, Memphis, Milwaukee, Washington, Seattle, and Denver. Several of the other new big cities, such as San Jose and Phoenix, are extremely fragmented, having numerous school districts within or partially within their municipal boundaries.

As a rule, then, the newer big cities outside the South are not coterminous with their school districts. This has implications for the much-discussed trend of urban mayors displacing local school boards. The chief advantage of mayoral control is said to be that the higher visibility of his or her office to city voters will make the mayor more accountable for the schools' successes and failures. The examples discussed by Frederick Hess (2008)—Baltimore, Boston, New York, Chicago, Philadelphia, and Washington—were all from the aforementioned older cities. Mayors of the newer big cities seldom govern territory that is perfectly congruent with a single school district, which makes granting mayoral control awkward if not entirely unconstitutional. For example, California passed legislation (at the behest of the city of Los Angeles) to establish mayoral control of the Los Angeles Unified School District. In an attempt to allay concerns about representation, the law gave the district's multiple cities population-weighted representation. This still gave control to the mayor of Los Angeles, which had more than 90 percent of the district's population. However, the entire plan was struck down by the state courts in *Mendoza v. State*, 57 Cal.Rptr.3d 505 (2007), and mayoral control of Los Angeles schools now appears to be a dead letter.

The supersize school districts of older central cities thus seem to be artifacts of their early, local monopoly on high schools. After 1920, the new big cities whose municipal boundaries moved into rural territory failed to have their school district boundaries moved along with them. The city of Houston, for example, has annexed most of the formerly unincorporated territory of Harris County, but the state did not change the school district boundaries so that Houston Independent School District would correspond to its municipal boundaries. (Houston mayors have lobbied for the change.) The same pattern persists in the other "new" cities of the West and Southwest. Suburban influence in the state legislatures—much increased by the reapportionment revolution of the 1960s (Reichley 1970)—seems to have kept the suburban districts independent. As will be discussed in chapter 6, this fragmentation may not simply benefit the suburbs. It may be better for cities themselves to have smaller school districts.

5.17 Racial Issues Inhibited City-Suburb Consolidation

One incentive for independence on the part of school districts in the suburbs is that they are less likely to be subject to racial desegregation orders because of *Milliken v. Bradley*, 418 U.S. 717 (1974). A U.S. District Court judge had ruled that the Detroit School District (which is coterminous with the city of Detroit) had maintained racially segregated schools. In response to the city's objection that an intradistrict remedy would only cause whites to move away, Judge Roth proposed to bus students in fifty-three suburban districts to and from Detroit. There was no evidence, however, that any of the suburban districts themselves had deliberately promoted segregation. On appeal, the U.S. Supreme Court reversed Judge Roth's attempt to bring the suburban refugees back into the Detroit school district. The Supreme Court disallowed desegregation remedies that crossed school district boundaries, unless the several districts themselves were proved to have conspired to create legally segregated schools. (The Supreme Court of Connecticut in *Sheff v. O'Neill*, 678 A.2d 1267 [1996], used state constitutional grounds to impose an interdistrict desegregation remedy in Hartford and its suburbs, but the case has not generated a following in other states, and its remedy has been rather slow moving in Connecticut itself.)

Milliken effectively insulated most suburban districts from interdistrict busing orders to cure central-city segregation. It is tempting to see *Milliken* as causal in the formation of suburban districts, and it surely is one reason it is difficult to get districts to merge further. The work of Alesina, Baqir, and Hoxby (2004), discussed in section 5.8, suggests that district fragmentation was partly informed by white suburbs declining to merge with districts that would have had more blacks. But the preeminence of racial motives is challenged by the fact that suburban district independence seems to be as fiercely defended in areas where race is not much of an issue. Smaller districts in Vermont and New Hampshire, two states with the lowest percentage of blacks, seem as disinclined to consolidate with the bigger cities as did the suburbs of Detroit. In 2006, Vermont's new commissioner of education proposed that the state's 284 school districts consolidate into sixty-three districts of at least 1,500 students, hardly a gargantuan size. The proposal nonetheless ran into a buzz saw of local opposition, and the 2007 legislature dropped its consolidation proposal as a result. The commissioner left his post soon thereafter.

Suburban reluctance to join with central-city districts also was well documented before *Milliken* in other areas. Two political scientists, both eager consolidationists, did personal surveys of residents of cities and suburbs in six northern metropolitan areas in the 1950s. The cities were Buffalo, Milwaukee, Dayton, Rochester (New York), Saginaw, and Rockford (Illinois). Basil Zimmer and Amos Hawley (1966) wanted to find out who favored and who opposed city-suburban school consolidation and for what reasons. Race did not appear to be an issue. (If it had been, Zimmer and Hawley, both politically progressive, would surely have brought it up.) Suburban residents were uniformly and strongly opposed to city-suburb consolidation because they thought school quality would decline and taxes would rise. A majority of central-city residents favored consolidation, but not by large margins. The survey indicated that city voters thought schools would get better if there were further consolidation, though they did not anticipate any tax savings. As in almost every survey about school quality, respondents in all locations thought that their own schools were fine. Whatever problems they saw with the system were somewhere else.

5.18 Causes and Implications of City-District Overlap

What can social science researchers take away from the interstate pattern of school district and municipal congruence? At the very least, the regional and state-to-state variation in these numbers should caution researchers who assume districts and cities are the same to look more closely at the states from which their samples are drawn. Moreover, it should be kept in mind that my study has looked only at municipal corporations: the cities, townships, villages, and boroughs that have their own elected officials. The total population of the 661 cities represented in the first table was 106 million in 2000. This amounts to only 38 percent of the U.S. population at the time, though the addition of the group from which the small-city sample was drawn would raise this total to about 50 percent. It excludes the non-urban population, and it excludes the substantial population that lives in urban areas who are not residents of any organized municipality.

In general, though, the evidence assembled here strongly suggests that cities and school districts are not strangers to one another, as the legal literature about school district formation and governance would usually have one believe. The degree of overlap is too strong for this pattern to have arisen by chance. This is confirmed by the few modern attempts to create new urban school districts that I have encountered. The city of Stafford, Texas (near Houston), managed to establish the only municipal school district in Texas in the 1980s. Kiryas Joel, a Hasidic Jewish community in New York, carved its own school district in 1989 from the town of Monroe to educate its handicapped children. Legislation in Utah in 2005 permitted the division of districts along city lines, though only one, the Jordan district has so far been divided. Saraland, Alabama, just north of Mobile, succeeded in creating its own school system in 2006 and will take over the schools within its city limits that are currently governed by the Mobile County school system. The cities of Carson and Lakewood in California both recently (and unsuccessfully) attempted to form districts along municipal lines. (The last two attempts will be discussed in greater detail in chapter 6.)

It should not be supposed, however, that school district formation was, as a historical matter, always politically guided by the municipality. That seems to have been the pattern of the early twentieth century, when city-sponsored high schools led the way to citywide consolidation into a single district. But it may not be the whole story in recent years, and occasional evidence points to causation in the other direction. I have encountered several instances in the Seattle area in which the school district was formed first, with the municipality subsequently forming around its borders (Fischel 2001, chapter 10). For example, the city of Federal Way, Washington, formed in 1990 around the borders of the district of the same name. ("The Federal Way" was the traditional name of the highway that ran through it). The city of Murray, Utah, was founded along preexisting school district lines (Gooderham 1977). Having a preexisting school district makes it easier for adults to organize to form a municipality from unorganized territory.

Another puzzle is why the largest urban school districts are so durable. These districts are often among the most problematical in terms of delivering the standard K–12 education. I have found very few observers of or even participants in the big-city school districts who are satisfied with them. But if few people like them, why can't the oversize districts be broken up into smaller districts? It is not logically necessary that big cities should have their own school districts rather than be divided into several smaller districts. Phoenix, San Antonio, and San Jose are counterexamples. This may be an instance in which the overlap of cities and school districts works to the disadvantage of the school district instead of, as I have argued, to the district's advantage. The advantage of overlap is that it makes it easier for the city to assist its district. Both political and administrative costs of city to district transfers (broadly conceived to include nonmonetary assistance) are reduced when there is substantial overlap between city and district boundaries. Indeed, the mayors of cities that are legally coterminous with their districts can more easily "take over" the management of the school when that seems warranted.

But it could be that these ties are also what make paring down the size of the biggest districts so difficult. City and school district relationships are especially strong when the extent of boundary overlap is strong. I will argue in the next chapter that this overlap allows adults to join more easily to make their municipality better. But these same social bonds may also make it especially difficult to cut the oversize district into more attractive pieces.

5.19 The Suburban School District Ratchet Effect

My foundational principle for explaining why suburban school district structures mimic rural structure is that school districts very rarely break up. Suburbs have accounted for most urban population growth since the 1920s. As suburban residents spilled over the central city boundaries, they entered previously established, rural consolidated school districts and took them as their own. But it seems likely that there would have been some conflict between the new suburbanites and the original residents of the rural district, who were most likely farmers. Demand for educational expenditures is highly income elastic, and the newcomers would often have demanded better schools than the original residents. Farmers may have resisted because they paid a disproportionate share of local property taxes. This would seem like an ideal opportunity to minimize conflict by dividing the original school district in two, one for the newcomers and one for the old timers. Each could get the level of spending and type of curriculum that it wanted. This would hardly have been unprecedented. The boundaries of one-room schools seem to have been fairly flexible, if one credits the stories about them that indicate that dissenting families would often simply join a different (though usually contiguous) district (Fuller 1982, 135).

This seemingly simple solution almost never happened after age-graded districts were established in rural areas. A fully-graded school system hardly ever broke up. One bit of evidence was described in section 3.1: the *number* of school districts in urban counties did not change during the latter part of the consolidation movement (after 1960), even as the number of districts in rural areas continued to decline drastically. This is less than conclusive, because stability in numbers could be consistent with a process of both consolidation and break-ups.

A more convincing approach would examine maps of districts over time. In the two states (Ohio and Illinois) in which I could locate early boundaries of suburban school districts near large cities, the graded districts near the cities look remarkably stable. Two states are hardly a great sample, but it is surprisingly difficult to locate school district maps from the period 1920–70, when the consolidation revolution was in full swing. Most of the attention of school reformers was on rural districts, not suburbs.

District maps of the metropolitan counties of Cleveland (Cuyahoga County) and Cincinnati (Hamilton) were served up in the aforementioned paper by Alesina, Baqir, and Hoxby (2004). They obtained maps that show school district boundaries in 1910 and 1926, publishing these for two metropolitan counties, Cuyahoga (Cleveland's county) and Hamilton (Cincinnati). In both areas, the district lines were radically transformed over that sixteen-year period. The earlier maps indicate a central-city district surrounded by tiny, most probably one- or two-room school districts. By 1926, both Hamilton County and Cuyahoga County are blanketed with regular, age-graded school districts. Some of the new districts were carved out of Cleveland, and Cincinnati seems to have annexed a few of its suburban districts, but most of the 1926 districts were formed along municipal and township lines in both counties.

The remarkable comparison is not 1910–26, when district boundaries changed a lot, but 1926–2000, when there was almost no change. (The Alesina, Baqir, and Hoxby article does not show the year 2000 maps, but they are easily available on the NCES map-viewer Web site.) The school district maps of Cuyahoga County and Hamilton County in 2000 look very much like their school district maps of 1926 despite the passage of three-quarters of a century. Closer examination indicates a few suburban consolidations during the period, but one thing stands out. All the consolidations appear to have been complete amalgams of two (sometimes three) previous districts. There are no examples of a 1926 district being split between two adjacent districts. School districts, at least age-graded school districts, appear to be atoms. They can join with other atoms to form molecules when properly coaxed, but the atoms (and the molecules) can be split only in the rarest of circumstances.

The problem with this comparison is that Ohio is not the ideal test of district durability. In Ohio, a metropolitan municipality is almost always within the bounds of a single school district. Thus the durability of school district boundaries could be thought of as no more than an artifact of the durability of municipal boundaries. (Though that begs the question of why municipal boundaries are usually indivisible.)

My only other map example is from Illinois for 1938. This was the product of a remarkable survey of government units in Illinois during the Depression (Illinois Tax Commission 1939). The atlas shows every government unit in the state by county, including all the school districts. Unlike those of Ohio, cities and their school districts in Illinois hardly ever overlap, with the very big exception of Chicago. In general, Illinois municipalities form and grow without much regard to school district boundaries.

My comparison of the Chicago-area maps of 1938 and 2000 revealed that the borders of the suburban elementary districts have been remarkably stable over time. (High school district boundaries were not as stable because in 1938 many elementary districts were not part of a specific high school district and simply paid for their graduates to attend the high school of their choice [Weaver 1944].) Almost none of the lines of the elementary districts in townships adjacent to Chicago in 1938 have changed. In a majority of cases, the close-in elementary districts have almost exactly the same borders as sixty-two years earlier, some even having the same district number. (Examples are Cicero District 99, Evergreen Park 124, Lincolnwood 74, and Oak Park 97.) Where there have been mergers, the new district almost always corresponds to the outer borders of the constituent districts. (An example is Evanston/Skokie District 65, which merged two elementary districts that were extant in 1938.) Only a few of the suburban Chicago mergers by 2000 had exterior boundaries that did not exist as part of the original districts in 1938, and several of those new boundaries are irregular shapes that follow streams or new highways. The consistent boundaries of the close-in Chicago elementary districts is strong confirmation of the atomistic stability of school districts. Once an age-graded (as opposed to one-room) school district is formed, it hardly ever splits into separate parts.

5.20 Conclusion: Geography Rules

The number of American districts declined precipitously from 1900 to 1970 in every state and then leveled off. This decline corresponded with the consolidation of rural, mostly one-room school districts, and the decline has slowed to a trickle since one-room schools became statistically extinct in 1972. The consolidation of rural districts was followed by a great deal of suburbanization. Older central cities, which had originally established city-run high schools, were by 1930 less able to annex their suburbs. Suburban residents took over the former rural districts that had earlier consolidated to facilitate age-graded schooling. In areas of high rural population density, the rural districts overtaken by suburbanites were relatively small, and so metropolitan areas in the North and well-watered parts of the West today have numerous competitive school districts. The South and the arid West have less fragmented structures because the rural districts their suburbanites inherited were large in land area. One of the consequences of the South's segregated rural schools was that the district had to be large.

School districts are clearly separate from municipalities in their functions and governance, but I have shown here that they retain a rough correspondence with their borders in most parts of the country, but especially in the North. The correspondence of districts with municipal boundaries is not perfect, but neither can it be called an "accident of geography." (The term is regularly invoked in school-finance litigation.) Indeed, there appear to be few durable accidents in political geography.

This chapter has made a case for thinking about school districts in a national rather than a state-by-state context. The generalizations about school districts that I have drawn are based primarily on political and population patterns that vary by region rather than by state. I have largely ignored the governance of school districts by local school boards and by state authorities. Political scientists such as Michael Berkman and Eric Plutzer (2005) do not have a high opinion of school board governance, though they do find from their survey evidence that the voters have no desire to give up their local boards. My impression is that elected governance and administrative structure are similar from one state to another. One indication of this is that the leading national treatise on education administration, *The Organization and Control of American Schools* (Campbell et al. 1990), is not organized along state lines.

The reason for this generic quality, I believe, is the need for districts and states to accommodate immigrants from other districts and states. States that tried to govern their schools in radically different ways would have found themselves at a disadvantage in attracting immigrants (including teachers) and thus lose jobs and tax base. Districts that set up unusual schemes that give much different educational outcomes—even if in some ways better—will be penalized by the property market. It may be that the true governors of local schools are the people who are not there yet.

CHAPTER SIX

Education Reforms and Social Capital in School Districts

When death comes to a small town, the school is usually the last thing to go. A place can lose its bank, its tavern, its grocery store, its shoe shop. But when the school closes, you might as well put a fork in it. — Timothy Egan, *New York Times*, December 1, 2003, p. 1

A major theme of the previous chapters has been that school districts are deliberately shaped communities. They are the product of a history of consensual unions, shaped by local voters' awareness that schools had to be acceptable to potential residents. Districts were sufficiently adaptable that they could make the transition from one educational technology—the tutorial-recitation method of the one-room school—to the age-graded method of instruction that we now take for granted. The transition is all the more remarkable because it was not widely discussed, let alone planned by a central committee. Educational leaders provided a menu of reforms involving consolidation of districts and a more standardized pedagogy, but local voters selected those that fit their circumstances.

The present chapter asks whether school districts are still relevant in American life. Even scholars who are sympathetic to the contributions of localism to American educational development question whether the school district system is still helpful. For example, Goldin and Katz (2008, 348), who regarded jurisdictional competition as one of the virtuous engines promoting the development of high school in the twentieth century, worry that now, "the system may not work well for many poor, inner-city residents who cannot easily relocate to new jurisdictions."

The problems of inner-city education, especially for African Americans, have generated two different responses since 1970. The first was the school-finance litigation movement, whose initial and most famous success was California's *Serrano v. Priest*, 96 Cal. Rptr. 601 (1971). The lawyers in these cases wrapped themselves in the banner of the landmark desegregation decision, *Brown v. Board of Education*, 347 U.S. 483 (1954), in attempting to provide for equal fiscal resources for inner-city residents. The second movement has been to provide families with school vouchers. These portable endowments would enable inner-city residents (and anyone else) to choose their own schools outside what their advocates regard as the failing public school system. Both these movements—equalization and vouchers—have a common disdain for local school districts.

School finance litigation has enjoyed considerable success in equalizing expenditures between city and suburb. This should have made school districts themselves less attractive to voters, and they should have embraced voucher proposals. I will argue in this chapter that the nearly universal rejection of vouchers as a general, statewide system was caused by voters' continuing attachment to school districts. The source of that attachment is not so much differentiation of education among districts, which is not especially large, but the social capital that schools provide for their communities. The empirical work in this chapter explains why schools are such an important source of local social capital.

Despite the success of litigation in reducing fiscal differences, large central-city districts remain among the most problematic in terms of student accomplishment, in part because, unlike most suburban districts, they are not subject to as much competitive pressure from their neighbors. The school-choice movement has sensibly turned its efforts to the largest districts, and residents of those districts do seem responsive to modified versions of the voucher vision. I conclude this chapter with a positive political reason for retaining some measure of local school district autonomy. It appears that voters without children in schools—typically the elderly—are considerably more motivated to support public education if it has a payoff for their local community.

6.1 The Public-Goods Puzzle of Local Public Schools

Why should American primary and secondary schools be provided by the local public sector and made equally and freely available only to those who reside in the community? The easy answer is that's the way it has been done for the last two centuries. As the earlier chapters of this book have demonstrated, however, American school districts are not bound by tradition. They implemented a radical change in their pedagogy between the nineteenth and twentieth centuries. In the process they consolidated so rapidly that district numbers declined from two hundred thousand in 1910 to twenty thousand in 1970. If the recent "tradition" implied by the consolidation trend were adhered to, school districts would have vanished by the end of the last century.

Schooling is probably the most used example of a local public good, but economists who reflect on it concede that it fits poorly into their technical definition of public goods. A public good is one that is subject to the nonexclusion principle or possesses the nonrival quality. An entrepreneur who seeks to profit by selling views of his overhead fireworks display will find he cannot *exclude* people who won't pay, and those who refuse to pay but enjoy watching can assuage their consciences by noting that their viewing the display does not subtract from ("is not *rival* with") anyone else's ability to see it.

Formal education has neither of these qualities. It is entirely possible to exclude nonpaying students, as is established by the existence of the private schools attended by about 10 percent of American children and by the "school censuses" that public-school districts undertake to root out students who falsely claim residence. (This is not the only purpose of a school census, which can also uncover truancy and aid in projecting enrollments.) That education is rival is evident from the continuing concern about class size. Bigger classes (more student consumers) do detract, at plausible margins, from the education of others (Boozer and Rouse 2001).

The economics literature falls back on two classes of arguments for the "publicness" of public schools. One is that there are spillover benefits to education that cannot be captured by those who are educated (Charles Benson 1961). The productivity of most workers is enhanced by the greater education of some. The extent to which this is true remains a matter of some debate. Educational attainment is closely correlated with lifetime earnings, which suggests that students themselves receive most of the benefits of schooling and thus do not need additional motivation. Even if we concede that there are uncaptured spillover benefits, however, it does not justify more than a subsidy to education. It does not explain why its *production* should be in the public sector, let alone the *local* public sector. Indeed, the spillover-benefits theory predicts that localities will provide too little education because local graduates are likely to move away (Lori Taylor 1992).

The other efficiency argument for public education is based on a supposed defect in the capital market (Gary Becker 1964). Because human capital cannot serve as its own security—the Thirteenth Amendment precludes that option—it is too costly for students to borrow against the future income that will result from educational investments. But again, even if this incomplete capital market is conceded, it argues for no more than a publicly financed subsidy to education, not for public provision. And both this and the spillover-benefits theory would warrant national public financing of education, not local or even state funding, and certainly not local provision.

Eric Hanushek (2002) points out that arguments for the external benefits of education are not much different from those for medical care. Health care has spillover benefits that may not be internalized (think infectious diseases), and long-term health investments may yield high returns that cannot be secured as collateral for lenders, causing individuals to underinvest in it. The institutional response to these potential defects in the market for medical care, however, has been largely to subsidize its purchase with grants and tax subsidies from the state and national governments, not to organize its production and most of its financing at the local level, as K–12 education is organized.

6.2 Alternatives to Local Provision and Financing Were Rejected by Voters

American policy entrepreneurs of both the left and the right seem to agree that education is not a local public good and that the present system requires significant changes. Their proposed reforms are, however, starkly different. The left sees a powerful argument against local financing and governance of education. A representative argument along this line was put forth by Leon Botstein (2000), president of Bard College, in an opinion column in the *New York Times* during a presidential election campaign. In the piece entitled, "Why Local Control?" Botstein could find no coherent reason to continue the "patchwork quilt of local governance." He dismissed school boards as too eager to fire school superintendents and regarded the electorate as too inclined to make children "victims of voters' frustration." He concluded, "A real 'education president' would be one who admits that our education crisis cuts across state lines, and that the solution is a federal system based on national standards and paid for with federal dollars." This is a long-standing view. Myron Lieberman (1960, 34) declared that "local control has clearly outlived its usefulness on the American scene." Matt Miller (2008) vigorously concurs in an article in *Atlantic Monthly* entitled, with tongue only partly in cheek, "First, Let's Kill All the School Boards."

Many economists would have some sympathy with these sentiments. Uniform funding by a national government would seem necessary to internalize the spillover benefits of education. The inefficiencies of the human-capital market require raising funds through national taxes to redistribute wealth through public education, assuming, as is reasonable, that capital-market constraints are more severe for the poor than the rich (Fernandez and Rogerson 1996). Nearly everyone agrees that redistributive taxes are best undertaken by the national government, because federal taxes can least easily be escaped by migration to lower-tax jurisdictions.

The political-right side of this argument might quibble about the extent of redistribution that is necessary, but its real beef with the left is about public *provision* of education (Edwin West 1965). The modern political right seeks to provide this good by simply subsidizing consumers' shopping for private schools with publicly financed education vouchers. In most proposals, the subsidy would come from state and federal funds, not local taxes. Voucher advocates argue chiefly for the benefits of competition that they see as being primarily in the private sector (Milton Friedman 1962; Chubb and Moe 1990). Although there is sometimes a nod to competition among local public school districts in the manner of Tiebout (1956), in which families are assumed to "vote with their feet" for their ideal school district, the main difference between the left and right among education reformers is whether the higher-government funds ought to be distributed to state-run schools or to privately run schools via vouchers. Neither side has much use for locally funded, locally run public schools.

Yet the public thinks otherwise. They vote with their feet and their wallets for localism, as is evidenced from the fact that improving local public schools almost always raises home values. They vote at the ballot box, too, rejecting in statewide referenda both conservative proposals to adopt state-funded voucher plans and liberal proposals to centralize financing of public education (Fischel 2001, 118; Terry Moe 2001, 359). Nobody loves local public schools but the people.

6.3 Tiebout Sorting and Efficiency Versus Equity

The odd thing about local public education is that Americans had figured out a way to provide it much like a private good. Ordinary citizens had done this many years (as described in chapters 2 and 3) before a group of economists developed a formal model that described it and ascribed to it some efficiency advantages (Tiebout 1956; Oates 1969; Hamilton 1975). Here is a sketch of the model: Given a stock of numerous and independent districts, a highly regulated supply of housing (by zoning), and a mobile population that can choose among many districts to live in, local public education was converted into an essentially private good. To get the benefits of the schools, you had to buy a home in the community whose property taxes covered the cost of education. You could not shirk from the property-tax burden by building a less valuable home or subdividing an existing structure; local land-use regulations would not permit it (Fischel 1992). Local schools, though nominally in the public sector, became more like a private good. Tuition for education quality differentials was extracted in the housing market, not at the schoolhouse door. Because education is in fact a private good at the local level, this aspect of the system is efficient.

Yet of course economic efficiency is hardly the only criterion by which a public school system can be judged. Public education is probably the most widely approved method of redistributing wealth. The ideal of "equality of opportunity" resonates more strongly among contemporary Americans than does equality of income and wealth. To say this ideal goes back to the origins of American public education would require the reader to forget what was said in earlier chapters about education—there wasn't much that was equal about one-room schooling and its successor districts. But it is abundantly clear from contemporary surveys that providing the poor with (almost) as much educational resources as the rich is a widely shared ideal, even if it is honored in the breach (Douglas Reed 2001, 121).

School districts present a challenge to the desire to promote educational equality. Within most districts, spending per pupil, adjusted for grade level and some other conditions such as handicaps, is presumably easy to equalize. Glaring inequalities among schools themselves would be noticed soon enough (though perhaps not in huge districts such as New York City [Iatarola and Stiefel 2003]), and the internal politics of the district and pressures from the state and perhaps the courts would remedy the situation.

Inequalities among districts, however, are more difficult to remedy. Each is an independent municipal corporation, and its governing directors and administrative staff answer to a local constituency. Its local tax base—almost always local real estate—is dedicated to its own students. Because property tax base is not distributed equally among school districts, some districts will find it politically less painful than others to raise funds for education. This is a long-standing condition. The inequalities of the property tax base—or of almost any local tax base—have been well known throughout American history. Almost all the early twentieth-century treatises on public education mention it and decry it (Cubberley 1919; Edwards and Richey 1938). There was no former Edenic equality from which late-twentieth-century education strayed.

Yet inequality in education has declined in the twentieth century. Goldin and Katz (2008, 339) summarize their comparison of the period from 1920 to 1990: "Thus, the actual inequality in per pupil expenditure was far greater in the past than today." Much of the reduction in educational inequality was brought about by the district consolidation movement, described in chapter 3. One-room school districts were consolidated and brought up to the standards of city schools by the carrot of increased state aid and thus less reliance on local property taxes (see table 3.1). Much federal aid in the 1960s and 1970s was given to school districts to induce and facilitate desegregation. Within this set of districts (the too small and the too segregated), the aid tended to equalize spending toward the mean of the state. Most of the small districts were in declining rural areas with insufficient wealth to fund a consolidated school district on their own. Desegregation was to a large degree achieved with the carrot of federal Title I funds, which were designed to be attractive to low-income districts in the South (Elizabeth Cascio et al. 2008).

6.4 Judicial Equalization Undermined Local Control

Up to the 1970s, the evolution of state and local school funding was chiefly the product of the interaction between local voters and the state legislature.

The political economy of state aid had two opposing forces, concentration of taxable wealth and demand for local control. Because taxable wealth and personal income often are concentrated in a few places, the majority of voters live in districts with less than the average of either measure of taxable wealth (Fernandez and Rogerson 2003). State aid to low-income and property-poor districts was thus always politically attractive as a way to redistribute wealth, though this took some care, since many poor people live in communities with large amounts of commercial and industrial property (Sonstelie, Brunner, and Ardon 2000; Fischel 2001, chapter 6). The attraction of this form of redistribution was enhanced by the development of a standardized system of education. Even representatives from wealthy districts were aware that education in other districts affected their own fortunes, and they were typically willing to have the state set a nontrivial floor on education spending (Arnold Meltsner et al. 1973).

The force opposing the growth of state aid was local control. As emphasized in chapter 3, all state legislatures are selected by contiguous geographic districts, which makes their members attentive to local concerns. Voters wanted additional funds from the state, but their representative knew that their constituents were reluctant to surrender fiscal control of their districts. The temptation to reach into another district's pockets was tempered by the anxiety that this would lead to a general increase in state supervision of public education. I thus regard the steady increase in the state share of school spending from 1920 to 1970 as a political balance between demands for local control and state funding.

That balance between state redistribution and local control was upset in the early 1970s with the *Serrano* decision, whose advocates sought to do much more equalization than voters and legislators were willing to do on their own (Elmore and McLaughlin 1982). After voters in several states had rejected initiatives to further equalize spending in the late 1960s (Paul Carrington 1973), reformers took their cause to the courts. Their efforts at the federal level were stymied by the U.S. Supreme Court, which in 1973 washed its hands of the issue in *San Antonio v. Rodriguez*, 411 U.S. 1 (1973), saying that education finance was a matter for the states. But as the Court specifically noted, the doors of the state courthouses remained open. Since then, legal reformers have fought a war of attrition against localism in the state courts (Michael Heise 1998).

This litigation has been remarkably successful in reducing inequalities *within* most states (Murray, Evans, and Schwab 1998). The largest remaining source of inequality in public education is actually among, and not within, the states (Rueben and Murray 2008). Nearly every state court has entertained these suits, and even when plaintiffs have not won in court, out-of-court settlements and defensive maneuvers by state-elected officials to forestall litigation have resulted in reductions in spending inequalities (Fischel 2001, chapter 6). Whether this has increased total resources for education is a matter of more debate, and some court-ordered gains seem to be paid out of reduced state expenditures on other services (Baicker and Gordon 2006).

As the earliest and most sweeping victory, *Serrano* has received the most attention from scholars (Henue 1986). The California Supreme Court's December 1976 ruling (135 Cal. Rptr. 345) required that variations in local property-tax bases could not be the basis (as they surely were before the decision) for variations in school spending. (The difference between property wealth and personal income was erroneously assumed by the court to be trivial because personal income data by district were not available before the court's first ruling in 1971 [McCurdy 1974].) As a result, the state had to provide resources so that spending per pupil would not vary among districts by more than one-hundred dollars. Compliance with this edict by California's legislature greatly equalized both school spending and local tax rates needed to finance it. (The best summary description of the *Serrano* litigation and the events that followed from it is still Judge Lester Olsen's 1983 trial court opinion, which was endorsed and reprinted in *Serrano v. Priest*, 200 Cal. App. 3d 897.)

The *Serrano*-driven reforms undermined the Tiebout system in which homebuyers could select their district and pay for schools via property taxes and mortgage payments. In doing so, *Serrano* transformed the school component of local property taxes from a fee-for-service into an excise tax that was unconnected to local spending. This aspect of the reform reduced the efficiency aspects of the property tax, since local voters were no longer rewarded with higher home values if they voted for cost-effective increases in school spending (Hoxby 1999). Voters further obliged the court—logically, I have argued—by cutting the property tax in half with Proposition 13 in 1978 (Fischel 1989; 2004b). Proposition 13 capped property taxes at 1 percent of value. The effective tax rate is actually lower—on the order of half that—because the constitutional amendment also rolled tax assessments back to 1975 levels and permitted only 2-percent annual increases in assessments until the property was sold (O'Sullivan, Sexton, and Sheffrin 1995).

6.5 Equal Spending and State Funding Made Vouchers More Logical

Some equalization advocates initially regarded Proposition 13 as a blessing because it forced the state of California to deal more thoroughly with *Serrano* (e.g., Alan Post 1979). They argued—correctly, according to Friedman and Wiseman (1978)—that only a state-funded system could meet both *Serrano's* equal-spending and common-tax-base requirements. California school finance has been almost entirely directed from Sacramento since 1978. This is both good and bad news. The good news is that the lowest spending school districts were raised in almost all cases to the state average, though most had not been much below the state average before *Serrano*. The bad news is that the highest-spending schools were pulled down to an average that has continuously lagged that of the rest of the nation, which appears to have induced a larger number of high-income families to choose private schools (Brunner and Sonstelie 2006). Almost everyone blames the chronic underfunding of California's public schools on Proposition 13 (Peter Schrag 1998).

As a result of *Serrano* and Proposition 13, no district could spend more than any other. Thus the supposed advantages of local schools for the rich suburbs and property-rich districts should have disappeared. Voters in those places should have been able to see the light of a voucher system. This was the expectation of John Coons and Stephen Sugarman (1978), whose earlier work supplied the intellectual basis for *Serrano* and related school-finance litigation (Coons, Clune, and Sugarman 1970). After *Serrano* accomplished what Sugarman called the "destruction of the old system" in order to "make the system rational" (*Los Angeles Times*, June 30, 1974), Coons and Sugarman entered the political arena to help build a new school-finance regime. They attempted to get a voucher initiative on the California ballot in 1979 but failed for lack of signatures (James Catterall 1982). A later initiative in California that did get on the ballot was nonetheless rejected by huge margins in 1993. This defeat, however, was blamed by voucher advocates on the substantial resources that opponents of vouchers—especially teacher unions—marshaled to defeat the initiative.

In 2000, another voucher initiative appeared on the California ballot. This time it had the support of a Silicon Valley billionaire, Tim Draper. A similar initiative in Michigan also had deep-pocket support. (Michigan had abolished local property taxation for schools by legislation in the early 1990s [Courant and Loeb 1997], and so would presumably also have been ripe for vouchers.) In both states, the provoucher forces spent at least as much as the antivoucher groups. But in both states, vouchers were again defeated by margins better than two to one (Moe 2001, 366). The national voucher movement has been moribund since these last defeats. Even the U.S. Supreme Court's decision in *Zelman v. Simmons-Harris*, 536 U.S. 639 (2002), which held that religious schools could be incidental parts of a voucher program, has failed to revive voucher proposals on a statewide level. (The development of a more selective approach to school choice will be discussed in section 6.21.)

The rejection of vouchers is sometimes explained as the product of public hostility to economic competition in traditional government services. This underestimates the public's tolerance for experimentation in the public sector. Housing vouchers as a substitute for public housing have been widely accepted. Proposals by economists to auction radio frequencies and air pollution permits (emissions trading) overcame initial public hostility. Plans to privatize waste disposal, prison management, and water supply are coolly evaluated on a case-by-case basis. Substituting vouchers for public schools should not seem all that unusual.

Surveys in California found that voucher proposals were most soundly rejected in those places where local public schools have maintained somewhat higher quality in the face of fiscal constraints (Brunner, Sonstelie, and Thayer 2001). Community residents in these places have managed to use private funds and a jury-rigged system of fees and "parcel taxes" to supplement Sacramento's meager offerings (Brunner and Sonstelie 1997). But why do California communities go to this kind of trouble to resuscitate local public schools? Why not just transfer their impressive fund-raising abilities to voucher-supported private schools? Why do the voters still like publicly managed schools so much?

6.6 The Answer Is "Community-Specific Social Capital"

Here's how I found out why California voters still prefer public schools. I spent a sabbatical year in Berkeley, California, during the academic year 1991–92. My son and only child was entering the eighth grade. Before going to California, I called friends in Berkeley who had children around that age and discovered that none sent their children to a public middle school in Berkeley. My wife and I decided instead to send our son to a tiny private school that happened to be just a block from the home we rented.

It looked perfect. But as the year progressed, we noticed something odd. We weren't getting to know very many people in the neighborhood. During a previous leave in Santa Barbara in 1985–86 (you notice a pattern), when our son was in second grade, he attended a nearby public school, and we had no trouble getting to know people in the area. But in Berkeley, all but our immediate neighbors remained strangers to us.

After a few months in Berkeley, we figured out what was different. Our son's schoolmates were drawn from all over the East Bay area. Indeed, the school (now defunct) had the grandiose name of East Bay Junior Preparatory School. Josh's school friends went home after school to widely spaced communities, and he seldom visited with them except for special, parent-arranged events. We got to know some of those parents on those occasions, but, since only two of Josh's schoolmates lived in Berkeley, we did not get to know people in Berkeley very well. The publicness of local public schools, I submit, is that they enable *parents* to get to know the other members of their community.

What's so important about that? More precisely, what is the nonexcludable, nonrival aspect of knowing your neighbors? It is that public schools increase the community's "social capital," to invoke a term given wide currency by Robert Putnam (2000). Social capital, as I will use the term, is one's network of friends and acquaintances. When bottom-up collective action is necessary, having established a network of personal relationships makes it much easier to organize and get the job done.

The social capital I am concerned with is what I call "community-specific social capital." This is not all the people you know, but the people you know within a given political community. Community-specific social capital facilitates collective action. If you know others in your community, you can more easily get them to sign a petition to do something about the dangerous intersection. It takes less effort to gather fellow gardeners to ask the city council to allow you to turn a derelict municipal lot into a community garden. It is more likely that neighbors will report a suspicious stranger entering your house if they know something about your life. Local school-board membership, which is usually an easily obtained political office, is often a stepping stone to municipal office, especially where the electorate of the district and the city overlap.

Public school's true public benefit—creating community-specific social capital—accrues mainly to a participatory view of local government (Lee Fennell 2001). It does not help much for governance that is removed from the neighborhood. Organized community groups are often the bane of higher governments. The neighborhoods are always interfering with the execution of regional plans and the placement of public facilities. Parent groups get in the way of school experiments like open classrooms and "whole language" reading. Homeowner groups insist that police pay attention to graffiti and excessive noise as well as to the major crimes that cops get promotions for solving. And homeowners can be formidable "NIMBYs"—antidevelopment activists whose motto is "Not In My Back Yard"—when developers seek rezonings that have even the remotest chance of diminishing their property values.

6.7 How Vouchers Undermine Community-Specific Social Capital

The publicness of local public schools is an argument against vouchers in the following sense. By enabling parents to select schools outside their communities and outside of local public supervision, vouchers work against the neighborhood and community networks that facilitate the bottom-up provision of local public goods. Community-specific social capital is more difficult to form if parents can easily send their children to schools in other communities. Maria Ferreyra (2007) simulated the effects of a metropolitan-wide voucher system. She found that it would induce substantial relocations of the school-age population. Some of this would be benign—the "back to the city" movement would be accelerated—but the relocations would surely disrupt the social-capital networks in most communities with viable public schools.

It is important to note that the aggregate amount of social capital (number of people each household knows) is *not* reduced by attendance at private schools that voucher programs might facilitate. Surveys indicate that the networks that adults and children acquire through schools are no less extensive in a private-school setting than in a public-school setting (Smith and Sikkink 1999). But in the voucher system, the social capital one gets from knowing people *outside* the community is not community-specific and is thus less valuable for producing local public goods.

The key to my argument is that a voucher system would allow students to cross municipal boundaries. This would not necessarily require longer trips to school. As will be discussed in the following section, large cities might be able to supply enough private schools within their borders to have a student body whose parents reside in the same municipality. But most suburbs and small towns would have to allow students to attend schools outside their borders. To offer vouchers but insist that they be used only within a small district's limits would undermine the opportunities for choice and the inducements to competition that are the primary virtues of a voucher system.

The cost of vouchers, then, is that their primary virtue—greater competition among suppliers—undermines another virtue, the community-specific social capital that local public schools provide. To phrase it in terms made famous by Albert Hirschman (1970), the tax-financed, local public school system makes "exit" (to private schools) more costly, which in turn promotes more "voice" within the community. Parents will inevitably seek to make their voices heard in their children's schools, wherever they are located. Public schools induce those within the same political jurisdiction to have a more effective common voice in self-governance in other community matters.

Some qualifications are in order. Many definitions of social capital focus on the good things that social capital may produce, such as trust, rather than the capital itself. In my view, social capital is simply the number of people you know. In contrast, James Coleman and Thomas Hoffer (1987) defined social capital as community norms and values that are transmitted to children from stable relationships among adults. Residential mobility undermines such relationships, and so Coleman and Hoffer regarded the fact that many families choose a residence on the basis of schools as detrimental to social capital formation. Tiebout's vote-with-your-feet system held no charms for them because mobility severs the deeper community roots that nurture social capital, as they defined it. For Coleman and Hoffer, then, suburban schools are no better for social capital than those in the biggest cities, and they disdained both when compared to traditional Catholic schools.

My approach to social-capital formation simply requires that people get to know one another. Investment in community-specific social capital is adding local names to your mental, paper, or electronic address book. (Trusting them is a separate outcome—and knowing who *not* to trust is as important as knowing those you do trust.) Sending your child to a local school adds those names more effectively than any other means. Because social capital is just all the people you know, I regard suburban and small-town schools as important and effective sources of social capital for their communities. In a survey of the Detroit metropolitan area, sociologist Aida Tomeh (1964) found that suburban residents had the highest levels of "informal group participation" in their communities. (See also Eric

Oliver [2000].) Indeed, for a mobile society, local public schools are among the most important ways of integrating newcomers into the community. Moving to a community and then using a voucher to send one's children to schools outside that community would undermine this function.

Public schools provide community-specific social capital mainly through the networks that parents establish. Children themselves also acquire a network of friends, and the benefits of knowing them last longer than the period of school attendance. But because people are so mobile after they leave school, their network of school friends is seldom *community-specific* social capital. Even if graduates do not move out of the metropolitan area in which they attended school, they are likely to have a number of municipalities in which they could reside. The social capital derived from any particular district's schools would be no greater than that derived from a private (voucher financed) school in the same metropolitan area.

As long as public-school parents have some reason to get to know other parents, it does not matter for my thesis what the schools teach as long as it does not drive families to other districts or to private schools. Religious education would be undesirably divisive in this respect, and American public schools have generally eschewed divisive religious observances, even before the U.S. Supreme Court banned the last vestiges of it (required Bible reading) in *Abington Township v. Schempp*, 374 U.S. 203 (1963). (Recall from section 2.6 that Congressional land grants for schools in the 1787 Land Act were favored over grants to churches because the multiplicity of sects would cause excessive controversy.)

6.8 Why Vouchers Are More Attractive in Big Cities

The most problematic aspects of American public education are geographic. As explained in chapter 4, migration by families limits the variety of pedagogies that can be adopted, providing both a floor and ceiling on educational quality. The low-side variations in school quality are almost all in the overly large districts, especially those within central cities of the largest metropolitan areas. The sources of their problems are usually said to be the concentration of low-income households, but that is a problem that is at least partly caused by low school quality. There has been a significant "back to the city" movement by middle-class families, but almost all those who make the move and have children in tow avoid using the public schools. Those who do use big-city schools are predominantly families with fewer geographic choices because of their poverty and their race.

The dysfunction of big-city schools is thus less about the quality of the clientele than the nature of city-school governance. In large-city districts, the majority-rule principle that characterizes most other districts is compromised by the influence of the unions and interest groups (Hoxby 1996). (I will discuss teacher union influence in section 6.17.) For now, I want to point out the difficulties that overly large school districts create for the formation of localized social capital. A comprehensive national study by Eric Oliver (2000) found that indicators of civic participation in American cities—voting, contacting local officials, and attending public meetings— were substantially less in larger municipalities, even after controlling for numerous demographic differences. His results were surprisingly insensitive to the size of the metropolitan area: other things equal, a city of 40,000 surrounded by rural territory had levels of civic participation similar to a suburban city of 40,000 in a large metropolitan area.

I will argue in this section that the adverse effect of city size on civic participation comes in part from large school districts. (Oliver did not address school districts.) My purposes are to show why vouchers are more attractive to big-city residents and to set up the empirical strategy for testing the social-capital hypothesis in the next section. One drawback of big school districts, I submit, is that parents get to know other parents less well. Schools themselves are larger in big districts. For example, the five hundred largest districts (the smallest of which in 1990 had about 14,000 students) have schools whose average size is 60 percent larger than that of schools in all remaining districts. Larger schools make it more difficult for parents to get to know one another because their children's classmates are more likely to change every year. School governance is more bureaucratized in larger districts, so parental input will be less. Romer, Rosenthal, and Munley (1992) found that smaller New York State school districts were reasonably attentive to the demands of local voters, but larger districts were governed by a more bureaucratic model.

With less parental influence on governance in big districts, there are fewer occasions for parents to interact with other parents at PTA or PTO meetings, school board meetings, and similar functions. And larger districts are more apt to send children out of neighborhoods to maintain racial balance or to receive more specialized education, so that parents of children in the same classroom live more distant from one another. It is well established that social capital is eroded by distance (Glaeser and

Sacerdote 2000). All these factors should reduce community-specific social capital in large school districts.

Vouchers are more compelling in larger American cities for reasons besides size. American suburbs are usually populated by people who have had a choice of several alternative communities. One of the most important reasons for choosing a community is its schools, and, because local residents know this, they try to provide an efficient level of education to maintain their home values. The advantages of this competitive system are attenuated in larger cities. Inner-city parents are poorer than average and are thus less likely to own a car, and their choice of communities is often further limited by racial prejudice. Residential immobility diminishes parents' ability to discipline unresponsive school officials by voting with their feet (William Hoyt 1999; David Brasington 2004).

In such a situation, a voucher program offers choices to big-city residents that have long been enjoyed by suburban residents. Indeed, the proliferation of charter schools may be an ad hoc way of undermining the monopoly of many big-city school districts, and there is some evidence that regular public schools do improve their performance when competition from vouchers or charter schools (to be discussed in section 6.21) is imminent.

A statewide voucher system, however, would undermine community-specific social capital in the suburbs and smaller cities. This is consistent with the evidence of Brunner, Sonstelie, and Thayer (2001), who found that homeowners in the better (mostly suburban) school districts in Los Angeles County were more opposed to California's 1993 voucher initiative than others. Brunner and Sonstelie (2003) found a similar pattern for the 2000 voucher initiative, which also failed by a large margin. They believe that voter opposition was caused by a fear that vouchers would undermine the public schools in which residents had invested heavily.

The most tangible manifestation of their school investment was the higher value of their homes. Brunner, Sonstelie, and Thayer (2001) suspected that it was residents' fear of a capital loss from a voucher system that made homeowners vote against it. This may explain the greater opposition to vouchers in the better districts, but the lopsided opposition by two-thirds of California's voters in both the 1993 and 2000 voucher initiatives would seem to require additional reasons. Even where public schools are not especially successful for students, they still have a payoff for adults. A desire to maintain the network of intracommunity links that public schools provide may account for voters' resistance to statewide voucher programs even in states where vouchers would seem to be most attractive.

6.9 Using District Size to Test for Social Capital Variations

The detrimental effect of large districts on social capital, described in the previous section, allows for an indirect test of the hypothesis that local public schools are valued as incubators of local social capital. My empirical strategy is to focus on variations in the size (number of students, not land area) of school districts among the forty-eight contiguous states, for which indexes of social capital are available. I use this interstate variation to determine whether bigger school districts reduce statewide measures of social capital.

In further support of my focus on district size, I note that voters in smaller districts in California disproportionately opposed the 1993 statewide voucher initiative. Jon Sonstelie (1995) estimated the extent of opposition to vouchers by school district for forty-two unified (K–12) school districts in Los Angeles County, the only county for which votes on the initiative were available by school district. Sonstelie derived estimates of the degree to which each district's voters opposed the 1993 voucher initiative. His resulting voucher-opposition index controlled for such differences among districts as childless households, private-school attendance, percent Catholic, household income, college graduates, race, ethnicity, political party, and employment in education. Figure 6.1 charts Sonstelie's estimates of voucher opposition (which I multiplied by minus 100, so that 240 on the vertical axis indicates the most opposition) for forty districts against their student enrollment. (I omitted Los Angeles and Long Beach because their huge enrollments—617,000 and 72,000, respectively—skew the diagram; their opposition indexes were 158 and 160, both below the median of the sample, indicating less than average opposition to vouchers, as my theory would predict.)

Opposition to vouchers was clearly greatest among the smaller districts, even after accounting for their other demographic differences. The simple correlation between the opposition index and enrollment in figure 6.1 is negative 0.52. It should be kept in mind, however, that voters opposed vouchers in the 1993 initiative in every district in this group. Statewide, 69.5 percent of voters opposed the voucher plan. The empirical work that follows is thus based on the idea that social capital is a *stronger* reason for

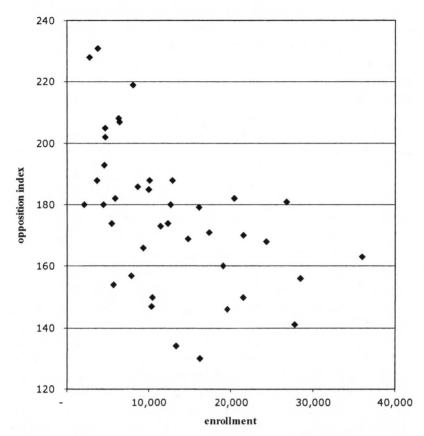

FIGURE 6.1. Opposition in California to voucher initiative in 1993. Adapted from Sonstelie (1995).

residents of smaller districts to oppose vouchers, not that bigger school districts are entirely lacking in social-capital benefits to their residents.

6.10 National Variations in Social Capital Are Related to School District Size

In the regression reported in table 6.1, the dependent variable is Robert Putnam's (2000) social capital index by state, excluding Alaska, Hawaii, and the District of Columbia. (Data are listed in Fischel [2006a]; census data are for 2000 and school district data are for 1997–98.) Putnam's index is a composite of fourteen elements from independent surveys that indicate whether people are likely to entertain friends, trust others, belong to civic clubs, volunteer their time, and vote regularly. My hypothesis is that interstate variations in his index of social capital can be accounted for in part by the size of the school districts (BIG DISTRICT) in the state and three statewide control variables: percentages of college graduates (COLLEGE), African Americans (BLACK), and the state's population in metropolitan areas (METRO). The three controls were found by Putnam to best explain state variation in his social capital index. The four variables account for almost two-thirds of the interstate variation in the social-capital index, an R-square that I consider reasonably large for these cross-section observations on the highly diverse states of the American union.

The key independent variable of table 6.1 is BIG DISTRICT, the percentage of public school children in the entire state who attend school in a district with more than twenty thousand students in the year 2000. There were 310 such districts (of more than fifteen thousand school districts in the entire United States), and 35 percent of the forty-eight states' public school children attend a school in a district of this size. The sign and significance level of the coefficient on this variable support my basic proposition.

A district with twenty thousand students would have a total population (adults and children) of about one hundred twenty-five thousand, given that public school children averaged about 16 percent of the nation's population. (Unified districts with enrollments around twenty thousand typically have three or four comprehensive high schools.) A problem with the twenty thousand cutoff is that seven states then have a zero for this variable. With a cutoff of fourteen thousand students, two of the seven states have finite (but still small) fractions, but the coefficient and the significance of the variable BIG DISTRICT drops considerably, most probably because the additional districts of fourteen to twenty thousand students in other states promote social capital rather than retard it. I experimented with other indicators of BIG DISTRICT including heavier weights for districts with more than thirty, fifty, and ninety thousand students, but none of the specifications did better than the twenty thousand cutoff. (Chapter 5 discussed measures of the "market structure" of school districts, but the issue examined in the present chapter is the effect of size itself, not competition among districts.) Note also that the voucher-opposition effect for the Los Angeles County districts in figure 6.1 does not have any appreciable variation for districts larger than twenty thousand. It looks as if all districts with more than twenty thousand students have the same detrimental effect on a state's social capital.

The three control variables are derived from Putnam's discussion of variations in his statewide indexes of social capital. The first is METRO which is the percentage of a state's population that is within Metropolitan Statistical Areas (MSAs). Social capital in general is lower in larger urban areas (Putnam 2000, 206). As anticipated, the coefficient on METRO is negative and statistically significant. As the correlation matrix indicates, this variable is correlated with BIG DISTRICT. But BIG DISTRICT is not simply a proxy for large metropolitan areas. Many large metropolitan areas are divided into small school districts. For example, Pennsylvania, which has 50 percent of its population in the Pittsburgh and Philadelphia MSAs has only 14 percent of its public school children in districts that enrolled more than twenty thousand pupils.

Social capital is also unarguably greater among the better educated, as measured by COLLEGE, the percentage of adults in the state who have four-year-college degrees. Social capital is lower in states with a large proportion of African Americans, and the coefficient on BLACK in the regression bears this out. As shown by Putnam's U.S. map (2000, 293), social capital is generally highest in states near the Canadian border and lowest in the states of the former Confederacy, which still have a disproportionate share of the black population. Putnam (2000, 294) explains the negative effect of BLACK as the legacy of slavery and segregation. This suggests some circularity, however, because, as I argued in chapter 5, segregation itself caused school districts to be too large. The negative effect of the variable BLACK may be more a manifestation of oversize (countywide) school districts in the South than low social capital on the part of blacks themselves.

The regression exercise in table 6.1 is consistent with the hypothesis that voters value public schools in part for their effect on social capital, which is valued in turn within the community for making true local public goods easier to provide. The regression does not examine how social capital maps into better local public goods. Putnam (2000, chaps. 18 and 21) makes a strong case for this intuitively plausible proposition, which has been confirmed in studies of Iowa cities (Tom Rice 2001), Swiss cantons (Markus Freitag 2006), and Flemish municipalities (Coffe and Geys 2005).

Only one of the fourteen elements of Putnam's social-capital index (the dependent variable for my regression) even mentions local schools, which offers some assurance that the dependent variable is not related by definition to the independent variables. But it also makes one wonder

TABLE 6.1 **OLS regression explaining variation in state-level indices of social capital (dependent variable: social-capital index [Source: Putnam 2000])**

R square = 0.659
Adjusted R square = 0.627
Observations = 48

Variable	Coefficients	Standard error	t Statistic
Intercept	1.948	0.4002	4.87
METRO	−0.009	0.0043	−2.14
BLACK	−0.039	0.0081	−4.82
COLLEGE	0.069	0.0178	3.89
BIG DISTRICT	−0.008	0.0038	−2.12

Descriptive statistic	Mean	Standard deviation	Minimum	Maximum	Median state
SOCIAL K INDEX	2.44	0.783	1.0 (NV)	4.14 (ND)	2.43 (MI)
METRO	64.5%	21.9	20.4% (ID)	100% (NJ)	67.5%
BLACK	10.73%	21.9	0.5% (MT)	36.6% (MS)	7.5%
COLLEGE	24.6%	4.65	17.3% (AR)	38.7% (CO)	23.9%
BIG DISTRICT	26.0%	22.6	0 (7 states)	88.0% (FL)	21.0%

Correlation	SOCIAL K	METRO	BLACK	COLLEGE
SOCIAL K INDEX	1			
METRO	−0.302	1		
BLACK	−0.694	0.243	1	
COLLEGE	0.330	0.467	−0.152	1
BIG DISTRICT	−0.480	0.521	0.369	0.154

how schools can be the incubator of social capital. What is it about having children and accessible (small district) local schools that makes adults more likely to entertain friends, be trusting, belong to civic clubs, volunteer their time, and vote regularly?

I submit that community contacts obtained through public schools have a local multiplier effect. (This is akin to the "social multiplier" of Glaeser, Sacerdote, and Scheinkman [2003].) The school-based network of adult acquaintances makes it easier to get other people to join a local organization or volunteer on a community project or attend a neighborhood picnic. Positive experiences from such activities create mutual bonds that increase people's sense of trust in others. Being recognized as members of the community ("the parents of Isabelle and Eloise") makes adults more inclined to participate in public life. Even people without children who live in such communities find it easier to do all those things, since getting to know a few people in the network facilitates getting to know the others who are already plugged in. Evidence for this was provided by Goolsbee and Klenow (2002), who found that learning about computers and related information technology spread from the schools to the rest of the community, enhancing its use even by households who did not have children in school. (Older readers may recall having asked a local teenager how to use some new electronic device.)

6.11 The Baby-Boomers' *Parents* Have the Most Social Capital

The previous section's statistical evidence connecting school district size and state social capital is supportive of the idea that public schools are a locus of social capital. But the evidence is hardly conclusive. It seems only to work with the cutoff of 20,000 students per district, and the rough congruence between school district boundaries and municipal boundaries (demonstrated in chapter 5) could mean that the real driver is small government units generally, not just small school districts. (Allcott et al. [2007] explain why smaller groups form stronger ties and offer some school-based evidence in support of it.) This would still be an interesting finding, but my theory would get a boost if there were a clearer connection between adult social capital and the number of school-age children they had.

I discovered this connection a few years ago when I watched Robert Putnam give a talk about the rise and decline of social capital in twentieth-century America. One of his principal graphs reminded me of something I had seen before. The bottom part in figure 6.2 is Putnam's longest-running measure of social capital, an index of participation by relevant groups of people in thirty-two national membership organizations. (For construction of this aggregated index, see Putnam [2001, 54, 426]. Its vertical axis in figure 6.2 is not labeled because the units have no special meaning.) This organization index is not Putnam's only time-series measure of social capital, but it is the only one that has reasonably accurate data that span the century, and its post-1945 trend tracks most other measures.

As figure 6.2 demonstrates, the rise and fall of the social-capital index almost exactly corresponds with the twentieth-century's most arresting demographic event: the rise and fall of average family size (total fertility). In popular parlance, the "baby boom" began in 1946 and is conventionally dated as ending in 1964. However, most demographers date it from the middle 1930s, when total fertility bottomed out. Total fertility peaked in

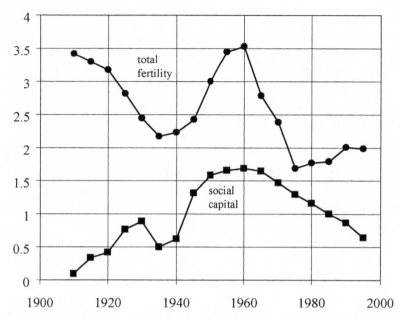

FIGURE 6.2. Twentieth-century U.S. total fertility and social-capital trends. White fertility was used because data for nonwhite fertility were not available before 1930 (Historical Statistics of the United States [2006, table Ab52–117]). Nonwhite fertility trend is similar but higher in earlier years. No data were available for 1915 and 1925 (points on this graph are linear interpolations). Social capital (lower series) is reprinted by permission from Putnam (2000, 54), an index of average membership rate in thirty-two chapter-based associations, with the index for 1900 reset to zero.

1955–59 at 3.69. It should be kept in mind that total fertility in the United States had been declining for most of the nineteenth century. Most demographers attribute this decline to the factors that contributed to urbanization and a modern, high-income economy, in which children are more likely to survive to adulthood. The increase in childbearing from 1935 to 1959 was thus an unusual event, and the decline in total fertility since then is a return to normal.

The group that Putnam identifies as having the most social capital, more than cohorts just before them as well as after them, are the *parents* of the children of the baby boom. He labels the cohort born between 1910 and 1940 "the long civic generation" (Putnam 1995, 674). Adults born in the years 1925–30 are singled out as the "culminating point of this civic generation." It was exactly this cohort that parented the baby boomers. They had more children per family than any other in the period since the

First World War. Because social capital does not deteriorate rapidly, the generation that parented the baby boom continues to lead in Putnam's indicators of civic engagement.

After 1959, total fertility began a continuous decline until it bottomed out in 1976 at 1.74, less than half its peak in the 1950s. It has rebounded since then, though only briefly exceeding the long-run replacement rate of 2.1. The decline in childbearing in the late 1950s meant that by the middle 1960s, there were fewer first graders than the year before, and the decline continued at least until 1981. With fewer children, adults have narrower avenues on which to meet others in their community.

The similarities in the two graphs in figure 6.2 are strongest from 1930 to the present. Membership organizations declined during the Great Depression, as did total fertility. Both increased from the bottom of the Depression and climbed continuously to 1960, after which both began to decline. The decline for social capital was less rapid than for total fertility, and total fertility bottomed out in the early 1970s, whereas social capital continued to decline. But social capital's less precipitous decline is likely accounted for by the fact that it is durable capital, and the older generation—Putnam's "long civic generation"—has only slowly abandoned its attachment to organizations.

The major divergence between the trends in fertility and organization membership is at the beginning of the twentieth century, when membership in organizations was rising but fertility was still falling. This seems explicable by the newness of the organizations in 1900—a time that marked the invention of the modern "franchise" organization, in which clubs would open chapters in various towns and cities (Putnam 2000, 384). Because it took time to spread this idea, the expansion of clubs during the 1900–1930 period is not surprising. The declining fertility in the 1900–1930 era marked the end of a long demographic transition from rural to urban. By 1930, however, American urbanization was nearly as complete as it was in 1960, so what we see after 1930 is the trend of births in an essentially urban society. The striking parallel between the two trends after 1930 is consistent with the view that parenthood is a wellspring of social capital for adults.

6.12 Smaller and Fewer Families Reduce Localized Social Capital

The two previous arrays of evidence—school district size and baby-boomer parents—offer aggregated evidence about school children and social capital. But such evidence could be conflating other trends with the social-capital indicators. In this section, I describe evidence from individual respondents. Bob Putnam again generously provided me with data that show the importance of family size on participation in social-capital–building activities. The data in table 6.2 below are from a national series of questions asked by the DDB-Needham advertising agency (described in Putnam 2000, 420). The numbers in the three right-hand columns refer to the average annual participation of married adults, not their children.

In general, the indicators of social capital are higher for adults who have more children, suggesting that larger families create more social capital. The exceptions are the largest families in the later periods and for entertaining at home. The substantial effect of family size on church attendance could, of course, have the causality reversed, as more religious people may have larger families. But other out-of-home activities—volunteering,

TABLE 6.2 **Family size and social capital**

Adult social-capital activity	No. of children at home	No. of events per year		
		1975–83	1984–90	1991–98
Volunteered	1	5.5	5.5	5.8
	2	7.6	7.1	7.5
	3	8.3	7.9	9.3
	4	8.2	8.6	10.0
	≥5	9.7	9.2	10.6
Worked on community project	1	2.4	1.9	1.7
	2	2.8	2.0	1.9
	3	2.9	2.2	2.1
	4	3.0	2.6	2.1
	≥5	3.4	2.2	1.6
Attended club meetings	1	7.9	5.9	4.7
	2	9.7	6.4	5.3
	3	9.8	6.8	5.8
	4	10.3	7.1	5.5
	≥5	10.7	6.4	5.1
Attended church services	1	22.7	21.7	20.9
	2	25.3	23.2	22.6
	3	27.6	25.7	25.3
	4	30.1	28.0	30.0
	≥5	32.8	30.8	28.7
Entertained at home	1	15.0	11.3	10.1
	2	14.4	11.3	10.0
	3	14.3	11.4	10.2
	4	13.8	10.4	9.7
	≥5	13.7	9.9	8.9

Source: DDB-Needham Survey, described in Putnam (2000, 420) and compiled by Robert Putnam for the author.

community projects, and club meetings—seem unlikely to induce people to have larger families. It is possible that people who have children are naturally more sociable—there is usually some sociability involved in the process—and Robert Schoen et al. (1997) infer from a survey that a desire to obtain social capital appears to be a reason that modern Americans do not forswear childbearing entirely. But these considerations seem unlikely to account for the foregoing comparisons, which are among people who have already made the child-bearing decision and differ in the number of offspring, not whether they have any at all.

Even if the direction of causality is not entirely clear, the DDB-Needham data support the aggregate evidence that children are the pathway to adult social capital. It is obvious from table 6.2, though, that community participation by parents does not increase in direct proportion to the number of children they have at home. In the most recent period, 1991–98, parents of four children volunteered ten times per year, compared to 7.5 times per year for parents with two children. The differences between two-child and four-child families are even smaller for other categories. Family size explains some but not all the secular decline in social capital.

Another demographic factor, however, augments the effect of declining family size after 1960. This is simply the decline in the number of households with *any* children at home after the baby boom ended. Table 6.2 does not measure this trend, since the DDB-Needham survey included only married couples who had children at home. There are two sources for this decline, both attributable to the aging of the baby boomers and their parents. By the 1980s, most children of the baby boom no longer lived with their parents. Thus their parents now became childless householders. At the same time, their young-adult children were slow in starting their own families and having children, at least compared to their parents at the same age. (A recent census report indicates that, for many more women than in previous generations, "slow" turned into "never" [Jane Dye 2008].)

The result of this was a substantial change in the nature of communities. Households with children at home constituted 45 percent of all households in 1970 (Fields and Casper 2001). The majority of baby-boom kids were still at home, and community life centered around children and schools. By 2000, the fraction had declined to 33 percent. Households without children at home outnumbered those with parents living with their minor children by a ratio of two to one. Moreover, most of the decline in households with children came from those most likely to form community-specific social capital, the two-parent family. In 1970, 40 percent of all

American households were married couples living with their own children. By 2000, only 24 percent of households were married couples with their own children at home.

In considering the social-capital effects of the increase in households without children, it is important to recall that households correspond by definition with occupied housing units. A community with 10,000 housing units in 1970 had almost one-half (45 percent) occupied by adults who had at least one school-age or preschool child. Thirty years later, that same community had only one-third of its housing occupied by adults who were likely to meet one another through child-oriented events. Many fewer of them would be mother-father units whose division of labor facilitates parent participation in schools and community-related activities. Combined with the aforementioned fact that those who nowadays do have children have fewer of them, the child-centered pathways between adults within the same community seem likely to have been cut by at least one-third between 1970 and 2000.

6.13 The School-Age Population Explains the Peak in Social Capital in the 1960s

I believe that Putnam's data about social capital support the idea that children are the widest avenue by which local social capital is formed. After the baby boom peaked in the late 1950s, adults tended to acquire less local social capital. However, Putnam regards this decline as part of a larger problem. As he frames the puzzle, "Why, beginning in the 1960s and 1970s and accelerating in the 1980s and 1990s, did the fabric of American community life begin to unravel?" (Putnam 2000, 184).

Putnam blames suburbanization, with its longer, asocial commuting times, and television for keeping people at home and alone. I would not rule these out as contributors, but the key issue here is timing. We need an explanation that accounts for three major observations about social capital: its rise from 1900, its peak in the 1960s, and its slow decline since that time. (The dip during the Great Depression probably reflects the corrosive effect of widespread unemployment on all social relationships, first documented in a classic study by Jahoda, Lazarsfeld, and Zeisel [1933].)

The problem with TV as an explanation for social capital's decline is that the timing is off by almost a decade. TV watching grew from near zero in 1948 to nearly universal by 1955 (Putnam 2000, 245), but most measures of social capital did not start declining until the mid-1960s. If people were taking a pass on attending a town meeting because they wanted to watch "Ozzie and Harriet," the decline should have started in the mid-1950s. Putnam suggests that TV did not affect the older generation as much as it did the younger, which could account for its delayed effect. But in the one natural experiment that he mentions, in which sociologists examined remote Canadian communities before and after TV arrived in the 1970s, people of all ages were equally affected (and social capital adversely affected) by the arrival of TV (Putnam 2000, 236).

Suburbanization is even more off in its timing as a cause of social capital's decline. The growth of suburbs was continuous throughout the twentieth century (Mieszkowski and Mills 1993). If longer commuting time was eroding social capital, the effect should have been noticed at least fifty years ago. Instead, social capital was booming through the 1950s, even as suburbanization and automobile usage increased dramatically.

There are a number of other explanations for long-term declines in social capital, including rising income inequality and increasing labor force participation by women (Kahn and Costa 2003). Although I would not claim that changes in the number of school-age children is the only explanation, it is the only one that does all three of the following: (1) It explains both social capital's rise and fall in the middle of the twentieth century; (2) it predicts its peak in the 1960s correctly; and (3) it offers a plausible behavioral reason for its decline: fewer kids to pull their parents into the community. Family size and women's labor force participation are no doubt jointly determined. Women with careers have typically had fewer children. However, this effect may be changing. Feyrer, Sacerdote, and Stern (2008) argue that women's increasing economic power will induce their husbands to do more child-rearing work, which in turn may increase women's willingness to have children. Perhaps the best way to promote community-specific social capital would be to get more dads to change diapers.

In the meantime, adults find alternative ways to build social capital without having school children around. The primary issue I am concerned with in this chapter, however, is not social capital generally, but the community-specific social capital that local public schooling promotes. Meeting people through work or clubs or athletic organizations or Web sites does build a network of acquaintances (my minimalist definition of social capital), but because people in those networks are apt to live in many different municipalities, it does little to help overcome free-rider problems in local governance.

6.14 Are Attendance Zones More Important than School Districts?

One of the questions that seminar audiences raised about my focus on social capital from school districts is that it overlooks the real source of neighborhood and community social capital: the school itself, not the district as a whole. Most districts with more than twenty thousand people (and thus about three thousand public-school children) would have more than one elementary school, and most districts of more than fifty thousand population (and about seven thousand five hundred school-age children) would have more than one high school. The usual rule for assigning children to schools in such districts is to divide the territory into contiguous attendance zones, and some studies show that schools matter more to homebuyers than the school district (Downes and Zabel 2002). Most attendance zones correspond to neighborhood divisions of some sort. This means that parents with children in different zones are less likely to encounter one another except at district-level events, such as school board meetings and interscholastic activities. So why isn't this book about attendance zones?

One reason is that attendance zones are more likely to change over time than school district lines, which are generally stable except when district enrollments decline substantially (chapter 5). When a school becomes obsolete, or when enrollments decline in one zone or rise in another, attendance zones usually change. This is not to say that change is uncontroversial. Few issues are more contentious within school districts than the closing of a neighborhood school. For a taste of it, consider Alan Peshkin's (1982) description of the political siege that resulted from attempts to close an Illinois district's village school and transfer students to a larger one in the same district. The stakes are not just emotional. Bogart and Cromwell (1997) found that closing neighborhood schools (because of declining enrollments) in Shaker Heights, Ohio, did depreciate home values near the schools, even though all children stayed within the much-admired Shaker Heights School District.

But the contentiousness of school closings does not extend beyond the district. Attendance zones are delineated by school districts, not state authorities. Residents of a particular zone have no special legal or political status within the district. As a result, homebuyers who spy a lone "good school" amid a sea of mediocre schools will feel a lot differently about the "good school" if all that protects it from merger with others is a locally generated attendance-zone line. If the "good school" is protected by a school district line, the buyer is more likely to pay a premium for a house located in that district. Conversely, if there is a distinctly "poor school" amid a district full of good schools, the prospective home buyer might reasonably expect that the district will be induced by internal politics to improve the quality of the poor school.

I should mention here that an influential and carefully done study that related home values to school quality used stable attendance zones, not school districts. Sandra Black (1999) examined differences in test scores of individual schools within Boston suburban districts to infer that test-score differentials were indeed capitalized in home values. The influence of school quality was relatively modest compared to previous studies that used interdistrict differences. The difference between the lowest quartile of test scores and the top quartile translated into a 6-percent premium for houses in the better schools' attendance zone.

This result may understate the effect of school *district* quality on home values. Black selected her schools precisely because the attendance-zone borders had hardly changed over the years. One reason for this stability may have been that school district officials saw to it that none of the schools within their purview became better than the others. (I witnessed in Santa Barbara a superintendent who reassigned an especially popular principal—he had years earlier been the principal of my son's school—to another school in her district for that reason.) Conversely, a lagging school might have received more attention from the superintendent, assigning it a new principal who was expert in turning schools around. So Black's study, although extremely clever in controlling for neighborhood and fiscal differences, seems like a lower-bound estimate of the impact of differences in school quality between districts, where a lagging school cannot call on the resources of another district.

6.15 West Bend's Odd (and Even) Solution to Attendance-Zone Controversy

Attendance zones are themselves usually drawn along neighborhood lines, except when a district is subject to desegregation concerns. Altering attendance zones for any reason is a fraught experience for a district. Sometimes it is easier to do if there are distinct communities that make up the district. When the Ohio school district of Willoughby-Eastlake (east of Cleveland) outgrew its old high school, it created two new high schools, one located in the city of Eastlake and the other in the city of Willoughby. (Both are in the same district, whose boundaries did not change.) The neighboring high schools are, naturally, "arch rivals" in interscholastic sports.

But usually creating new high schools is not so simple. School districts that want to create an additional high school without dividing the community might consider the example of West Bend, Wisconsin. It has two high schools, West Bend West and West Bend East. I stumbled on this example in a Web search of school districts and originally thought it was a mistake, since both are at the same address. Then I began to suspect that it was a joke, like a Garrison Keillor set-up for a story about his fictional hometown, Lake Wobegon. But the two West Bend high schools are real and, in their way, more imaginative than fiction.

The high schools share the same address because they are actually in a single building but are run as separate schools. The building was constructed in 1970 with the two-separate high schools in mind; it was not a merger of an old and a new building. The two high schools have different faculty, classrooms, and principals. Graduation ceremonies are held on the same day but at different times. There is almost no daily crossover between the schools. Each fields a separate set of athletic teams and conducts separate extracurricular activities, although they do take advantage of some scale economies by having a common swimming pool, combined theatrical presentations, and a few jointly offered specialized courses.

Even more interesting is how students are assigned to each school. It is not by geographic attendance zones. It is by birthday. Families whose eldest child's birthday is on an even-numbered day of the month are assigned to West Bend West High School, and odd-numbered birthdays go to West Bend East. The eldest-child rule is so siblings are not on divided schedules or on opposing sports teams. Like the Ohio high schools of Willoughby and Eastlake, the two West Bend schools do play against each other in sports, though one guesses that community passions are muted at the West Bend contests, since your next-door neighbor's kids could be on the other team.

The reason for this system, as it was reported to me in an e-mail from one of the schools' principals, Cassandra Schug, was primarily egalitarian. The two schools were created so that the growing and geographically diverse district, which contains the city of West Bend and a large rural area around it, would not have too large a high school. But the school board did not want to risk having one part of the community divided against another, so they settled on the odd-even birthday assignment.

I have tried to think of social-science experiments involving the West Bend schools and their method of dividing students. It's almost like "separated at birth" twins, and state-mandated test scores are reported for each school and *are* slightly different. But the most interesting social-science fact seems to be that this high school system is unique. It began in 1970, but it has inspired no imitators in Wisconsin or anywhere else in the United States. A Korean colleague, Jong Kim, once told me that public school attendance in Seoul is also determined by factors personal to the student rather than his location in the city. He explained that this was done for the same reasons as in West Bend—not wanting to have one neighborhood feel it was better than others. (The Korean system afforded the opportunity to study "peer group" effects in randomly assigned schools [Changhui Kang 2007], and, yes, peers do affect their compatriots' success.) And there are American magnet, charter, and vocational schools that attempt to defy the determinism of geography. (West Bend is 97 percent white, so race was not a special issue.) But I was assured by my West Bend correspondent that no other American school district has undertaken a similar experiment in creating two comprehensive, medium-sized high schools and assigning students randomly to each, and I have not encountered another in my own searches.

I suspect that the reason that other districts have not embraced this idea is that it actually undermines community-specific social capital. If all schools were divided this way, parents of children in the same neighborhood would have fewer occasions to meet one another and form the bonds that make communities work better. If one's children are attending a different school than those of the family down the block, there are fewer occasions to meet those adults. When it comes time to round up the neighbors to do something about that dangerous intersection, the number of people one can comfortably ask to attend the hearing or do some political legwork is cut in half by the West Bend odd-even system.

There are some offsetting social-capital benefits to West Bend's system. If West Bend had divided its high schools into city and rural attendance zones, people in one area would be less likely to know anyone in the other area via children's contact. So in one sense, West Bend's social capital is extended to a wider area. But this extension is somewhat less useful in local affairs. The rural part of the school district is outside the corporate limits of the city of West Bend. Residents of the incorporated village of Jackson, contained in the West Bend school district but seven miles south of the city, will know a bit less about half of their Jackson-village neighbors with high school–age children. West Bend city residents will know more people in the rural area, but they are of little help in dealing with issues in the city of West Bend.

In reality, things cannot be that problematic in West Bend, because the elementary and middle school attendance areas are based on contiguous neighborhoods. West Bend apparently does not want to extend its social experiment down to the first eight grades. And it may be a tribute to the already high levels of social capital in West Bend (states in the upper Midwest generally lead in Putnam's indicators of social capital) that it had the pluckiness to embark on this experiment. But it is perhaps anxiety about eroding neighborhood and municipal social capital in the other 15,000 school districts around the nation that makes the West Bend solution one of those exceptions that prove the rule. Children in the same neighborhood almost always are entitled to attend the same public school.

Reluctance by growing school districts to adopt the West Bend solution also may account for why large districts have, on average, larger schools. Most currently large districts probably began with a small number of students but a large land area. (Chapter 5 demonstrated that rural district lines of the past usually determined the area of suburban districts.) As the district grew in population, the old school would be outgrown. It might have been ideal to create two or more new schools of moderate size, but that would require redistricting the attendance zones. This would disrupt neighborhoods bonded by school-generated relationships, and parents would complain about the redistricting. The path of least resistance for the school board might be to create a larger school (or add wings to the old school) and not change attendance zones. If this story is valid, it would appear that social-capital connections tend to undermine themselves, since I argued in section 6.8 that larger schools themselves tend to undermine social capital.

6.16 Fiscal Problems Retard the Division of School Districts

If large school districts are less congenial to social capital and are, as some research indicates, less effective as educational institutions (Hoxby 2000; Driscoll, Halcoussis, and Svorny 2003), why are there still so many large districts? My history of school district formation in chapter 3 found that it was largely consensual. If the school district is now too large, why don't the local voters agree to break it up?

Creation of new school districts should not be confused with administrative decentralization. The huge Los Angeles Unified School District established eleven "minidistricts" in 2000 in an effort to decentralize its operations, and they may have slightly improved the district's academic performance (Banzhaf and Bhalla 2008). But this was purely administrative decentralization, which created a separate superintendent for each minidistrict. None of the minidistricts had an independently elected governing body or independent ability to raise revenue. In a more serious effort at decentralization, New York City in the 1960s established nominally independent local districts within the city, and these did have locally elected boards that could hire some administrators and staff. However, all were fiscally dependent on the larger district, and most national statistics continued to report New York as a single district. The ability of New York's "community boards" to allocate money that they did not have to raise from their constituents probably contributed to the widespread corruption that led to the system's demise (Lydia Segal 1997). The last vestiges of the plan ended with a resumption of mayoral control in 2002.

I have looked for modern instances of substantial school districts being formed from larger districts, and very few examples have come to my attention. (The few I located were formed around a preexisting municipality, as mentioned in section 5.18.) The paucity of district breakups generally mirrors that of municipalities, so the reasons for school district indivisibility may be the same as those for cities, though that only broadens the mystery.

One possible reason for the scarcity of school district divisions is that the fiscal balance sheet seldom works out. Often the part of the district that seeks to withdraw has better access to taxable property, either in the form of more valuable homes or more valuable nonresidential uses. Because in most cases the breakup must be mutually acceptable, engineering a suitable division is difficult. Legislation in Utah in 2005 permitted the division of districts along city lines. The lone instance so far is the division of the Jordan District, which is the state's largest and covers the southern suburbs of Salt Lake City. It will be divided along the banks of the Jordan River starting in 2009. Given the contentiousness about the fiscal transfers following the vote to split (e.g., *Deseret News*, August 2, 2008), the resulting districts might as well be called "Israel" and "Palestine." Dividing a pie that has been thought of as common property for many years is not easy to do.

Fiscal issues that would retard the creation of new districts in most states would seem to be much less of a problem in California. As a result of *Serrano* and Proposition 13 (as described in section 6.4 above), California school districts are essentially funded by the state government. The funding is based on enrollments and is remarkably equal among almost all the state's one thousand districts (Brunner and Sonstelie 2006, 66). The fiscal barriers to forming a new school district should, as a result, be substantially less than in states in which much funding remains local. A California district with twenty thousand students could be broken into two districts with ten thousand students each, and both districts would still receive the same funding per pupil as the larger district. The situation seems unlikely to change because no politician in California dares to tamper with Proposition 13 and the California Supreme Court is unlikely to revisit the *Serrano* decision. Given this situation, California should be ripe for the creation of smaller districts.

6.17 Lakewood Attempted to Form Its Own School District

A recent attempt to create a new and smaller school district occurred in Lakewood, an independent city that is part of the Los Angeles Urbanized Area. Its journey to cityhood in 1954 made its name synonymous with a particular form of municipality. Its plan for incorporation was municipal minimalism (Gary Miller 1981). Lakewood's founders proposed to residents that the new city would not actually provide its own services. It would purchase them from Los Angeles County and private providers. The idea worked, and scores of other cities emulated what has continued to be called the "Lakewood Plan" for incorporation. Much of Orange and Los Angeles Counties' suburban territory became covered with Lakewood Plan municipalities until a 1964 law made incorporation more difficult.

What Lakewood's founders either overlooked or could not do was to form a school district along its new borders. School district lines had been drawn when Lakewood and nearby communities were still farm fields or small towns. Most of Lakewood was encompassed by what is now the Long Beach Unified School District, but about one-third of the city's territory was in three other unified school districts: Paramount, ABC, and Bellflower. In none of these districts were Lakewood residents anywhere close to being the majority partner. Lakewood residents could vote for school board members in each district of which they were a part, but their voices were relatively small in each of them, especially in Long Beach Unified, which is the third largest in the state.

In terms of my categories for city and school district overlap from chapter 5, Lakewood qualifies as "fragmented" without so much as a second look. Lakewood would, under my theory of community-specific social capital, be a good candidate for formation of a school district along municipal lines. Moreover, the creation of a new school district in this case would increase school district competition, not reduce it, since Lakewood is a relatively small part of the southern Los Angeles County area, with a land area of about nine square miles and a population of eighty thousand in the census of 2000. (By contrast, consolidation of school districts along the municipal boundaries of San Jose, Phoenix, or Houston—all fragmented—would reduce district choice within their respective Urbanized Areas.) Lakewood's attempt to form its own district thus seemed to be a good example of late-date creation of a community that would enhance local social capital and add to school district choice.

Lakewood's other advantage for my purpose is that its attempt to carve out a new district was fairly recent, and I could talk with the person who headed the effort. Todd Rogers was an officer in the Los Angeles County Sheriff's Department and a resident of Lakewood. In 1996 he had preschool children, and he began the movement to organize the Lakewood Unified School District. I made an appointment to meet him at a diner in Lakewood on September 21, 2005. Since we were strangers and he was not in uniform (he was now a captain), I told him on the phone that I would be the guy wearing the blue baseball cap. He said he would be the guy who looked like a cop.

Rogers told me he had passed out some handbills in Lakewood announcing a meeting at a local pizza parlor to form a committee to look into forming a new school district. He hoped a dozen people might show up. Instead several hundred showed up, many more than could fit in the restaurant. The organizing committee that was created from that meeting, with Rogers at its head, got the Lakewood city council to hire a consultant to see how an independent district might be formed. (I supplemented and checked the information I got from my interview with archived newspaper reports from the Long Beach *Press-Telegram*.)

California, like other states, channels school district reorganization through a procedure that is a mix of bottom-up initiative and top-down controls. Formation of a new district requires a petition signed by at least 10 percent of the registered voters within the area of the proposed district. (Some minor transfers of land between districts can bypass this process.) Lakewood easily surpassed this minimum with more than 25 percent of its voters signing petitions to create the proposed Lakewood Unified School District. The proposed district included all the city of Lakewood plus a nearby small, unincorporated area that was in the ABC Unified District.

I asked Rogers what caused the city to want to form its own district along city lines. He had, since the attempt began, become a member of the Lakewood City Council, but he denied in all his Joe-Friday sincerity that his school district activity was the product of political ambitions. Aside from the general concern about having little say in the governance of their respective districts, Lakewood residents had two specific concerns. The first was that one of the city's districts, Paramount Unified, was so troubled that very few parents who lived in that section of the city sent their children to Paramount schools. They either sent them to private schools or arranged for interdistrict transfers to other public-school districts. Such transfers are contingent on space availability, and it appears that families with children simply avoid that area of Lakewood.

The other specific problem was the declining number of school-age children in Lakewood. As an avowedly family-friendly city, Lakewood had originally attracted families with many children, and its school enrollments expanded with the baby boom in the 1950s and the "echo" of the baby boom in the 1980s. But, as in many other mature communities, the echo has petered out, and many of the schools built in Lakewood would be half empty if they depended on neighborhood children to fill them up. About twenty-four thousand children attend schools located within the borders of the city, but only about twelve thousand came from Lakewood as of the late 1990s. With a large and growing immigrant population, Long Beach supplies almost half the school children in Lakewood.

The problem, according to Captain Rogers, was that Long Beach was using Lakewood as something of dumping ground for problem students, kids who were expelled from schools closer to their homes or who otherwise just did not fit in. The importation of large numbers of students from outside the city meant that schools in Lakewood no longer had much of a neighborhood feel. Parents of some children in Lakewood itself no longer felt comfortable with their local schools.

As the reader might have guessed, Lakewood's population is largely non-Hispanic white (63 percent in 2000). The city of Long Beach is 45 percent non-Hispanic white, and so it is reasonable to suppose that many of those bused to Lakewood are Hispanic. (Both cities' populations are about 12 percent Asian, and blacks constitute about 15 percent of Long Beach and 7 percent of Lakewood.) Rogers and the organizing committee's Web site emphatically denied that their effort is about race or ethnicity, and they did their best to repel any politically incorrect supporters. The Lakewood committee's sensitivity to the issue may have been one reason it sought to include in the proposed district a small area outside the incorporated boundaries of the city of Lakewood, since that area brought up the numbers of minorities.

Lakewood's most obvious logistical problem as a school district would have been how to fill its schools. A newly incorporated district in California inherits all the schools within its boundaries. (Unlike Lakewood's proposal, most new incorporations in California have been "unifications" of several elementary-school districts into the area of the high school district that served them, and so local enrollments and building assignments are unchanged.) The Lakewood organizing committee proposed that all the existing students in the district would be "grandfathered" into the schools; there would be no mass expulsion of non-Lakewood students. But the committee could not bind the future school board to such policies, and the promise of grandfathering existing students, even if it could be binding, would not affect potential students from outside of Lakewood. In meeting this argument, Rogers (as newspapers reported it) fell back on simple rationality. Lakewood would not want to leave schools empty if there were students who wanted to attend, and each student, under California's fiscal formula, came with the same amount of funds. But it was clear that Lakewood wanted some say in how those schools would be filled up. (The Lakewood organizers undoubtedly knew that California interdistrict transfer rules would not allow Lakewood to select *individual* students from outside the district. Their main concern was that Long Beach Unified's administrators were systematically moving problem students to Lakewood.)

6.18 School District Breakups Are Prevented by the State Education Establishment

As a management-level officer in the nation's largest county police force, Captain Rogers was well acquainted with the logistics of bureaucracy and ways of public-sector employee unions. He nonetheless appeared to be quite disappointed, not to say bitter, about the treatment that the Lakewood organizing committee received at the hands of the county and state education establishment. They opposed Lakewood at every turn. The county committee rejected the proposed incorporation, as did the state.

The state committee had nine preexisting criteria, each of which the proposed district had to meet in order for the state to order a local election (California Department of Education 2006). Just who would vote in the election is also up to the state committee. If it was only the residents of the proposed school district, it would presumably have a better chance of passing than if the reorganization had to be approved concurrently by each of the four school districts. I was somewhat surprised that voting within the proposed district alone was even an option, but the state's administrators could by this power enable or scuttle a proposed district.

The nine criteria could be summarized as requiring that any new district meet—at least approximately—the requirement for Pareto superiority, which holds that as long as someone is better off and no one else worse, the action should be judged an improvement. Creation of a new district must not increase the costs of other units; education programs in the remaining and new districts must not be disrupted; and property should divided so as to "result in an equitable division" with the old district. Interestingly, the rules require that the new district be "organized on the basis of substantial community identity," but it cannot be "primarily designed to result in a significant increase in property value causing financial advantage to property owners." (The latter was probably to discourage tax-base seeking, a motive that is now mooted by the post-1978 equalizations.)

The real sticking point for most urban districts in California is the criterion that requires that a new district not create additional racial or ethnic imbalances among school districts. This creates a functional catch-22. A proposed district that is homogenous will have little trouble persuading residents to vote for it, but the state is likely to block it because the remaining district may thereby be more segregated. A proposed district that is heterogeneous will get state approval, but its very heterogeneity will make it difficult to get voter support. That appears to have been what happened to Carson, California, a near neighbor to Lakewood. Its proposal to carve out a new district along city lines and withdraw from the Los Angeles Unified School District did not have much problem with the county and state process. Only voters within the proposed district had to approve it. (The most recent city to have escaped from Los Angeles Unified was Torrance in 1948.)

Carson was a highly diverse community whose major minorities were Mexican and African Americans. But after the proposed district obtained state approval to hold an incorporation election (which was denied to Lakewood), the factions within Carson fell to bickering among themselves about who would serve on the first school board. A well-funded and concerted effort by the Los Angeles teachers union campaigned against it (David Boaz 2001). The proposal to create a separate district was defeated by a lopsided margin (three to one) in the local vote. (The work of Rose and Sonstelie [2004] suggests a reason for union opposition to secession: in the California school districts that they examined, teacher unions had a bigger impact on district pay policies in larger districts.)

Lakewood never got the chance to have a vote. The county committee that reviewed the proposal rejected it on most criteria. All the districts from which Lakewood would have withdrawn vigorously opposed it. However, the fact that more than 25 percent of Lakewood voters had signed the district petition allowed it to be sent to the state committee on school district reorganization. Lakewood was turned down there, too. Captain Rogers was especially unhappy with this process, and I would infer from his remarks that it responded to teacher-union opposition more than what he thought were the merits of the case. (Rogers had trained to be a school teacher before beginning his law-enforcement career.)

So this looks like a situation that runs contrary to my conclusion that the voters call the shots about school district formation. Keep in mind that my earlier claim was about district consolidation, not district breakups. School district consolidations still occur only with the consent of all districts involved in California. In 2005, the Penryn Elementary School District (twenty-six miles northeast of Sacramento) voted to consolidate with neighboring Loomis Elementary School District. Penryn was a one-school district whose enrollments were declining, but it resisted state efforts to consolidate until a local board member took it upon himself to convince voters that it was in their interest to do so. But consolidation also required a separate affirmation by the voters in the Loomis district. Mutual consent for consolidation is still the rule.

One could condemn the teacher unions and state bureaucrats for foiling Lakewood in what looks like an innocent attempt to create more local social capital and better schools. The proposed Lakewood district seems to have had everything going for it on that account. The district would be smaller, it would create stronger bonds among community residents, and both conditions would have created better schools. These better schools would have attracted families with children, and so the problem of empty buildings in Lakewood would only be temporary. The better schools would in turn make Lakewood's neighbors redouble their efforts to improve their schools. Keep in mind that every district in California is entitled to the same public resources per pupil, so there's no excuse for educators in what would be the neighboring districts of Paramount, ABC, Bellflower, and Long Beach to fail to respond. It is difficult to banish the thought that the prospect of that competition was the source of their opposition.

From this point of view, the failure of large districts in all places to break up is due to a political ratchet effect. Local control applies for decisions to consolidate, but state control and the organized education establishment prevent effective reversals. It certainly looks that way from the Lakewood saga, but the failed vote in Carson prevents me from jumping to that conclusion. Carson voters could have escaped what may be the most unpopular school district in California, Los Angeles Unified. There would have been no fiscal penalty (or gain) from doing so. Yes, the Los Angeles teacher unions did campaign strenuously against withdrawal, but voters in the privacy of their booths still had to make the choice.

The large turnout in the Carson election (about ten thousand votes were cast) would seem to make irrelevant the electoral participation of local teachers, which Terry Moe (2006) found could be influential in ordinary (low turnout) school board elections in California. Spending money to oppose a vote is no guarantee that voters will be induced to follow, and Carson voters had plenty of information before the election about the merits of having their own district. Todd Rogers, Lakewood's organizer, dismissed Carson's failure with a grimace and assurance that it would not have happened in Lakewood. He surely knows his community better than me, but I suspect the organizers in Carson would have said the same thing prior to their attempt to form an independent district. So perhaps in school districts (as in municipalities), history is destiny. The events of the past may be etched in the social fabric so deeply that present-day reformers cannot turn it around.

6.19 Is Support for Schools Threatened by "the Gray Peril?"

The inflexibility of school district boundaries may be one reason that reformers are so impatient with them. The centralizers would have the state run the schools directly. The decentralizers would give parents vouchers to send their children to the schools they want, regardless of where they live. School districts are in both camps regarded as dinosaurs that are irrelevant to modern concerns. I will argue that there are some reasons to maintain some degree of local school district fiscal discretion.

The trend in total fertility shown in figure 6.2 indicates that the fraction of school-age children in the population is not likely to rise. In this respect, the United States is similar to other high-income nations, whose birth rates by any measure have declined in the last forty years (Feyrer, Sacerdote, and Stern 2008). American birth rates are not as low as in most European countries, but much of that is accounted for by the larger percentage of recent immigrants in the American population. If history is any guide, the offspring of those immigrants will have smaller completed families than their parents.

The implications of this demographic trend for education are complex. On the one hand, fewer school-age children implies that the education industry will shrink. This could be desirable in that resources once required to educate children can be reallocated to other productive public goods like health, parks, and transportation. On the other hand, the demand for education *per child* is likely to be greater. This is for both personal and social reasons. Parents in general are predicted to demand more education per child if they have only one or two (Gary Becker 1981). Even if one does not accept that the demand for child "quality" is larger if there are fewer per family—what am I, says the fifth in the birth order, chopped liver?—it is arithmetically true that income per family member is larger if the denominator is smaller. More wealth per child almost always facilitates more education. It is also socially desirable for parents to invest more in their children as birth rates decline, since the smaller cohorts of the future labor force will have to shoulder a larger burden for old-age support as well as for other public expenditures. Carrying that burden will be easier if the younger cohort is well educated.

The pessimistic political story about this is that an older population, one without children in schools, will be less inclined to support public education. James Poterba (1997; 1998) summarized this position and provided evidence in support of it. Poterba found that states with an older population had lower spending per pupil. He also noted studies of counties in Florida showing that those with a larger proportion of elderly voters were less supportive of school bond issues. Projecting these results into the future, Poterba warned of what might be called the "gray peril" to education: voters in an aging America are less apt to support public education, especially since an increasing fraction of families with children in school are from a different ethnic or racial background than the majority of the elderly.

The diminished support by the elderly would seem to commend a strategy that moves school financing further away from local districts. Districts with an especially high proportion of elderly voters would continually vote against school budgets and bond issues in situations where there was discretion to do so. Removing school finance from the district level to the state and national level would submerge such pockets of resistance into the larger polity. Indeed, removing school-spending decisions from the legislative sphere and into the courtroom might seem preferable on these grounds, since state legislatures would respond disproportionately to the preferences of the elderly. The school-finance litigation movement could rejuvenate itself on a new basis, that of preventing unconstitutional discrimination against school-age children by their grandparents. (I write this last with tongue in cheek, but I have heard academic lawyers argue that children deserve special judicial protection because they cannot vote.)

6.20 "Elder Voters" Have a Stake in Local School Districts

The centralization solution, however, is not supported by more recent studies, most of which were generated in response to Poterba's challenge to consider more nuanced evidence about the elderly and political support for schools. Harris, Evans, and Schwab (2001) examined the same data as Poterba but at the school district level. They found that school districts with elderly voters were more supportive of education at the local than at the state level. They proposed that elderly homeowners favored local school spending because it enhanced their home values, and their interaction variable (homeowners who were elderly) supported that. Capitalization studies by Ladd and Murray (2001) and Mayer and Hilber (2009) also support the idea that older voters are like other homeowners at the local level. I will call this the "elder-voter hypothesis," in shameless imitation of my coinage of the "homevoter hypothesis." Elder voters are more interested in schools in their community than in the state as a whole.

The elder-voter hypothesis is also supported by survey evidence. Political scientists Michael Berkman and Eric Plutzer (2005) used a question from the General Social Survey that was asked of respondents in the four decades from the 1970s to the 2000s: "Are we spending too much, too little, or about the right amount on improving the nation's education system?" Although their question directs the respondent to national rather than local conditions, the responses seem consistent with the elder-voter hypothesis. The older generation of voters was less supportive of school spending at any given time (say, 1980) than the general population, but as each cohort approached retirement age, their support for public education went up, not down. This is consistent with an earlier finding of elder-voter behavior in Michigan by Bergstrom, Rubinfeld, and Shapiro (1982). They inferred that older voters were more inclined to support local education because it would enhance the sale price of homes that they expected to sell soon.

Berkman and Plutzer discovered that the real bias of the "elderly" is actually by older cohorts. For example, those born in the 1920s always were less supportive of school spending at all times than those born in the 1940s, but as each group aged, they became more supportive. Thus in the General Social Surveys in the 1970s, 50 percent of the respondents born in the 1920s thought school spending was too low at the time of the survey, but 58 percent of those born in the 1940s thought it was too low. By the 1990s, support for schools from those born in the 1920s grew to 58 percent of the cohort, and support from the 1940s birth cohort grew to 68 percent. With only a few exceptions, more recent cohorts were more favorable toward school spending, and support for spending grew as each cohort neared retirement age.

Berkman and Plutzer dug deeper into these data and looked at the state of residence of the respondents. They found that elderly respondents in states with more reliance on *local* school taxes (that is, property taxes) were considerably more supportive of education spending. Their finding would seem to defy the conventional wisdom that older voters oppose the property tax. Some opposition could have been defused by tax breaks for older homeowners, and expansion of such programs could account for some of the growing support by older voters over time. But most such programs are modest in size and seem unlikely to account for much of the trend that Berkman and Plutzer found.

Other opinion-poll research is consistent with the elder-voter hypothesis. A 2002 statewide poll by the Public Policy Institute of California asked respondents two questions about their support for spending on school capital projects. One addressed a real referendum that sought support for a state-funded bond issue to benefit school districts all over the state. The second asked whether voters would vote for a *local* bond issue for the same purposes. Respondents gave their age and other demographic information. Edward Balsdon and Eric Brunner (2004) analyzed these data and found considerable support for the elder-voter hypothesis: older voters were more inclined to favor expenditures at the local level than at the state level. It was true that Balsdon and Brunner, like almost all others, found that older voters were less favorably disposed toward spending than those with children in schools at both the state and local level. (And it is not clear that the spending favored by voters with school-age children is the benchmark for efficiency.) The critical finding, however, is that older voters are more supportive at the local level for all schools, not just for the wealthy few.

The usual explanation for the elder-voter phenomenon is financial: childless voters are motivated solely by the capitalization effect, which they realize when they move (Brueckner and Joo 1991). I am skeptical of this as a sole explanation for two reasons. One is that the fraction of home-buyers with children has been going down in recent years. As a result, the capitalization of school quality in home values should be of diminishing importance in the housing market. Moreover, differences among school district taxes and spending have become less, not greater, so there should be less concern about tax capitalization. But, as sources cited in section 2.1 indicate, the capitalization effect seems as robust in studies using very recent sales as it was forty years ago, when many more homebuyers had children in tow.

The other reason for my skepticism is that school districts' educational quality seems to be overcapitalized. Recent studies have shown that home values seem too high in better districts relative to the apparent value-added by local schools (Bayer, Ferreira, and McMillan 2007). This suggests that there is some quality about school districts besides education that appeals to homebuyers. One answer to the "overcapitalization" puzzle is that higher school spending or test scores are signals to buyers about the existence of a high-class community (Jesse Rothstein 2006). It is not the schools, goes this argument; it is the snooty zoning laws and other restrictions that are really the attraction to those desiring an exclusive residential enclave. But that role for school districts seems too indirect. Homebuyers do not need to check school records to find high-income communities. They can look at the census data on local income (available from their real estate salesperson) if they cannot discern it from a quick drive around the community.

School districts, on my account, provide benefits to existing residents well before they sell their homes. The elderly benefit because schools augment their community-specific social capital. The childless gain from this because residents with school-age children create a network from which all residents gain. Economics researchers have sometimes expressed surprise that the elderly and other childless do not migrate to the lowest-cost school districts. The costs of moving are said to be the main barrier to such sorting.

It could be, though, that childless households do not want to relinquish the social capital they have in their own district. That could, of course, be called a moving cost, but that's very much the point. Elderly residents who do not move for this reason do not want to trash their local schools. Their reluctance to sell their homes where social capital is high can help explain why the school district premium is larger than would be expected if it was only about education. Communities with "good schools" also have more social capital, and this benefits the elder voters as much as the younger voters.

6.21 Charter Schools Build Inner-City Social Capital

I argued in earlier sections that the "big reform" movements have not achieved their goals. The school finance equalization movement did succeed in achieving more equal expenditures—legislative defiance of the courts is hard on a state's bond rating—but this has done little to increase educational resources for the inner-city minorities that the lawyers originally wanted to help (Rueben and Murray 2008). Serious evaluations of these reforms find almost no gains in student achievement after their implementation (Husted and Kenny 2000).

Perhaps because of its meager results, the school-finance litigation movement has changed its goals somewhat. Instead of seeking to equalize property tax bases or per-pupil expenditures, many recent cases have sought to insure an "adequate" education for all public-school children (Peter Schrag 2003). This in principle could direct more resources to inner-city schools despite their sometimes larger tax bases and expenditures. In *Campaign for Fiscal Equity v. New York*, 744 N.Y.S.2d 130 (2003), New York's highest court ordered the legislature to increase state aid to New York City's schools, despite the fact that the city spends more per pupil than the average for the rest of the state. But many other state courts continue to embrace the equalization schemes of the original *Serrano* advocates. Clothing their decisions in the new language of "adequacy" does little to hide the fact that judicial supervision of public education undermines the bottom-up self-governance that continues to be a one of the virtues of public education (Fischel 2002).

Following the defeat of statewide voucher proposals in 2000, school-choice advocates also have revised their game plan. Instead of sweeping, statewide reforms, voucher advocates have become more selective in their goals (d'Entremont and Huerta 2007). Experiments in vouchers continue in large cities. The evidence that these plans improved education is complicated and contested—one has to account for the reaction of public schools as well as the voucher-receiving schools. Summarizing her analysis of three modest-sized voucher programs in Arizona, Michigan, and Milwaukee, Wisconsin, Caroline Hoxby (2003, 339) concluded that "regular public schools increased productivity by raising achievement, not by lowering spending while maintaining achievement." Howell and Peterson (2006) present a largely upbeat view as well as an accessible description of the evidence. They find in particular that African American students get the most benefit from voucher programs. Rouse and Barrow (2009) are more guarded, issuing what might be called a Scotch verdict on the evidence: not proved.

The other modification of the school-choice movement has been to embrace charter schools, which had previously been disdained as not offering enough choice and being beholden to the public-school establishment. Charter schools are created by contracts with government. They receive public funds and agree to educate students along certain lines and achieve certain goals. They are usually exempt from many of the regular school district's rules for hiring and management, but their life expectancy is determined by their continuing success in meeting their goals. Charter schools are typically governed by parent groups, and a considerable minority are run by for-profit teaching corporations. Many appeal to distinct ethnic or linguistic groups, which has caused some controversy (*New York Times*, January 12, 2009). They currently enroll about one million students. This is about the same number as are said to be homeschooled, and vastly more than the approximately fifty thousand students who receive vouchers (d'Entremont and Huerta 2007, 41). Although one million is only 2 percent of the school-age population, it represents a phenomenal growth for charter schools since their inception in Minnesota in 1990.

Charter-school students are usually drawn from the school district in which they are located, and the district often has some control over their establishment. Out-of-district students are sometimes allowed to apply to charter schools, but most administrative rules give preference to students who reside in the local district. This is critical to their success, in my opinion, as it means that successful charter schools can add to the home values and to the community-specific social capital of a single district. If charter schools were in practice open to all comers, the ability of a locale to benefit from their success would be limited, and so would local support for charter schools.

Most charter-school enrollment has been in central cities (Ryan and Heise 2002). Suburban districts have been reluctant to accommodate them, as they regard them as unwanted competition for what most suburban residents regard as satisfactory schools and because, as I have argued, they would undermine the social-capital role of public schools. Central-city districts have been more receptive, most likely because charter schools are seen as the best way to improve schools and attract city-inclined households to send their children to public schools. Charter schools are thus the mild-mannered heroes of the school-choice movement. Like many low-key heroes, their success is not flashy. The evidence that they improve test scores is even more difficult to confirm than the effects of vouchers.

One finding, however, seems to be widely accepted: *parents* are more satisfied with their children's schools in both charter schools and the much smaller group of voucher-financed schools (Rouse and Barrow 2009, 34). This suggests that vouchers and charter schools are contributing to community social capital in the cities that have adopted them. For the larger districts, then, vouchers and charter schools may *increase* local social capital because of the greater parental involvement in private-school activities and governance. Mark Schneider et al. (1997) found from a study in New York and New Jersey that intradistrict school-choice programs did increase parental social capital.

Parental satisfaction with charter schools also represents an example of ongoing political adaptation in American public education. Oversized school districts are almost impossible to break up, and full-scale privatization of education is politically unacceptable. Charter schools represent an intermediate, largely homegrown way of mitigating the effects of oversize and often-dysfunctional city school districts. No one can foresee how far this reform movement will go—perhaps it will lead to a more permanent decentralization, perhaps it will fall back into the arms of the big-city bureaucracy—but the charter movement should be seen as another in a long line of local government responses to the evolving demands of education.

6.22 Conclusion: Places Trump Placelessness

This chapter asks why Americans prefer locally managed public schools over the apparently more rational alternatives of subsidies to private education or direct control of schools by the state. The most persuasive of the purely economic explanations is the influence of home values on local voters. Many studies have found that voters in better school districts are more supportive of local public schools. They don't want a general system of vouchers, and they don't want to surrender local control to state authorities, even when very little fiscal autonomy remains. But capitalization explains *differences* in property values. It explains why community A with good schools would vote by a greater margin against vouchers than community B, which has mediocre schools. But it does not explain why voters in both A and B as well as the rest of the alphabet of communities would almost always reject voucher proposals and struggle mightily against other forces that would erode local autonomy.

The gravitational force that holds Americans to local public school districts requires more than incremental explanations. I have proposed one in this chapter: local voters like their public schools because they are the social glue that holds the community together. Propositions like this are difficult to prove with the ordinary tools of economics. The circumstantial evidence assembled in this chapter is broadly supportive of my hypothesis: social capital does appear to be more robust in states with more intimate school districts. Residents of smaller districts in California were more attached to public schools—as shown by their disproportionate opposition to vouchers—than residents of larger school districts. Social capital's twentieth-century rise and decline closely parallel the fraction of school-age children in the population. And surveys indicate that families with more at-home children participate more actively in their communities.

This chapter has touched on two contemporary trends that could undermine the relevance of school districts. The school-finance litigation movement has had considerable success in reallocating fiscal authority, but it has, contrary to expectations, done little to undermine public attachment to their local school districts. The failure of large-scale voucher reforms is likewise evidence that voters prefer local districts. The relative success of charter schools (compared with vouchers) is, in my mind, confirmation of the importance of place-based school reforms.

Charter schools have been most popular with voters and parents in the problematic, oversize school districts of large central cities. The extreme difficulty of breaking up these oversize districts has led voters not to support vouchers, which would embrace placelessness, but to create within-district charter schools. These schools offer central-city residents the benefits of participation in their schools and their governance. The scarcity of charter schools in suburban districts is evidence that residents there are satisfied with their local school districts.

I have ignored completely two other trends, homeschooling and Web-based education. I think it is unlikely that either of these will displace school districts as the dominant organization of primary and secondary education in the United States. Their common element is placelessness. Students and their parents are disconnected from their other political community. For some, this rootlessness may be a benefit—they are indifferent or even hostile to the local community. But I think the number of such people is relatively small. For most people, disconnecting with their local schools is the product of poor compromises. They prefer to keep themselves and their neighbors in the local school district. No one wants to put a fork in it.

References

Section numbers indicate location within this book.

Able, J. F. 1923. *Consolidation of Schools and Transportation.* Bulletin 41, U.S. Bureau of Education. §3.15

Akagi, Roy Hidemichi. 1924. *The Town Proprietors of the New England Colonies; a Study of their Development, Organization, Activities and Controversies, 1620– 1770.* Philadelphia: Press of the University of Pennsylvania. §2.4

Alesina, Alberto, Reza Baqir, and Caroline Hoxby. 2004. "Political Jurisdictions in Heterogeneous Communities." *Journal of Political Economy* 112:348–96. §§5.8, 5.9, 5.12, 5.17, 5.19

Alexander, Carter. 1921. "Comparative State School Aids." *Elementary School Journal* 21:522–28. §3.2

Allard, Scott W., Nancy Burns, and Gerald Gamm. 1998. "Representing Urban Interests." *Studies in American Political Development* 12:267–302. §3.13

Allcott, Hunt, Dean Karlan, Markus M. Mobius, Tanya S. Sosenblatt, and Adam Szeidl. 2007. "Community Size and Network Closure." *American Economic Review, Papers and Proceedings* 97:80–85. §6.11

Anderson, Wilbert L. 1906. *The Country Town.* New York: Baker and Taylor. §3.4

Angus, David L., Jeffrey E. Mirel, and Maris A. Vinovskis. 1988. "Historical Development of Age-Stratification in Schooling." *Teachers College Record* 90:211–36. §§2.12, 3.6, 3.21

Bachman, Frank P. 1933. "Present Status of Elementary School Teaching." *Peabody Journal of Education* 10:281–92. §§2.15, 3.3

Baicker, Katherine, and Nora Gordon. 2006. "The Effect of State Education Finance Reform on Total Local Resources." *Journal of Public Economics* 90:1519–35. §6.4

Balsdon, Edward M., and Eric J. Brunner. 2004. "Intergenerational Conflict and the Political Economy of School Spending." *Journal of Urban Economics* 56:369–88. §6.20

Banzhaf, H. Spencer, and Garima Bhalla. 2008. "Do Households Value School Effectiveness? A Natural Experiment." Working paper, Department of Economics, Georgia State University. §6.16

Barber, Marshall A. 1953. *The School House at Prairie View*. Lawrence: University Press of Kansas. §2.12

Barron, Hal S. 1992. "And the Crooked Shall Be Made Straight." *Journal of Social History* 2:81–104. §2.11

———. 1997. *Mixed Harvest: The Second Great Transformation in the Rural North, 1870–1930*. Chapel Hill: University of North Carolina Press. §§3.12, 3.14, 3.17

Barzel, Yoram, and Tim R. Sass. 1990. "The Allocation of Resources by Voting." *Quarterly Journal of Economics* 105:745–71. §2.2

Battersby, Sarah, and William A. Fischel. 2007. "The Competitive Structure of Urban School Districts in the United States." Working paper, Dartmouth College Economics Department. §5.9

Baxter, Donald Weir 1959. "The History of Public Education in Daggett County, Utah and Adjacent Areas." Masters thesis, Department of Educational Administration, Brigham Young University. §2.5

Bayer, Patrick, Fernando Ferreira, and Robert McMillan. 2007. "A Unified Framework for Measuring Preferences for Schools and Neighborhoods." *Journal of Political Economy* 115:558–638. §6.20

Beadie, Nancy. 2008. "Tuition Funding for Common Schools: Education Markets and Market Regulation in Rural New York, 1815–1850." *Social Science History* 32:107–33. §2.20

Becker, Gary S. 1964. *Human Capital: A Theoretical and Empirical Analysis, with Special Reference to Education*. New York: Columbia University Press. §6.1

———. 1981. *A Treatise on the Family*. Cambridge: Harvard University Press. §6.19

Bedard, Kelly, and Elizabeth Dhuey. 2008. "Is September Better than January? The Effect of Minimum School Entry Age Laws on Adult Earnings." Working paper, Department of Economics, University of California, Santa Barbara. §4.14

Benson, Charles S. 1961. *The Economics of Public Education*. Boston: Houghton Mifflin. §6.1

Bergstrom, Theodore C., Daniel L. Rubinfeld, and Perry Shapiro. 1982. "Micro-Based Estimates of Demand Functions for Local School Expenditures." *Econometrica* 50:1183–205. §6.20

Berkman, Michael B., and Eric Plutzer. 2005. *Ten Thousand Democracies: Politics and Public Opinion in America's School Districts*. Washington: Georgetown University Press. §§3.17, 5.20, 6.20

Berry, Christopher, and William Howell. 2007. "Accountability and Local Elections: Rethinking Retrospective Voting." *Journal of Politics* 69:844–58. §3.17

Berry, Christopher, and Martin West. 2005. "Growing Pains: The School Consolidation Movement and Student Outcomes." Working paper, Harris School of Public Policy, University of Chicago. §3.21

Black, Sandra E. 1999. "Do Better Schools Matter? Parental Valuation of Elementary Education." *Quarterly Journal of Economics* 114:577–99. §6.14

Blair, John P., and Samuel R. Staley. 1995. "Quality Competition and Public Schools: Further Evidence." *Economics of Education Review* 14:193–98. §§5.10, 5.12

Boaz, David. 2001. "Unions vs. Education: Teachers Unions Beat the Latest Reform Initiative." *National Review*, November 20, 2001. §6.18

Boex, L. F. Jameson, and Jorge Martinez-Vazquez. 1998. "Structure of School District in Georgia: Economies of Scale and Determinants of Consolidation." Report No. 16, Andrew Young School of Policy Studies, Georgia State University. §§5.7, 5.9

Bogart, William T., and Brian A. Cromwell. 1997. "How Much More Is a Good School District Worth?" *National Tax Journal* 50:215–32. §6.14

Bolton, Charles C. 2000. "Mississippi's School Equalization Program, 1945–1954: "A Last Gasp to Try to Maintain a Segregated Educational System." *Journal of Southern History* 66:781–814. §§5.6, 5.8

Bond, Horace Mann. 1932. "Negro Education: A Debate in the Alabama Constitutional Convention of 1901." *Journal of Negro Education* 1:49–59. §5.5

———. 1934. *The Education of the Negro in the American Social Order*. Reprint, New York: Octagon Books, 1966. §§3.21, 5.6

Boozer, Michael, and Cecilia Rouse. 2001. "Intraschool Variation in Class Size: Patterns and Implications." *Journal of Urban Economics* 50:163–89. §6.1

Botstein, Leon. 2000. "Why Local Control?" *New York Times*, September 19, p. A31. §6.2

Bradbury, Katharine L., Karl E. Case, and Christopher Mayer. 2001. "Property Tax Limits, Local Fiscal Behavior, and Property Values: Evidence from Massachusetts under Proposition 2 1/2." *Journal of Public Economics* 80:287–311. §2.1

Brasington, David M. 2004. "House Prices and the Structure of Local Government: An Application of Spatial Statistics." *Journal of Real Estate Finance and Economics* 29:211–31. §6.8

Brasington, David, and Donald R. Haurin. 2006. "Educational Outcomes and House Values: A Test of the Value Added Approach." *Journal of Regional Science* 46:245–68. §2.1

Brueckner, Jan K., and Man-Soo Joo. 1991. "Voting with Capitalization." *Regional Science and Urban Economics* 21:453–67. §6.20

Brunner, Eric J., and Jon Sonstelie. 1997. "Coping with *Serrano*: Voluntary Contributions to California's Local Public Schools." *1996 Proceedings of the Eighty-Ninth Annual Conference on Taxation*. Washington: National Tax Association. §6.4

———. 2003. "Homeowners, Property Values, and the Political Economy of the School Voucher." *Journal of Urban Economics* 54:239–57. §6.8

———. 2006 "California's School Finance Reform: An Experiment in Fiscal Federalism." In *The Tiebout Model at Fifty*, ed. William A. Fischel, 55–93. Cambridge: Lincoln Institute of Land Policy. §§6.5, 6.16

Brunner, Eric J., Jon Sonstelie, and Mark Thayer. 2001. "Capitalization and the Voucher: An Analysis of Precinct Returns from California's Proposition 174." *Journal of Urban Economics* 50:517–36. §6.5

Bullock, Henry A. 1967. *A History of Negro Education in the South: From 1619 to the Present*. Cambridge: Harvard University Press. §§5.5, 5.6

Burchfield, Marcy, Henry G. Overman, Diego Puga, and Matthew A. Turner. 2006 "Causes of Sprawl: A Portrait from Space." *Quarterly Journal of Economics* 121:351–97. §5.9

Burton, David L. 2000. *A History of the Rural Schools in Greene County, Missouri*. Springfield: University of Missouri Extension Center. §§3.8, 3.19

California Department of Education. 2006. *District Organization Handbook*. Sacramento: California Department of Education. §6.18

Campbell, Macy. 1927. *Rural Life at the Crossroads*. Boston: Ginn and Company. §§2.16, 3.3, 5.4

Campbell, Roald F., Luvern L. Cunningham, Raphael O. Nystrand, and Michael D. Usdan. 1990. *The Organization and Control of American Schools*. 6th ed. New York: Macmillan. §§3.13, 5.7, 5.13, 5.20

Carlson, Avis. 1979. *Small World . . . Long Gone*. Yarmouth: John Curley and Associates. §3.10

Carney, Mabel. 1912. *Country Life and the Country School*. Chicago: Row, Peterson. §2.10

Carrington, Paul D. 1973. "Financing the American Dream: Equality and School Taxes." *Columbia Law Review* 73:1227–60. §6.4

Carstensen, Vernon. 1962. "A Century of the Land-Grant Colleges." *Journal of Higher Education* 33:30–37. §2.7

Cascio, Elizabeth, Damon Clark, and Nora Gordon. 2008. "Education and the Age Profile of Literacy into Adulthood." *Journal of Economic Perspectives* 22:47–70. §4.15

Cascio, Elizabeth, Nora Gordon, Ethan Lewis, and Sarah Reber. 2008. "From *Brown* to Busing." *Journal of Urban Economics* 64:296–325. §6.3

Catterall, James S. 1982. "The Politics of Education Vouchers." PhD diss., School of Education, Stanford University. §6.5

Cheney, May L. 1888. "The Schools of California." *Overland Monthly* 12:82–87. §§2.12, 3.13, 4.9

Chubb, John E., and Terry M. Moe. 1990. *Politics, Markets, and America's Schools*. Washington: Brookings Institution. §6.2

Church, Robert L., and Michael W. Sedlak. 1976. *Education in the United States: An Interpretive History*. New York: Free Press. §§4.4, 4.10

Coffe, Hilde, and Benny Geys. 2005. "Institutional Performance and Social Capital: An Application to the Local Government Level." *Journal of Urban Affairs* 27:485–501. §6.10

Coleman, James S., and Thomas Hoffer. 1987. *Public and Private High Schools: The Impact of Communities*. New York: Basic Books. §6.7

Conant, James B. 1959a. *The American High School Today: A First Report to Interested Citizens*. New York: McGraw-Hill. §3.21

————. 1959b. *The Child, the Parent, and the State.* Cambridge: Harvard University Press. §3.21

Coons, John E., William H. Clune III, and Stephen D. Sugarman. 1970. *Private Wealth and Public Education.* Cambridge: Harvard University Press. §6.5

Coons, John E., and Stephen D. Sugarman. 1978. *Education by Choice: The Case for Family Control.* Berkeley: University of California Press. §6.5

Cooper, Harris, Barbara Nye, Kelly Charlton, James Lindsay, and Scott Greathouse. 1996. "The Effects of Summer Vacation on Achievement Test Scores: A Narrative and Meta-Analytic Review." *Review of Educational Research* 66:227–68. §4.1

Cordier, Mary H. 1992. *Schoolwomen of the Prairies and Plains: Personal Narratives from Iowa, Kansas, and Nebraska, 1860s–1920s.* Albuquerque: University of New Mexico Press. §2.15

Courant, Paul N., and Susanna Loeb. 1997. "Centralization of School Finance in Michigan." *Journal of Policy Analysis and Management* 16:114–36. §6.5

Courchesne, Gary L. 1979. "The Growth of Public Education in Holyoke, 1850 to 1873." *Historical Journal of Western Massachusetts* 7:15–24. §§2.19, 4.11

Cremin, Lawrence A. 1965. *The Wonderful World of Ellwood Patterson Cubberley: An Essay on the Historiography of American Education.* New York: Bureau of Publications, Teachers College, Columbia University. §3.11

————. 1970. *American Education: The Colonial Experience, 1607–1783.* New York: Harper and Row. §§2.4, 2.16, 2.19

————. 1980. *American Education: The National Experience, 1783–1876.* New York: Harper and Row. §§2.17, 2.19

Cuban, Larry. 1984. *How Teachers Taught: Constancy and Change in American Classrooms, 1890–1980.* New York: Longman. §§2.12, 3.8

Cubberley, Ellwood P. 1914. *Rural Life and Education: A Study of the Rural-School Problem as a Phase of the Rural Life Problem.* Boston: Houghton Mifflin. §§3.3, 3.16, 4.12, 5.7

————. 1919. *Public Education in the United States: A Study and Interpretation of American Educational History.* Boston: Houghton Mifflin. §§2.20, 2.21, 3.6, 3.8, 3.11, 5.16, 6.3

Cunha, Flavio, and James Heckman. 2007. "The Technology of Skill Formation." *American Economic Review* 97:31–47. §4.15

Dabney, Charles W. 1936. *Universal Education in the South.* Chapel Hill: University of North Carolina Press. §§3.4, 3.21

Dafflon, Bernard. 2003. *Fiscal Federalism in Switzerland.* University of Fribourg, Switzerland. §4.8

David, Paul A. 1985. "Clio and the Economics of Qwerty." *American Economic Review* 75:332–37. §4.2

David, Paul T., and Ralph Eisenberg. 1961. *Devaluation of the Urban and Suburban Vote.* Charlottesville: Bureau of Public Administration, University of Virginia. §3.13

Davis, Calvin O. 1916. "High School Standings of Pupils from Graded and Ungraded Elementary Schools." *Educational Administration and Supervision* 2:159–74. §3.10

Davison, Oscar W. 1950. "Education at Statehood." *Chronicles of Oklahoma* 28:63–80. §§2.9, 2.16, 5.12

Day, Jennifer C., and Amie Jamieson. 2003. *School Enrollment: 2000.* Census 2000 Brief C2KBR-26. Washington: U.S. Census Bureau. §4.3

Dehring, Carolyn A., Craig A. Depken, and Michael R. Ward. 2008. "A Direct Test of the Homevoter Hypothesis." *Journal of Urban Economics* 64:155–70. §2.1

Denenberg, Dennis. 1979. "The Missing Link: New England's Influence on Early National Education Policies." *New England Quarterly* 52:219–33. §2.4

d'Entremont, Chad, and Luis A. Huerta. 2007. "Irreconcilable Differences? Education Vouchers and the Suburban Response." *Educational Policy* 21:40–72. §6.21

Donald, David Herbert. 1995. *Lincoln.* New York: Simon & Schuster. §2.17

Donohue, John J., III, James J. Heckman, and Petra E. Todd. 2002. "The Schooling of Southern Blacks: The Roles of Legal Activism and Private Philanthropy, 1910–1960." *Quarterly Journal of Economics* 117:225–68. §5.8

Douglas, Davison M. 1995. *Reading, Writing and Race: The Desegregation of the Charlotte Schools.* Chapel Hill: University of North Carolina Press. §§5.6, 5.7

———. 2005. *Jim Crow Moves North: The Battle over Northern School Segregation, 1865–1954.* Cambridge: Cambridge University Press. §§2.21, 5.8

Downes, Thomas A., and Jeffrey E. Zabel. 2002. "The Impact of School Characteristics on House Prices: Chicago 1987–1991." *Journal of Urban Economics* 52:1–25 §§2.1, 6.14

Driscoll, Donna, Dennis Halcoussis, and Shirley Svorny. 2003. "School District Size and Student Performance." *Economics of Education Review* 22:193–201. §6.16

Duncombe, William, and John Yinger. 2007. "Does School District Consolidation Cut Costs?" *Education Finance and Policy* 2:341–75. §5.9

Dye, Jane Lawler. 2008. *Fertility of American Women: 2006.* Current Population Reports, P20–558. U.S. Census Bureau. §6.12

Easterlin, Richard A., George Alter, and Gretchen A. Condran. 1978. "Farms and Farm Families in Old and New Areas: The Northern States in 1860." In *Family and Population in Nineteenth Century America*, ed. Tamara K. Hareven and Maris A. Vinovskis, 22–84. Princeton: Princeton University Press. §2.21

Edwards, Newton, and Herman G. Richey. 1938. *The Extent of Equalization Secured Through State School Funds.* Staff Report No. 6, U.S. Advisory Commission on Education. Washington: Superintendent of Documents. §6.3

Eggleston, Edward. 1871. *The Hoosier Schoolmaster.* New York: Orange Judd. §2.13

Elazar, Daniel J. 1988. "Land and Liberty in American Society: The Land Ordinance of 1785 and the Northwest Ordinance of 1787." *Publius* 18:1–29. §2.6

Ellsworth, Clayton S. 1956. "The Coming of Rural Consolidated Schools to the Ohio Valley, 1892–1912." *Agricultural History* 30:119–28. §§3.3, 3.9

Elmore, Richard F., and Milbrey W. McLaughlin. 1982. *Reform and Retrenchment: The Politics of California School Finance Reform.* Cambridge: Ballinger. §6.4

Ely, James W., Jr. 1992. *The Guardian of Every Other Right: A Constitutional History of Property Rights.* New York: Oxford University Press. §2.10

Fairfax, Sally K., Jon A. Souder, and Gretta Goldenman. 1992. "The School Trust Lands: A Fresh Look at Conventional Wisdom." *Environmental Law* 22:797–910. §§2.5, 2.9

Faragher, John M. 1986. *Sugar Creek: Life on the Illinois Prairie.* New Haven: Yale University Press. §§2.5, 2.7, 5.5

Fennell, Lee Anne. 2001. "Beyond Exit and Voice: User Participation in the Production of Local Public Goods." *Texas Law Review* 80:1–87. §6.6

Fernandez, Raquel, and Richard Rogerson. 1996. "Income Distribution, Communities, and the Quality of Public Education." *Quarterly Journal of Economics* 111:135–64. §6.2

———. 2003. "Equity and Resources: An Analysis of Education Finance Systems." *Journal of Political Economy* 111:858–97. §6.4

Ferrie, Joseph. 1997. "Migration to the Frontier in Mid-Nineteenth Century America: A Re-Examination of Turner's 'Safety-Valve'." Working paper, Department of Economics, Northwestern University. §3.7

Ferreyra, Maria Marta. 2007. "Estimating the Effects of Private School Vouchers in Multidistrict Economies." *American Economic Review* 97:789–817 §6.7

Feyrer, James, Bruce Sacerdote, and Ariel Dora Stern. 2008. "Will the Stork Return to Europe? Understanding Fertility within Developed Nations." *Journal of Economic Perspectives* 22:3–22. §§6.13, 6.19

Fields, Jason, and Lynne M. Casper. 2001. *America's Families and Living Arrangements.* U.S. Census Bureau, Current Population Report P20–537. Washington: U.S. Census Bureau. §6.12

Finkelstein, Barbara. 1989. *Governing the Young: Teacher Behavior in Popular Primary Schools in Nineteenth-Century United States.* Philadelphia: Falmer Press. §§2.12, 2.14, 2.21

Fischel, William A. 1981. "Is Local Government Structure in Large Urbanized Areas Monopolistic or Competitive?" *National Tax Journal* 34:95–104. §5.10

———. 1989. "Did *Serrano* Cause Proposition 13?" *National Tax Journal* 42:465–74. §6.5

———. 1992. "Property Taxation and the Tiebout Model: Evidence for the Benefit View from Zoning and Voting." *Journal of Economic Literature* 30:171–77. §6.4

———. 2001. *The Homevoter Hypothesis.* Cambridge: Harvard University Press. §§2.1, 5.13, 5.18, 6.2, 6.4

———. 2002. "School Finance Litigation and Property Tax Revolts: How Undermining Local Control Turns Voters Away from Public Education." In *Developments in School Finance, 1999–2000*, ed. William J. Fowler, Jr., 77–128. Washington: National Center for Education Statistics. §6.21

———. 2004a. "An Economic History of Zoning and a Cure for Its Exclusionary Effects." *Urban Studies* 41:317–40. §5.16

———. 2004b. "Did John Serrano Vote for Proposition 13? A Reply to Stark and Zasloff, 'Tiebout and Tax Revolts: Did *Serrano* Really Cause Proposition 13'?" *UCLA Law Review* 51:887–932. §6.4

———. 2006a. "Why Voters Veto Vouchers: Public Schools and Community-Specific Social Capital." *Economics of Governance* 7:109–32. §6.10

———. 2006b. "Will I See You in September? An Economic Explanation for the Standard School Calendar." *Journal of Urban Economics* 5:236–51. §4.8

Fischer, Claude S. 2002. "Ever-More Rooted Americans." *City and Community* 1:177–99. §§2.17, 4.11

Fishlow, Albert. 1966. "The Common School Revival: Fact or Fancy" In *Industrialization in Two Systems*, ed. Henry Rosovsky. New York: Wiley. §2.19

Fitzgerald, Deborah K. 2003. *Every Farm a Factory: The Industrial Ideal in American Agriculture*. New Haven: Yale University Press. §§3.3, 3.22

Fogel, Robert W. 1989. *Without Consent or Contract: The Rise and Fall of American Slavery*. New York: Norton. §5.5

———. 2005. "Changes in the Physiology of Aging during the Twentieth Century." National Bureau of Economic Research, Working Paper 11233. §4.15

Foght, Harold W. 1910. *The American Rural School: Its Characteristics, Its Future, and Its Problems*. New York: Macmillan. §§3.3, 3.4

Frantz, Douglas, and Catherine Collins. 1999. *Celebration, U.S.A.* New York: Holt. §2.4

Freitag, Markus 2006. "Bowling the State Back In: Political Institutions and the Creation of Social Capital." *European Journal of Political Research* 45:123–52. §6.10

Friedman, Lee S., and Michael Wiseman. 1978. "Understanding the Equity Consequences of School Finance Reform." *Harvard Educational Review* 48:193–226. §6.5

Friedman, Milton. 1962. *Capitalism and Freedom*. Chicago: University of Chicago Press. §6.2

Frost, Norman. 1921. *A Comparative Study of Achievement in Country and Town Schools*. Teachers College Contributions to Education No. 111. New York: Teachers College, Columbia University. §3.20

Fuller, Wayne E. 1982. *The Old Country School: The Story of Rural Education in the Middle West*. Chicago: University of Chicago Press. §§2.5, 2.9, 2.13, 2.19, 2.20, 3.1, 3.4, 3.9, 3.12, 3.16, 3.18, 3.21, 5.19

Galenson, David W. 1992. "Precedence and Wealth: Evidence from Nineteenth Century Utah." In *Strategic Factors in Nineteenth Century American Economic History*, ed. Claudia Goldin and Hugh Rockoff. Chicago: University of Chicago Press. §2.17

Garofano, Anthony, and Jennifer Sable. 2008. *Characteristics of the 100 Largest Public Elementary and Secondary School Districts in the United States: 2004–05* (NCES 2008–335). Washington: National Center for Education Statistics, Institute of Education Sciences, U.S. Department of Education. §5.1

Gates, Paul W. 1968. *History of Public Land Law Development*. Washington: U.S. Government Printing Office. §§2.2, 2.6, 2.7

Gaumnitz, Walter H. 1940. *Are the One-Teacher Schools Passing?* Pamphlet No. 92. Washington: U.S. Department of Interior, Office of Education. §§3.19, 5.3, 5.6

Glaab, Charles Nelson, and A. Theodore Brown. 1967. *A History of Urban America.* New York: Macmillan. §§3.7, 5.13

Glaeser, Edward L, and Bruce I. Sacerdote. 2000. "The Social Consequences of Housing." *Journal of Housing Economics* 9:1–23. §6.8

Glaeser, Edward, Bruce Sacerdote, and José Scheinkman. 2003. "The Social Multiplier." *Journal of the European Economic Association* 1:59–467. §6.10

Glasco, Laurence. 1978. "Migration and Adjustment in the Nineteenth-Century City: Occupation, Property, and Household Structure of Native-born Whites, Buffalo, New York, 1855." In *Family and Population in Nineteenth Century America,* ed. Tamara K. Hareven and Maris A. Vinovskis. Princeton: Princeton University Press. §2.21

Glines, Don E. 1995. *Year-Round Education: History, Philosophy, Future.* San Diego: National Association for Year-Round Education. §4.11

Gold, Kenneth M. 1997. "Mitigating Mental and Moral Stagnation": Summer Education and American Public Schools, 1840–1990." PhD diss., Department of History, University of Michigan. §§4.2, 4.4

———. 2002. *School's In: The History of Summer Education in American Public Schools.* New York: Peter Lang. §4.2

Goldin, Claudia. 1998. "America's Graduation from High School: The Evolution and Spread of Secondary Schooling in the Twentieth Century." *Journal of Economic History* 58:345–74. §§3.18, 5.16

Goldin, Claudia, and Lawrence F. Katz. 2003. "The 'Virtues' of the Past: Education in the First Hundred Years of the New Republic." NBER Working Paper 9958. §§2.22, 3.11

———. 2008. *The Race between Education and Technology.* Cambridge: Harvard University Press. §§1.4, 2.14, 2.17, 2.18, 2.20, 2.21, 4.12, 4.15, 6.0, 6.3

Gooderham, Marie E. 1977. *History of Granite School District, 1904–1976.* Salt Lake City: Granite School District. §§3.19, 5.18

Goodman, Allen G., and Thomas G. Thibodeau. 1998. "Housing Market Segmentation." *Journal of Housing Economics* 7:121–43. §2.1

Goodman, John L., Jr. 1993. "A Housing Market Matching Model of Seasonality in Geographic Mobility." *Journal of Real Estate Research* 8:117–37. §4.10

Goolsbee, Austan, and Peter J. Klenow. 2002. "Evidence on Learning and Network Externalities in the Diffusion of Home Computers." *Journal of Law and Economics* 45:317–44. §6.10

Gordon, Nora. 2002. "Essays in the Economics of Education." PhD diss., Harvard University, Economics Department. §3.1

Graham, Patricia Albjerg. 1974. *Community and Class in American Education, 1865–1918.* New York: Wiley. §§3.6, 3.8, 3.11, 3.20, 5.6

Greene, Margaret E., and Jerry A. Jacobs. 1992. "Urban Enrollments and the Growth of Schooling: Evidence from the U.S. Census Public Use Sample." *American Journal of Education* 101:29–59. §3.21

Gulliford, Andrew. 1991. *America's Country Schools*. Washington: Preservation Press. §4.2

Hamilton, Bruce W. 1975. "Zoning and Property Taxation in a System of Local Governments." *Urban Studies* 12:205–11. §§5.13, 6.3

Hanushek, Eric A. 1998. "Conclusions and Controversies about the Effectiveness of School Resources." *Federal Reserve Bank of New York Policy Review* (March): 11–27. §4.15

———. 2002. "Publicly Provided Education." In *Handbook of Public Economics*, ed. Alan J. Auerbach and Martin Feldstein. Amsterdam: North-Holland. §6.1

Hanushek, Eric A., John F. Kain, and Steven G. Rivkin. 2004. "Disruption versus Tiebout Improvement: The Costs and Benefits of Switching Schools." *Journal of Public Economics* 88:1721–46. §4.2

Hanushek, Eric A., and Dongwook Kim. 1995. "Schooling, Labor Force Quality, and Economic Growth." NBER Working Paper 5399. §4.15

Hanushek, Eric A., and Ludger Woessmann. 2008. "The Role of School Improvement in Economic Development." *Journal of Economic Literature* 46:607–68. §4.15

Harlan, Louis R. 1958. *Separate and Unequal: Public School Campaigns and Racism in the Southern Seaboard States 1901–1915*. Chapel Hill: University of North Carolina Press. §§5.6, 5.7, 5.8

Harris, Amy R., William N. Evans, and Robert M. Schwab. 2001. "Education Spending in an Aging America." *Journal of Public Economics* 81:449–72. §6.20

Heise, Michael. 1998. "Equal Educational Opportunity, Hollow Victories, and the Demise of School Finance Equity Theory: An Empirical Perspective and Alternative Explanation." *Georgia Law Review* 32:543–631. §6.4

Henke, Joseph T. 1986. "Financing Public Schools in California: The Aftermath of *Serrano v. Priest* and Proposition 13." *University of San Francisco Law Review* 21:1–39. §6.4

Henry, Nelson B., and Jerome G. Kerwin. 1938. *Schools and City Government*. Chicago: University of Chicago Press. §5.13

Herrick, Mary J. 1971. *The Chicago Schools: A Social and Political History*. Beverly Hills: Sage. §3.6

Hess, Frederick M. 2008. "Looking for Leadership: Assessing the Case for Mayoral Control of Urban School Systems." *American Journal of Education* 114:219–45. §5.16

Hibbard, Benjamin H. 1924. *A History of the Public Land Policies*. New York: Macmillan. §2.4

Hill, Robert S. 1988. "Federalism, Republicanism, and the Northwest Ordinance." *Publius* 18:41–52. §2.3

Hinsdale, Burke A. 1898. *Horace Mann and the Common School Revival in the United States*. New York: Charles Scribner's Sons. §§2.16, 3.6

Hirschman, Albert. 1970. *Exit, Voice and Loyalty: Responses to Decline in Firms, Organizations, and States*. Cambridge: Harvard University Press. §6.7

Homel, Michael W. 1990. "Two Worlds of Race? Urban Blacks and the Public Schools, North and South, 1865–1940." In *Southern Cities, Southern Schools*, ed. David N. Plank and Rick Ginsberg, 237–61. New York: Greenwood Press. §5.8

Hooker, Clifford P., and Van D. Mueller. 1970. *The Relationship of School District Organization to State Aid Distribution Systems.* Minneapolis: Educational Research and Development Council of the Twin Cities Metropolitan Area. §§3.1, 3.15, 3.21, 5.2, 5.7

Hosseini, Khaled. 2003. *The Kite Runner.* New York: Riverhead Books. §4.7

Houseman, Susan. 2007. "Outsourcing, Offshoring, and Productivity Measurement in U.S. Manufacturing." *International Labour Review* 146:61–80. §4.15

Howell, William G., and Paul E. Peterson. 2006. *The Education Gap: Vouchers and Urban Schools.* Washington: Brookings Institution. §6.21

Hoxby, Caroline M. 1996. "How Teachers' Unions Affect Education Production." *Quarterly Journal of Economics* 111:671–718. §5.9

———. 1999. "The Productivity of Schools and Other Local Public Goods Producers." *Journal of Public Economics* 74:1–30. §6.4

———. 2000. "Does Competition Among Public Schools Benefit Students and Taxpayers?" *American Economic Review* 90:1209–38. §§5.9, 5.10, 5.12, 6.16

———, ed. 2003. *The Economic Analysis of School Choice.* Chicago: University of Chicago Press for NBER. §6.21

Hoyt, William H. 1999. "Leviathan, Local Government Expenditures, and Capitalization." *Regional Science and Urban Economics* 29:155–71. §6.8

Huppert, George. *Public Schools in Renaissance France.* 1984. Urbana: University of Illinois Press. §4.0

Husted, Thomas A., and Lawrence W. Kenny. 2000. "Evidence on the Impact of State Government on Primary and Secondary Education and the Equity-Efficiency Tradeoff." *Journal of Law and Economics* 43:285–308. §6.21

Hyman, Harold M. 1986. *American Singularity: The 1787 Northwest Ordinance, the 1862 Homestead and Morrill Acts, and the 1944 G.I. Bill.* Athens: University of Georgia Press. §2.6

Iatarola, Patrice, and Leanna Stiefel. 2003. "Intradistrict Equity of Public Education Resources and Performance." *Economics of Education Review* 22:69–78. §6.3

Illinois Tax Commission. 1939. *Atlas of Taxing Units.* Chicago: Illinois Tax Commission and Works Progress Administration. §5.19

Iwamoto, Sumiko, and Keiko Yoshida. 1997. "School Refusal in Japan: The Recent Dramatic Increase in Incidence Is a Cause for Concern." *Social Behavior and Personality* 25:315–20. §4.14

Jahoda, Marie, Paul F. Lazarsfeld, and Hans Zeisel. 1933. *Marienthal: The Sociography of an Unemployed Community.* Trans. ed., Chicago: Aldine, Atherton, 1971. §6.13

Japan Cabinet Office. 2001. *Public Opinion Poll on What University Education Should Be Like in the Future.* Tokyo: Government of Japan Public Relations. §4.6

Jenning, Joe. 1927. "Origin of the Enrolment of the County White High Schools in Tennessee." *School Review* 35:530–33. §3.10

Johnson, Marcia L., and Jeffrey R. Johnson. 1996. "Daily Life in Japanese High Schools." *Japan Digest* (Indiana University National Clearinghouse for United States-Japan Studies) October. §4.6

Jorgenson, Lloyd P. 1956. *The Founding of Public Education in Wisconsin*. Madison: State Historical Society of Wisconsin. §§2.11, 3.13, 5.7

Kaestle, Carl F., ed. 1973. *Joseph Lancaster and the Monitorial School Movement: A Documentary History*. New York, Teachers College Press. §3.6

———. 1983. *Pillars of the Republic: Common Schools and American Society, 1780–1860*. New York: Hill and Wang. §§2.11, 2.16, 2.19, 2.20, 2.21, 3.14, 4.2, 4.9

Kaestle, Carl F., and Maris A. Vinovskis. 1980. *Education and Social Change in Nineteenth-Century Massachusetts*. Cambridge: Cambridge University Press. §2.22

Kahn, Matthew E., and Dora L. Costa. 2003. "Understanding the Decline in Social Capital, 1952–1998." *Kyklos* 56:17–46. §6.13

Kane, Thomas J., Douglas O. Staiger, and Gavin Samms. 2003. "School Accountability Ratings and Housing Values." In *Brookings-Wharton Papers on Urban Affairs*, ed. William Gale and Janet Pack, 83–137. Washington: Brookings Institution. §2.1

Kang, Changhui. 2007. "Classroom Peer Effects and Academic Achievement: Quasi-Randomization Evidence from South Korea." *Journal of Urban Economics* 61:458–95. §6.15

Kansas State Historical Society. 1893. *The Columbian History of Education in Kansas*. Topeka: Hamilton Printing. §3.8

Katz, Michael B. 1968. *The Irony of Early School Reform: Educational Innovation in Mid-Nineteenth Century Massachusetts*. Cambridge: Harvard University Press. §3.11

Kaufmann, Jeffrey Allen. 2000. "Teaching Practices of Iowa Rural Teachers in the 1930s: An Oral History Approach." PhD diss., University of Iowa. §3.18

Keith, Jeanette. 1995. *Country People of the New South: Tennessee's Upper Cumberland*. Chapel Hill: University of North Carolina Press. §§3.3, 3.19

Kendrick, Muriel S., ed. 1976. *Our Yesterdays: An Anthology of Memories and History*. Concord: New Hampshire Retired Teachers Association. §3.20

Kenny, Lawrence W., and Amy B. Schmidt. 1994. "The Decline in the Number of School Districts in the United States—1950–1980." *Public Choice* 79:1–18. §§3.1, 5.2

Key, V. O. 1949. *Southern Politics in State and Nation*. New York: Vintage Books. §5.5

Knight, Edgar W. 1913. *The Influence of Reconstruction on Education in the South*. New York: Teachers College, Columbia University. §5.5

Kremer, Michael, Nazmul Chaudhury, F. Halsey Rogers, Karthik Muralidharan, and Jeffrey Hammer. 2006. "Teacher Absence in India: A Snapshot." *Journal of the European Economic Association* 3:658–67. §2.13

Ladd, Helen F. 1975. "Local Education Expenditures, Fiscal Capacity, and the Composition of the Property Tax Base." *National Tax Journal* 28:145–58. §5.16

Ladd, Helen, and Sheila Murray. 2001. "Intergenerational Conflict Reconsidered: County Demographic Structure and the Demand for Public Education." *Economics of Education Review* 20:343–57. §6.20

Lassonde, Stephen. 2005. *Learning to Forget: Schooling and Family Life in New Haven's Working Class, 1870–1940*. New Haven: Yale University Press. §§2.19, 3.20

Lazerson, Marvin. 1971. *Origins of the Urban School: Public Education in Massachusetts, 1870–1915*. Cambridge: Harvard University Press. §3.21

Leight, Robert L., and Alice Duffy Rinehart. 1999. *Country School Memories: An Oral History of One-Room Schooling*. Westport: Greenwood Press. §§3.1, 3.10, 3.20

Leloudis, James L. 1996. *Schooling the New South: Pedagogy, Self, and Society in North Carolina, 1880–1920*. Chapel Hill: University of North Carolina Press. §§2.16, 3.8, 4.11, 5.5

Leslie, Bruce. 2001. "Where Have All the Academies Gone?" *History of Education Quarterly* 41:262–70. §§2.19, 3.8

Lieberman, Myron. 1960. *The Future of Public Education*. Chicago: University of Chicago Press. §6.2

———. 1997. *The Teacher Unions*. New York: Free Press. §3.14

Liebowitz, Stanley J., and Stephen E. Margolis. 1990. "The Fable of the Keys." *Journal of Law and Economics* 33:1–25. §4.2

Link, William A. 1986. *A Hard Country and a Lonely Place: Schooling, Society, and Reform in Rural Virginia, 1870–1920*. Chapel Hill: University of North Carolina Press. §§3.9, 3.17, 3.21, 5.5

———. 1992. *The Paradox of Southern Progressivism, 1880–1930*. Chapel Hill: University of North Carolina Press. §§3.3, 5.5, 5.6

Linklater, Ardo. 2002. *Measuring America: How and Untamed Wilderness Shaped the United States and Fulfilled the Promise of Democracy*. New York: Walker. §§2.4, 2.5, 2.10

Madison, James H. 1984. "John D. Rockefeller's General Education Board and the Rural School Problem in the Midwest, 1900–1930." *History of Education Quarterly* 24:181–99. §3.12

Mann, Horace. 1847. *Report of Massachusetts Board of Education*. Boston: Dutton and Wentworth. §2.16

Manning, Diane. 1990. *Hill Country Teacher: Oral Histories from the One-Room School and Beyond*. Boston: Twayne. §2.15

Margo, Robert A. 1990. *Race and Schooling in the South, 1880–1950: An Economic History*. Chicago: University of Chicago Press. §5.6

———. 1991. "Segregated Schools and the Mobility Hypothesis: A Model of Local Government Discrimination." *Quarterly Journal of Economics* 104:61–73. §5.6

Martin, John Frederick. 1991. *Profits in the Wilderness: Entrepreneurship and the Founding of New England Towns in the Seventeenth Century*. Chapel Hill: University of North Carolina Press. §2.4

Martinez-Vazquez, Jorge, Mark Rider, and Mary Beth Walker. 1997. "Race and the Structure of School Districts in the United States." *Journal of Urban Economics* 41:281–300. §5.8

Mauhs-Pugh, Thomas J. 2003. "12,000 Little Republics: Civic Apprenticeship and the Cult of Efficiency." Working paper, Green Mountain College, Poultney, Vermont. §2.20

Mayer, Christopher, and Christian Hilber. 2009. "Why Do Households without Children Support Local Public Schools? Linking House Price Capitalization to School Spending."*Journal of Urban Economics* 65:74–90. §6.20

Mazurkiewicz, Albert J. 1965. *First Grade Reading Using Modified Co-Basal versus the Initial Teaching Alphabet.* Bethlehem: Lehigh University. §4.13

McClusky, Frederick D. 1920a. "Introduction of Grading into the Public Schools of New England, Part I." *Elementary School Journal* 21:34–46. §3.6

———. 1920b "Introduction of Grading into the Public Schools of New England, Part II." *Elementary School Journal* 21:132–45. §3.6

McCurdy, Jack. 1974. "School Funding Ruling: A Setback for the Poor?" *Los Angeles Times*, June 30, pt. I, p. 3. §6.4

McGuffey, Verne. 1929. *Difference in the Activities of Teachers in Rural One-Teacher Schools and of Grade Teachers in Cities.* New York: Teachers College, Columbia University. §3.18

McKenzie, Evan. 1994. *Privatopia: Homeowner Associations and the Rise of Residential Private Government.* New Haven: Yale University Press. §2.2

McKinnon, Jesse. 2001. *The Black Population: 2000.* Census 2000 Brief. Washington: U.S. Bureau of the Census. §5.8.

McMillen, Bradley J. 2001. "A Statewide Evaluation of Academic Achievement in Year-Round Schools." *Journal of Educational Research* 95:67–74. §4.1

Meier, Kenneth J., Joseph Stewart, Jr., and Robert E. England. 1989. *Race, Class, and Education: The Politics of Second-Generation Discrimination.* Madison: University of Wisconsin Press. §5.8

Meltsner, Arnold J., Gregory W. Kast, John F. Kramer, and Robert T. Nakamura. 1973. *Political Feasibility of Reform in School Financing: The Case of California.* New York: Praeger. §6.4

Menefee-Libey, David, Benjamin Diehl, Keena Lipsitz, and Nadia Rahimtoola. 1997. "The Historic Separation of Schools from City Politics." *Education and Urban Society* 29:453–73. §5.13

Mieszkowski, Peter, and Edwin S. Mills. 1993. "The Causes of Metropolitan Suburbanization." *Journal of Economic Perspectives* 7:135–47. §6.13

Miller, Gary J. 1981. *Cities by Contract: The Politics of Municipal Incorporation.* Cambridge: MIT Press. §§5.13, 6.17

Miller, John E. 1998. *Becoming Laura Ingalls Wilder: The Woman Behind the Legend.* Columbia: University of Missouri Press. §§2.17, 3.4

Miller, Matt. 2008. "First, Kill All the School Boards." *Atlantic Monthly*, January. §6.2

Moe, Terry M. 2001. *Schools, Vouchers, and the American Public.* Washington: Brookings Institution. §§1.3, 6.2, 6.5

———. 2006. "Political Control and the Power of the Agent." *Journal of Law, Economics, and Organization* 22:1–29. §§5.9, 6.18

Moffitt, John C. 1946. *The History of Public Education in Utah.* Salt Lake City: Desert News Press. §§3.6, 3.13, 3.19, 5.2

Monroe, Paul, ed. 1913. *A Cyclopedia of Education.* New York: Macmillan. §2.19

———. 1940. *Founding of the American Public School System.* New York: Macmillan. §§2.10, 2.16, 2.20, 2.21

Motomura, Hiroshi. 1983. "Preclearance under Section Five of the Voting Rights Act." *North Carolina Law Review* 61:189–246. §5.8

Murray, Sheila E., William M. Evans, and Robert M. Schwab. 1998. "Education-Finance Reform and the Distribution of Education Resources." *American Economic Review* 88:789–812. §6.4

Myer, John W., David Tyack, Joan Nagel, and Audri Gordon. 1979. "Public Education as Nation-Building in America: Enrollments and Bureaucratization in the American States, 1870–1930." *American Journal of Sociology* 8:591–613. §§3.11, 4.11

Myrdahl, Gunnar. 1944. *An American Dilemma: The Negro Problem and Modern Democracy*. New York: Harper. §5.6

National Center for Education Statistics. 2004. *International Outcomes of Learning in Mathematics Literacy and Problem Solving: PISA 2003 Results From the U.S. Perspective*. NCES 2005–003. Washington: U.S. Department of Education. §4.15

National Commission on School District Reorganization. 1948. *Your School District*. Washington: National Education Association. §§3.5, 3.15, 3.16, 3.17

Nelson, Lowry. 1949. "The American Rural Heritage." *American Quarterly* 1:225–34. §2.10

Nelson, Margaret K. 1983. "From the One-Room Schoolhouse to the Graded School: Teaching in Vermont, 1910–1950." *Frontiers: A Journal of Women Studies* 7:14–20. §3.18

New Hampshire Department of Public Instruction. 1910. *Program of Studies for the Elementary Schools of New Hampshire*. 2d ed. Manchester: John B. Clarke. §3.20

New Hampshire State Board of Education. 1920. *Biennial Report*. Concord. §4.9

New Hampshire Superintendent of Public Instruction. 1880. *Forty-Fourth Annual Report*. Concord. §4.9

———. 1900. *Fifty-First Annual Report*. Concord. §3.9

Nicolaides, Becky M. 2002. *My Blue Heaven: Life and Politics in the Working-Class Suburbs of Los Angeles, 1920–1965*. Chicago: University of Chicago Press. §5.16

Oates, Wallace E. 1969. "The Effects of Property Taxes and Local Public Spending on Property Values: An Empirical Study of Tax Capitalization and the Tiebout Hypothesis." *Journal of Political Economy* 77:957–71. §§2.1, 6.3

Oliver, J. Eric. 2000. "City Size and Civic Involvement in Metropolitan America." *American Political Science Review* 94:361–73. §§6.7, 6.8

Olson, James C, and Ronald C. Naugh. 1997. *History of Nebraska*. 3d ed. Lincoln: University of Nebraska Press. §3.13

Onuf, Peter S. 1987. *Statehood and Union: A History of the Northwest Ordinance*. Bloomington: Indiana University Press. §§2.3, 2.6

O'Sullivan, Arthur, Terri A. Sexton, and Steven M. Sheffrin. 1995. *Property Taxes and Tax Revolts: The Legacy of Proposition 13*. Cambridge: Cambridge University Press. §6.4

Perlmann, Joel, and Robert A. Margo. 2001. *Women's Work? American Schoolteachers, 1650–1920*. Chicago: University of Chicago Press. §§2.14, 2.15

Peshkin, Alan. 1982. *The Imperfect Union: School Consolidation and Community Conflict*. Chicago: University of Chicago Press. §6.14

Pischke, Jørn-Steffan. 2003. "The Impact of Length of the School Year on Student Performance and Earnings: Evidence from the German Short School Years." NBER Working Paper 9964. §§4.8, 4.12

Post, Alan 1979. "Effects of Proposition 13 on the State of California." *National Tax Journal* 32 (June supplement):381–85. §6.5

Poterba, James M. 1997. "Demographic Structure and the Political Economy of Public Education." *Journal of Policy Analysis and Management* 16:48–66. §6.19

———. 1998. "Demographic Change, Intergenerational Linkages, and Public Education." *American Economic Review* 88:315–20. §6.19

Putnam, Robert D. 1995. "Tuning in, Tuning out: The Strange Disappearance of Social Capital in America." *PS: Political Science and Politics* 28:664–83. §6.11

———. 2000. *Bowling Alone: The Collapse and Revival of American Community*. New York: Simon and Schuster. §§6.6, 6.10, 6.11, 6.12, 6.13

———. 2001. "Social Capital: Measurement and Consequences." *Isuma, Canadian Journal of Policy Research* 2:41–51. §6.11

Racine, Philip N. 1990. "Public Education in the New South: A School System for Atlanta, 1868–1879." In *Southern Cities, Southern Schools*, ed. David N. Plank and Rick Ginsberg. New York: Greenwood Press. §5.6

Rakoff, Todd D. 2002. *A Time for Every Purpose: Law and the Balance of Life*. Cambridge: Harvard University Press. §4.4

Randall, Samuel S. 1851. *The Common School System of the State of New York*. Troy: Johnson and Davis. §2.21

———. 1871. *History of the Common School System of the State of New York*. New York: Ivison, Blakeman, Taylor, 1871. §2.20

Ravitch, Diane. 1974. *The Great School Wars: New York City, 1805–1973*. New York: Basic Books. §3.11

———. 1995. "The Search for Order and the Rejection of Conformity: Standards in American Education." In *Learning from the Past: What History Teaches Us About School Reform*, ed. Diane Ravitch and Maris Vinovskis, 167–90. Baltimore: Johns Hopkins University Press. §2.12

———. 2001. "American Traditions of Education." In *A Primer on America's Schools*, ed. Terry M. Moe, 1–14. Stanford: Hoover Institution Press. §3.11

Reavis, George H. 1920. *Factors Controlling Attendance in Rural Schools*. Teachers College, Columbia University Contributions to Education, No. 108. New York: Teachers College, Columbia University. §3.3

Reed, Douglas S. 2001. *On Equal Terms: The Constitutional Politics of Educational Opportunity*. Princeton: Princeton University Press. §6.3

Reed, Thomas Harrison. 1926. *Municipal Government in the United States*. New York: The Century Fund. §5.13

Reese, William J. 1995. *The Origins of the American High School*. New Haven: Yale University Press. §§2.16, 2.19, 3.6, 3.10, 3.13

———. 1998 "Urban School Reform in the Victorian Era." In *Hoosier Schools*, ed. William J. Reese, 29–52. Bloomington: Indiana University Press. §§3.6, 3.8

———. 2005. *America's Public Schools: From the Common School to "No Child Left Behind."* Baltimore: Johns Hopkins University Press. §§2.12, 2.21

Reichman, Uriel. 1976 "Residential Private Governments: An Introductory Survey." *University of Chicago Law Review* 43:253–306. §2.2

Reichley, A. James. 1970. *The Political Constitution of the Cities*. Englewood Cliffs: Prentice-Hall. §§3.13, 5.16

Reischauer, Edwin O., and Marius B. Jansen. 1995. *The Japanese Today: Change and Continuity*. Cambridge: Harvard University Press. §4.6

Reps, John W. 1965. *The Making of Urban America: A History of City Planning in the United States*. Princeton: Princeton University Press. §2.10

Reynolds, David R. 1999. *There Goes the Neighborhood: Rural School Consolidation at the Grass Roots in Early Twentieth-Century Iowa*. Iowa City: University of Iowa Press. §§2.18, 3.3, 3.8, 3.18, 4.9, 4.12

Rice, Thomas W. 2001. "Social Capital and Government Performance in Iowa Communities." *Journal of Urban Affairs* 23:375–89. §6.10

Richardson, D. S. 1883. "Putting in the Summer Professionally." *Overland Monthly and Out West Magazine*. August. §2.14

Richardson, John G. 1984. "Settlement Patterns and the Governing Structures of Nineteenth-Century School Systems." *American Journal of Education* 92:178–206. §5.5

Rickard, Garrett E. 1947. "Establishment of Graded Schools in American Cities. Part I." *Elementary School Journal* 67:575–85. §§3.6, 3.12

———. 1948. "Establishment of Graded Schools in American Cities. Part II." *Elementary School Journal* 68:326–35. §§3.6, 3.12

Romer, Thomas, Howard Rosenthal, and Vincent G. Munley. 1992. "Economic Incentives and Political Institutions: Spending and Voting in School Budget Referenda." *Journal of Public Economics* 49:1–33. §§5.9, 6.8

Rose, Heather, and Jon Sonstelie. 2004. "School Board Politics, District Size, and the Bargaining Power of Teachers' Unions." Working paper, Economics Department, University of California at Santa Barbara. §§5.4, 5.9, 6.18

Rosenberg, Gerald K. 1991. *The Hollow Hope: Can Courts Bring about Social Change?* Chicago: University of Chicago Press. §5.8

Rosenberry, Lois Kimball Mathews. 1909. *The Expansion of New England: The Spread of New England Settlement and Institutions to the Mississippi River, 1620–1865*. Boston: Houghton Mifflin. §§2.11, 5.7

Rosenbloom, Joshua L. 1996. "Was There a National Labor Market at the End of the Nineteenth Century? New Evidence on Earnings in Manufacturing." *Journal of Economic History* 56:626–56. §4.10

Rothstein, Jesse M. 2006. "Good Principals or Good Peers? Parental Valuation of School Characteristics, Tiebout Equilibrium, and the Incentive Effects of Competition among Jurisdictions." *American Economic Review* 96:1333–50. §6.20

Rouse, Cecilia E., and Lisa Barrow. 2009. "School Vouchers and Student Achievement: Recent Evidence, Remaining Questions." *Annual Review of Economics* 1: n.p. §6.21

Rueben, Kim, and Sheila Murray. 2008. "Racial Disparities in Education Finance: Going Beyond Equal Revenues." Brookings Discussion Paper No. 29. §§6.4, 6.21

Rutan, Douglas Edwin. 1996. "The History of the Meridian [Idaho] School District." EdD diss., University of Idaho. §5.4

Ryan, James E. 2004. "The Tenth Amendment and Other Paper Tigers: The Legal Boundaries of Education Governance." In *Who's in Charge Here? The Tangled Web of School Governance and Policy*, ed. Noel Epstein. Washington: Brookings Institution. §3.13

Ryan, James E., and Michael Heise. 2002. "The Political Economy of School Choice." *Yale Law Journal* 111:2043–136. §6.21

Sass, Tim R., and Stephan L. Mehay. 1995. "The Voting-Rights Act, District Elections, and the Success of Black Candidates in Municipal Elections." *Journal of Law and Economics* 38:367–92. §5.8

Schneider, Mark, Paul Teske, Melissa Marschall, and Christine Roch. 1997. "Institutional Arrangements and the Creation of Social Capital: The Effects of Public School Choice." *American Political Science Review* 91:82–93. §6.21

Schnore, Leo F., and Gene B. Petersen. 1958. "A Crowding Hemisphere: Population Change in the Americas." *Annals of the American Academy of Political and Social Science* 316:60–68. §3.3

Schoen, Robert, Kim J. Young, Constance A. Nathanson, Jason Fields, and Nan Marie Astone. 1997. "Why Do Americans Want Children?" *Population and Development Review* 23:333–58. §6.12

Schrag, Peter. 1998. *Paradise Lost: California's Experience, America's Future*. New York: New Press. §6.5

———. 2003. *Final Test: The Battle for Adequacy in America's Schools*. New York: New Press. §6.21

Segal, Lydia. 1997. "The Pitfalls of Political Decentralization and Proposals for Reform: The Case of New York City Public Schools." *Public Administration Review* 57:141–49. §6.16

Sher, Jonathan P., and Stuart A. Rosenfeld. 1977. *Public Education in Sparsely Populated Areas of the United States*. Washington: Department of Health, Education, and Welfare, Education Division, National Institute of Education. §3.11

Skandera, Hanna, and Richard Sousa. 2002. "Mobility and the Achievement Gap." *Hoover Digest* 2002:3. §4.11

Smith, Christian, and David Sikkink. 1999. "Is Private Schooling Privatizing?" *First Things* 92:16–20. §6.7

Smith, Marion Bush. 1938. *A Sociological Analysis of Rural Education in Louisiana*. Baton Rouge: Louisiana State University Press. §3.21

Smith, Maude W., Fern E. Bickford, Deland A. Davis, and Henry J. Otto. 1937. "Age-Grade and Grade-Progress Data for Children in One-Room Rural Schools." *Elementary School Journal* 37:336–43. §§3.21, 4.14

Smith, T. Lynn. 1966. "The Redistribution of the Negro Population of the United States, 1910–1960." *Journal of Negro History* 51:155–73. §5.7, 5.8

Snyder, John P. 1969. *The Story of New Jersey's Civil Boundaries, 1606–1968.* Trenton: Bureau of Geology and Topography. §3.16

Soltow, Lee, and Edward Steven. 1981. *The Rise of Literacy and the Common School in the United States: A Socioeconomic Analysis to 1870.* Chicago: University of Chicago Press. §§3.21, 4.2

Sonstelie, Jon. 1995. "School Finance Reform and the Voucher: An Analysis of Precinct Returns from California's Proposition 174." Working paper, Department of Economics, University of California, Santa Barbara. §6.9

Sonstelie, Jon, Eric Brunner, and Kenneth Ardon. 2000. *For Better or for Worse? School Finance Reform in California.* San Francisco: Public Policy Institute of California. §6.4

Sonstelie, Jon C., and Paul R. Portney. 1980. "Take the Money and Run: A Theory of Voting in Local Referenda." *Journal of Urban Economics* 8:187–95. §2.1

Sparkman, William E. 1994. "The Legal Foundations of Public School Finance." *Boston College Law Review* 35:569–95. §2.8

Spry, John A. 2005. "The Effects of Fiscal Competition on Local Property and Income Tax Reliance." *Topics in Economic Analysis and Policy* 5:1–18. §5.16

Stark, Kirk J. 1992. "Rethinking Statewide Taxation of Nonresidential Property for Public Schools." *Yale Law Journal* 102:805–34. §2.16

Starr, Edward C. 1926. *A History of Cornwall, Connecticut, a Typical New England Town.* New Haven: Tuttle, Morehouse & Taylor. §3.3

Stephan, Edward. 1995. *The Division of Territory in Society.* http://www.edstephan .org/Book/contents.html. §5.13

Strang, David. 1987. "The Administrative Transformation of American-Education: School-District Consolidation, 1938–1980." *Administrative Science Quarterly* 32:352–66. §§3.1, 3.11

Stratton, Joanna L. 1981. *Pioneer Women: Voices from the Kansas Frontier.* New York: Simon and Schuster. §§2.5, 2.22

Swett, John. 1900. *American Public Schools: History and Pedagogics.* New York: American Book Company. §2.15

Swift, Fletcher H. 1911. *A History of Public Permanent Common School Funds in the United States, 1795–1905.* New York: Holt. §§2.7, 2.9, 2.20

Swift, Samuel. 1859. *History of the Town of Middlebury.* Middlebury: A. H. Copeland. §2.11

Taylor, Howard C. 1922. *The Educational Significance of the Early Federal Land Ordinances.* New York: Columbia University Teachers College. §§2.2, 2.6, 2.7, 2.9

Taylor, Lori L. 1992. "Student Emigration and the Willingness to Pay for Public-Schools: A Test of the Publicness of Public High-Schools in the United-States." *Public Finance-Finances Publiques* 47:131–52. §6.1

Teaford, Jon C. 1979. *City and Suburb: The Political Fragmentation of Metropolitan America, 1850–1970.* Baltimore: Johns Hopkins University Press. §5.16

———. 1984. *The Unheralded Triumph: City Government in America, 1870–1900.* Baltimore: Johns Hopkins University Press. §3.11

Theobald, Paul. 1993. "Country School Curriculum and Governance: The One-Room School Experience in the Nineteenth-Century Midwest." *American Journal of Education* 101:116–39. §§2.5, 2.14

Thornbrough, Emma Lou. 1965. *Indiana in the Civil War Era.* Indianapolis: Indiana Historical Society. §2.16

Thrun, F. M. 1933. *Rural School Organization in Michigan.* Special Bulletin No. 229, Agricultural Experiment Station, Michigan State College, East Lansing. §3.9

Tiebout, Charles M. 1956. "A Pure Theory of Local Expenditures." *Journal of Political Economy* 64:416–24. §§2.1, 5.0, 5.9, 6.2, 6.3, 6.4, 6.7

Tomeh, Aida K. 1964. "Informal Group Participation and Residential Patterns." *American Journal of Sociology* 70:28–35. §6.7

Tyack, David B., ed. 1967a. *Turning Points in American Educational History.* Lexington: Xerox College Publications. §2.12

———. 1967b. "The Common School Crusade." In *Turning Points in American Educational History*, ed. David B. Tyack. Lexington: Xerox College Publications. §2.19

———. 1974. *The One Best System: A History of American Urban Education.* Cambridge: Harvard University Press. §3.11

Tyack, David B., and Larry Cuban. 1995. *Tinkering Toward Utopia: A Century of Public School Reform.* Cambridge: Harvard University Press. §§1.0, 2.4, 3.5, 3.12, 4.13

Tyack, David B., and Elisabeth Hansot. 1992. *Learning Together: A History of Coeducation in American Public Schools.* New York: Russell Sage Foundation. §2.11, 2.14

Tyack, David, and Thomas James. 1986. "State Government and American Public Education: Exploring the 'Primeval Forest.'" *History of Education Quarterly* 26:39–69. §§3.11, 3.13

———. 1987. "Education for a Republic: Federal Influence on Public Schooling in the Nation's First Century." In *This Constitution: A Bicentennial Chronicle.* Washington: American Political Science Association and American Historical Association. §2.8

Tyack, David B., Thomas James, and Aaron Benavot. 1987. *Law and the Shaping of Public Education, 1785–1954.* Madison: University of Wisconsin Press. §§2.8, 3.13, 5.6, 5.7, 5.8, 5.16

Tyack, David, Robert Lowe, and Elisabeth Hansot. 1984. *Public Schools in Hard Times: The Great Depression and Recent Years.* Madison: University of Wisconsin Press. §3.11

Tyler, William S. 1895. *A History of Amherst College During the Administrations of Its First Five Presidents.* Amherst: Amherst College. §4.4

United States Bureau of the Census. 1960. *Public Schools System in 1960.* State and Local Government Special Studies No. 44. Washington: The Bureau. §3.1

———. 1976. *Historical Statistics of the United States: Colonial Times to 1970.* Washington: The Bureau. §4.10

United States Commissioner of Education. 1910. *Report.* Washington: U.S. Commissioner of Education. §3.2

van Ark, Bart, Mary O'Mahony, and Marcel P. Timmer. 2008. "The Productivity Gap between Europe and the United States: Trends and Causes." *Journal of Economic Perspectives* 22:25–44. §4.15

Vermont Department of Education. 1921. *The State Course of Study of Vermont. Part One for Rural and Elementary Schools*. Montpelier: State Board of Education. §3.8

Vinovskis, Maris. 1985. *The Origins of Public High Schools: A Reexamination of the Beverly High School Controversy*. Madison: University of Wisconsin Press. §§3.11, 4.12

Vinovskis, Maris A., and Richard M. Bernard. 1978. "Beyond Catharine Beecher: Female Education in the Antebellum Period." *Signs* 3:856–69. §2.11

Weaver, Leon H. 1944. "School Consolidation and State Aid in Illinois." In *Illinois Studies in the Social Sciences*, vol. 27, no. 4. Urbana: University of Illinois Press. §§3.5, 3.16, 5.19

Weiler, Kathleen. 1998. *Country Schoolwomen: Teaching in Rural California, 1850–1950*. Stanford: Stanford University Press. §2.15

Weiss, Joel, and Robert S. Brown. 2003. "Telling Tales Over Time: Constructing and Deconstructing the School Calendar." *Teachers College Record* 105:1720–57. §4.11

Wells, William H. 1877. *The Graded School*. New York: A. S. Barnes & Burr. §§3.6, 3.7

West, Edwin G. 1965. *Education and the State: A Study in Political Economy*. London: Institute of Economic Affairs. §6.2

———. 1967. "The Political Economy of American Public School Legislation." *Journal of Law and Economics* 10:101–28. §§2.21, 3.11

White, Merry. 1988. *The Japanese Overseas: Can They Go Home Again?* New York: Free Press. §4.6

Wickersham, James P. 1886. *History of Education in Pennsylvania*. Lancaster: Inquirer Press. §§2.4, 3.16

Wiewora, Nathaniel H. 2007. "'Pure Religion of the Gospel . . . Together with Civil Liberty': A Study of the Religion Clauses of the Northwest Ordinance and Church-State in Revolutionary America." Master's thesis, Department of History, Florida State University. §2.6

Wilson, Charles H., Sr. 1947. *Education for Negroes in Mississippi since 1910*. Boston: Meador Publishing. §§4.2, 5.6, 5.7

Wright, Gavin. 2006. *Slavery and American Economic Development*. Baton Rouge: Louisiana State University Press. §5.5

Zanzig, Blair R. 1997. "Measuring the Impact of Competition in Local Government Education Markets of the Cognitive Achievement of Students." *Economics of Education Review* 16:431–41. §§5.9, 5.10

Zimmer, Basil George, and Amos H. Hawley. 1966. *Resistance to Reorganization of School Districts and Government in Metropolitan Areas*. Cooperative Research Project No. 1044 with the U.S. Office of Education. Providence: Brown University. §5.17

Index

Authors are indexed in the References.